MUHAMMAD AND THE CHRISTIAN

By the same author

This Year in Jerusalem (DLT 1982)
The Call of the Minaret (OUP 1956)
The Event of the Qur'ān (Allen & Unwin 1971)
The Mind of the Qur'ān (Allen & Unwin 1973)
The Wisdom of the Sufis (Sheldon 1974)

MUHAMMAD AND THE CHRISTIAN

A Question of Response

KENNETH CRAGG

Darton, Longman and Todd
London

ORBIS BOOKS
Maryknoll, New York 10545

First published in 1984 by
Darton, Longman and Todd Ltd
89 Lillie Road, London SW6 1UD
and Orbis Books
Maryknoll, New York 10545

ISBN 0 232 51599 9 (DLT)
ISBN 0-88344-349-X (Orbis)

Phototypeset by Input Typsetting Ltd, London SW19 8DR
Printed in Great Britain by
Anchor Brendon Ltd
Tiptree, Essex

CONTENTS

quarrels; the ultimate question of the sovereignty of God.

PREFACE

'There is an issue that disturbs Muslims more than any other in their approach to Christians,' wrote a participant in the 1975 Seminar convened at Tripoli, Libya, by President Qaddafi, to bring together representatives from the great Islamic University, Al-Azhar in Cairo, and from the Vatican and elsewhere. 'It is,' he went on, 'the silence and reserve of Christians regarding Muḥammad. He is for Muslims the last and greatest of the Prophets. Christian reticence on this subject surprises and scandalizes them. They do not understand why we refuse to grant Muḥammad the respect they themselves grant to the person of Jesus.'

But do we so refuse? If we link the two 'respects' the answer is, indeed, difficult. But, if we may distinguish them, need it follow that either scandalous rejection or puzzling silence are the only Christian options?

It is the aim of this study to offer at least one Christian's view of a resolution of the problem, a resolution which, no more than tentative, remains loyal to Christian criteria while outlining a positive response to Muḥammad. As Hamlet said to his players we must 'use all gently,' if we are not to 'make the judicious grieve'. That is always the case in religious study.

Muslims themselves, of course, have been involved in long and deep issues about the Prophet's status in a divine economy. His all-embracing stature came to personify what Islam understood itself to be.

Given the background of enmity, his inclusive authority, exclusively institutionalized in Islam, shaped a long legacy of mutual alienation between Muslims and Christians which successive political factors have sharpened. In consequence there has been scant occasion for open and positive reckoning either with the other. The Islamic significance of Muḥammad has been opaque to Christians, if not also anathema, while, for the most part, the Christian significance of Jesus has been seen to warrant disavowal of the Qur'ān. Rejections have been reciprocal. Christians felt they were faced with an impossible supercession of the finality in which they trusted, where Muslims claimed a more ultimate finality presented as corrective and fulfilment. As that claim could in no way be merely a matter of chronology but essentially one of content, only impasse could persist within communal loyalties so deeply at odds.

Yet in that very impasse was the incentive by which either laid controversial obligation on the other. It was as if their very disparities ruled out neutrality. One might almost express the situation in a paraphrase of the words: 'Ye believe in God, believe also . . .' (John 14:1), only that the verse would be continued in radically different ways.

The inquiry of this book, therefore, is into the God-and-Muḥammad fact of believing, as it presents itself to the God-and-Christ fact of believing. It would take another book to reverse the two and attempt some exploration into Jesus and the Muslim. There is more than enough at stake for one study in trying to bring together Muḥammad and the Christian.

Perhaps 'Muḥammad and *a* Christian' would be a more modest title, since any authorship is personal. Even so, there *are* broad areas of Christian criteria which a single writer might aim to present. It will be the exercise of bringing them to bear in this form which many will discount. A book which intends mediating interpretation will obviously arouse mixed reaction. There will be those in both faiths whom it is certain to disconcert. Some from the Muslim side will deny its goodwill and reprove its efforts after decisions of thought about Muḥammad which do not begin and end within the dogma of Islam. These will dispute the sincerity of the venture and even disallow any Christian estimates of Muḥammad which do not belong with the history, the devotion, the ideology which – it will be said – only Islamic experience can know. Such Muslims will disallow it altogether.

On the Christian side too, there will be readers and reviewers stolidly sceptical of its positive purpose, disapproving of commitment in any sense to acknowledgement of Muḥammad. These see him only as false, a usurper or displacer of Jesus. They may query why that displacement is not here more passionately voiced. For in their view it extinguishes any feasible recognition of the Qur'ān as in any way consonant with Christian discipleship.

Further, it may be assumed that secular sociology and academic orientalism will give the book's concern short shrift. Comparativists will insist that there is no true scholarship which does not first eliminate personal religion from its operation. Those who see religions only as social phenomena, functions of the human psyche, will suspect a treatment of Islam which is genuinely alive to absolute claims. And, by contrast, there may well be readers wistful for transcendent meaning, who will nevertheless have already concluded, either to their dismay or their comfort, that differing religious presentations of it are incapable of inter-relationship.

Well aware of these, and other, contrasted doubts or denials of its enterprise, I have in this book set myself the duty of reflecting on a duly Christian response to the perennial request of Muslims for 'acknowledgement' of the Prophet Muḥammad. The book attempts to answer out of careful regard to the many aspects of Muḥammad's role in Islam and with a realism alive both to Muslim experience and to the demands of the contemporary situation in the world. The undertaking may well fail of conclusions that satisfy: it can hardly fail of incentives to sustain it – given that Lordship to which 'in the Name of the merciful Lord of mercy' Muslims submit every work of mind or heart or pen.

Kenneth Cragg
July 1983

ACKNOWLEDGEMENTS

The author and publishers are grateful to the following for permission to reproduce extracts from copyright sources:

Clarendon Press, Oxford: *Centuries, Poems, and Thanksgivings* by Thomas Traherne.
Faber and Faber Ltd, London, and Harcourt Brace Jovanovich Inc. New York: "Choruses from 'The Rock' " in *Collected Poems, 1909–1962* by T. S. Eliot (copyright 1936 by Harcourt Brace Jovanovich Inc.; copyright © 1963, 1964 by T. S. Eliot).
The Journal of Economic and Social History of the Orient, Leiden: 'Some Reports Concerning Mecca' by M. L. Kister.
John Murray Ltd, London: *Discourses of Rumi*, translated by A. J. Arberry.
SPCK, London, and Paulist Press, New York: *Muslim Devotions* by C. E. Padwick.
The University of Chicago Press: *The Venture of Islam*, vol. 1, by Marshall Hodgson. © 1974 by University of Chicago Press.

Passages from the Qur'ān quoted in this book are the author's own translation.

1

READY FOR THE QUESTION

A Christian 'recognition' of the Prophet of Islam has long been a concern, indeed a demand, of Muslims in their exchanges with Christians. 'Why do you not acknowledge our Prophet?' is a familiar question, and an insistent one on occasions of what is currently called 'dialogue', or between disciples of the two monotheisms in their day-to-day relationships. An adequate response from the Christian side is certainly owed. Yet it bristles with problems and issues, not lightly to be resolved. So taxing are the things at stake that it is easy to see how the question has been shelved in diffidence or foreclosed in dogma.

Not least among the difficulties is the further question whether Muslims really want an answer from within the terms in which Christians, if they are intelligently sincere, would need to broach it. Religion has to do with final loyalties. Does not something essential go out of these if we allow them to be subject, especially by outsiders, to criteria of assessment external to their authority as inwardly received?

Among Muslims, in the main, the apostolate of Muḥammad is not for debate or inquiry, but for acceptance. Islam, as the name implies, presupposes unreserved commitment. Thus it is disturbing for the ordinary Muslim to have it made the theme of an acknowledgement, or of pondering – if acknowledgement is withheld – which reserves a critical freedom, which scrutinizes and discriminates and makes detached decisions. These imply some autonomy of mind remaining to the individual. Such reservation of will seems to place the absoluteness of religion within a personal option, and without the absolute dimension all religion – and not least Islam – feels compromised. For the absolute, in trust and in ultimacy, is what religion is about. Indeed, 'absolute' only says in syllables of Latin origin what *islām* says in Arabic. Islam, literally 'unfettered' by reserve, expects submission to truth criteria entirely and squarely within the authority of the faith that offers them. So understood, the prophethood of Muḥammad is the fact of the *Shahādah*, or witness of faith, co-equal with the unity of God. It is to be affirmed, not discussed.

It does not, therefore, anticipate a situation in which the uncommitted temper takes it into supposedly 'impartial' consideration. For 'partiality' will be in the very nature of such abstract and external viewing.

Here is the first hurdle the Christian has to take in determining a Christian attitude to Muḥammad and which the Muslim has to take in engaging with the other's response. Neither has an easy or a congenial task. Both can quickly fall or fail at the first hurdle. The hope of success can hardly be unilateral. There will need to be a mutual readiness to convince, and be convinced, of good faith. The Muslim, as the insider where the Prophet is involved, will need to bear his distrust of the Christian's unpersuadedness, while that unpersuadedness will have to demonstrate its *bona fides* as reverent and sincere. Both must live with a situation in which the one holds to criteria which the other either excludes or believes to have been already fully satisfied. Both must be gentle and honest with the manifest dispute about the criteria themselves. Each will need to renounce the suspicion that the sought relationship is merely a more subtle form of vested interest in which strong temptation keeps company with legitimate concern.

Some, aware of these tensions, will see the whole enterprise of relationship as misguided and futile. Religions, they will say, are specifics best left to their differing histories and their segregated faith-systems, hopefully practising tolerance but never venturing to translate their own ethos into the idiom of another. On this view, it will be either naive or hopeless to think that Muḥammad is assessable in terms proper to the Buddha or that the Prophet of the Qur'ān can rightly be aligned with the Jesus of the Gospels. Mecca, plainly, was not Galilee, nor Medina Jerusalem. The seventh century cannot be matched with the first, nor the Quraish with Caesar and Pilate, nor the Ka'bah with the synagogue. Therefore it is wisdom to leave the several faiths to their own world-views, their historical matrix and their characteristic mood and mind. One should not look to their contemporary societies for any common reaction to the present world. Their futures must be conceded to be as separate as their pasts.

On this logic we should pursue our study no further. The question of Muḥammad for Christians need not be answered because it cannot properly be put. Or, differently stated, the only feasible answer is to refuse one. Yet Muslims continue to look for a response and to press the duty of it upon the Christian conscience and spirit. For all its tense implications they assume it to be a right and necessary obligation, theirs to require and ours to meet. They are certainly not content to privatize Islam as meant only for themselves. Nor can Christians occupy a 'Jesus territory' with 'No admission' posted on their borders. The very claims which recruit inward allegiance assume external relevance. On every count of human community and of current history, not to say truth-reach, it seems plain that faiths – or at least these two – are not to be isolated and that, therefore, neither Muḥammad nor Jesus can be communally monopolized. That it matters to Christians about Muḥammad, and to Muslims about Jesus, must follow inescapably from the significance of the central figures as their custodian communities have known them. So we are back with the Muslim-to-Christian question, however strenuous the duties it imposes in the phrasing and the facing.

Yet the paradox persists. Custodian communities there are and tenacious they remain. Privacies in religion cannot well be claimed, truth-wise. But they are strongly practised, cult- and culture-wise. Dogma as the structure for truth easily becomes its usurper. Interior tradition and the complex of language, memory, habit, and history erect formidable barriers of identity which have to be painfully penetrated by the would-be reconciler and the 'alien' mind.

For the Christian 'alien' attempting an insider's study of Muḥammad the first of these barriers has been the *Sīrah*, or biography of the Prophet. By New Testament criteria it contains many features of a sharply, even bitterly, political kind. These prove immediately daunting to assumptions framed in the school of Gethsemane. Muḥammad emerges from the portrayal of the earliest Muslim historians themselves as assuming far too readily and practising far too freely the sanction of power. Temple Gairdner's *Ecce Homo Arabicus* may be taken as a passionate, yet also sensitive, expostulation with Islam from this angle.[1]

[1] W. H. Temple Gairdner, *Ecce Homo Arabicus*, Cairo, 1918. Gairdner was deeply committed to Christian apologetics but served by a genuine scholarship and warmed with strong personal love. In this tract he put into powerful form his impatience with what he saw as historically unwarranted idealization of Muḥammad. The actual truth of the Prophet's militancy should not be obscured because it was directly in line with the arbitrary exaltation of supreme Will, in Islamic theology. It is only in the retrospect of sixty years since Gairdner that a Christian theology can see Islam in more conciliatory terms.

This will concern us more fully in chapter 2, where its thrust may perhaps, in measure, be countered in historical assessment of all that is here at stake in the politics of religion. The present point is to realize how the historical merits of this issue lead into still deeper question as to history itself, and the place that 'fact' may be expected to occupy in the sphere of faith. There is certainly a sense in which belief about a personality or a situation, even if it be historically inaccurate or ethically suspect, nevertheless becomes itself a new 'fact' to be reckoned with as such. Every religion contains this issue. Islam is no exception. Beliefs become a positive element in the phenomenon of religious history and themselves constitute the form in which ideals and emotions are powerfully engaged and fulfilled. There is, therefore, not only the Muḥammad of the *Sīrah*, of the uninhibited early historians and chroniclers who are unabashed by features sure to appal their modern readers. There is also the Muḥammad of the believer's image, the Muḥammad who, as the Tijāniyyah Order of Sufi mystics tell us, takes his seat at the centre of the circle where they gather in the remembrance of God. There is the Muḥammad of sweet and rich devotion, enshrining within himself the very focus of spiritual aspiration. Will the 'bare' historian, pursuing strict historical fact, in modern terms, not seem, and be, a sort of devil's advocate if he pleads against such aspiration the veto of a distant record? At all events, he will be pitting one sort of actuality against another and it must remain an open question whether the annalist's is more vital than the disciple's.

Such are the deep waters into which we are taken by our task. The debate, to put it in formal terms, between the historicist and the phenomenologist, between the past as event and the past as myth-through-faith, is a difficult one. It is fine to affirm with Edwin Calverley:

> Serious students know that they are serving the highest religious duty when they acknowledge facts that can be verified. Whenever a previous belief or doctrine they have accepted conflicts with the facts they have learned, then they make their belief conform to the truth. Unfounded religious convictions bring discredit and defeat at the end upon both the believer and his religion.[2]

But the question remains whether there is a 'verification' in experience which is not countermanded by investigative scholar-

[2] Edwin E. Calverley in *The Muslim World*, xxii, 1 (1932), p. 67.

ship. Or, again, perhaps we may legitimately set against 'facts that we have learned,' ideals that we have 'associated'. Will 'conformity to the truth' be only in respect of history or also in respect of meaning? And what shall we do if these conflict? And what, again, if that conflict is not inwardly our own but belongs with the integrity and spiritual experience of another's religion with which we aspire to relate? In what sense are religious convictions 'unfounded' if, albeit historically questioned, they are lived in sincerely and intensely? We shall only be ready for the ultimate question here if we can appreciate the Muslim even as we inquire about Muḥammad. In chapters to follow we shall attempt to undertake both obligations.

In introductory terms, in this chapter, it is possible to see one way of reconciling the issue we have posed. It has to do with a matter at stake about the Prophet of the Qur'ān which is neither political nor devotional, but which bears strongly on the Christian attempt at the verdict Muslims request. It has the happy potential of being the means of bringing the historical and the ideological into closer relation and so, in turn, of drawing Muslim and Christian into riper mutual sympathy. It has to do, as chapter 6 will explore, with the nature of prophetic consciousness.

For those qualms, if we may so describe them, of the historians of religion when they turn to Islam, do not have to do only, or even primarily, with the dark areas of *Ecce Homo Arabicus*. Intelligent and perceptive apologia can perhaps handle these along the lines of chapter 2, especially if we transcend the *animus* that has so long and so understandably accompanied such stories as the massacre of the Banū Qurayẓah and the confiscations and intimidations that went with the Prophet's political success after his establishment in Medina. These abide and with them the ethical revulsion they arouse. Yet we must beware of either incriminating, or vindicating, the Prophet in over hasty terms that do not stay to take the measure of still more vital questions.

Among these, certainly, is that of the mode of revelation, or *Waḥy*, as the term is, within the heart and mind of the Prophet. Christian 'acknowledgement' of Muḥammad must deeply interest itself in whether the traditional view of *Waḥy*, as Muslims have held it, does or does not do justice both to the real phenomenon of the Prophet and to the nature of revelation itself. If it were to be possible, for example, to think of Muḥammad much more within the pattern, say, of Amos in the Bible – in respect, that is, of what prophetic experience meant – then we should have a much livelier 'dialogue', and, incidentally, a much more vigorous and productive approach, whether theirs or ours, to the contents of the Qur'ān.

As it is, orthodoxy within Islam on this point clings to belief in the illiteracy of the Prophet and the 'miracle' of the Scripture in arbitrary terms. It holds to the unnecessary dogma that the more a thing is God's the less it is man's, that divine employment of prophetic messengership means an abeyance of personal powers and qualities. Hence the emphasis on 'literal illiteracy' (if the phrase may be allowed) and on the belief that celestial dictation, rather than inward travail, verifies the Qur'ān as the divine Word.

One must have a ready sense of the religious yearning for certainty and authenticity which lies behind this faith as to Muḥammad, though these need not be unsatisfied on a more active view of what his role must have been. There are also many indications within the Qur'ān itself that his role was, indeed, active and personal, and that prophetic instrumentality in no way obviates deep human engagement. Such indications, which will be examined in chapter 6, are, of course, entirely in line with intelligent convictions about language, locale and context, as these are necessarily caught up in the incidence, not to say the very possibility, of divine revelation within human ken.

Thus a significant part of a Christian response to the request for 'acknowledgement' of Muḥammad will be concerned with his inner experience, and this question will have more final importance than the political and military involvements of the faith in Quranic revelation. It must be, as far as possible, a common study with Muslims, ours here being perhaps the role of encouragement to venture, and of reassurance about the 'security' of the essential message of the Qur'ān, as something not merely intact, but reinforced, after authentic reckoning with what could be meant by the confession: *Muḥammadun Rasūl Allāh*.

There is a sense in which all these urgent and crucial issues, as now sketched, having to do with the personality, history and career of the Prophet, are preparatory. The ultimate area of Christian response, given an honest reckoning with all the foregoing, will be the content of the Qur'ān itself. Indeed the question of a Christian acknowledgement of Muḥammad resolves itself into that of a Christian response to the Islamic Scripture. It is safe to say that Muḥammad himself would not have it otherwise. Nor could any faithful Muslim. For the Qur'ān is the *locus standi*, the Book of its Prophet and its people.

Accordingly, in chapter 7, we will turn to a Christian 'appreciation' of the Book of Islam, using the term in a genuine and in no way patronizing sense. Such positive Christian reckoning with the Qur'ān is long overdue, trapped as we have too long been in abstracts about 'authority', 'validity', and 'finality', or deterred by evident tensions with our own theology which we have not been free either to renounce or overcome. Certainly, as chapter 8 will demonstrate, no renunciation of what is contrary is here in mind. But these controversies and arguments have too long dominated the relationships and obscured the potentials that are positive. It is to these that we must first give ourselves, if we are to do final justice to discipleship in Christ.

Patience and perception will discover how ample they are. It must be assumed here that the Christian who is minded for this enterprise will be aware of the technical problematics that confront him in the Qur'ān and be able, if not to surmount them, at least to understand them. First among them is the compromise of the Arabic stature which translation entails. There is the further problem of chronology, or rather the disregard for it, and the difficulty of living with the fact that the Qur'ān is for recital rather than mere perusal, so that its sequences, refrains, strophes and accents have this in view rather than a studied logic. A Christian may hope to surmount these obstacles if he first has their measure. In Jalāl al-Dīn Rūmī's metaphor, the Qur'ān, like a Damascus brocade, has an under and an upper side and must be read accordingly.

Given that discernment, which we need not stay here to educate, a fascinating design of meaning emerges, central to which are the reality, sovereignty and unity of God. The Qur'ān affirms with entire emphasis the old Latin truth, *Non Deus nisi Deus solus* ('Not God, unless God alone'). Luther's cry; 'Let God be God', is its supreme demand and theme. Unity, or *Tauḥīd*, first repudiates all pseudo-worship. In that repudiation, that *Lā Ilāha illa* . . . of the negative part of the *Shahādah*, is the necessary prelude to the affirmation of *Allāh*. Islam negates the idols to affirm the Unity. Seeing that idolatries, false absolutes of various and devious kinds, remain the besetting evil of contemporary society everywhere, this staunch insistence of Islam on the reality of God speaks vitally to our condition.

There are, to be sure, acute problems for the theologian in the Islamic doctrine of God and in its characteristic 'distancing' of the divine/human relationship. But these, critical as they are, do not detract from the relevance of this most resolute of theisms. It is within, rather than against, this witness to the divine Lordship that the Christian can find community with Muslims and may ground his estimation of Muḥammad. It will be our concern later to grapple with all that is at stake in this. The immediate point is that, from this angle and with this dimension, the Qur'ān can become the Christian's territory in a positive sense.

A variety of other significances follow. Take the *Bismillāh* itself, the invocation of the Name of *Al-Raḥmān al-Raḥīm*, so constantly reiterated in the Muslim Scripture. Its theme of the divine mercy has a double meaning – mercy as definitive of the divine nature and mercy as characteristic of the divine action in and for mankind. In that sequence in the sense of the *Bismillāh* we must set the whole enterprise of creation, the fact of revelation and guidance, the genesis of prophethood and man's experience of the bounty of nature and the benediction of society. Here belong the many 'signs' of the Qur'ān which alert a scientific intelligence and also bespeak a religious reverence. The focus at one and the same point in nature of the instinct to 'technologize' and the impulse to religious awe and grateful wonder is a precious clue to the Quranic esteem of man. It belongs with the Qur'ān's account of the human 'caliphate', or 'dominion', over things and under God.

That account, of course, involves the central 'perhaps', the *La'alla*, of the Book. The *islām* of the Muslim, in these terms, is at once a summons and an option. His proper vocation requires his willed consent. His due fulfilment hinges on his personal decision *for* the recognition of the divine claim – a recognition which must belong within the fabric of his mortal span and his earthly setting, both understood as the gift of the divine grace. These are aspects of the human meaning with which any intelligent compassion can be glad to be associated. Esteem of them by any reader will properly encourage him to think receptively on the prophetic spokesmanship that teaches them.

This, however, is not to ignore the genuine problems as to the Islamic reading of humanity which still persist for the Christian student of the Qur'ān. Yet they are not of a sort legitimately to deny or to cancel the significant positive 'anthropology' of the Muslim Scripture and its bearing on contemporary experience.

When we have in this way soberly – if also eagerly – maximized Quranic meanings of this order there remain formidable reasons for Christian reservation. In many quarters such reservation may well effectively prevent any will to set out on quests of sympathy at all. These reasons we must honestly explore in chapter 8. Many will be deterred, either initially or finally, by the whole question of authority, and inhibited from embarking on any open relation to the content of the Qur'ān until they have satisfied themselves about its status, and the claims that Islamic dogma makes for it. They may fail to see that this in itself is a position of frustration, since the status question cannot be 'satisfied' without a will to attention. But it will be better to neglect, at least for a while, the dogmatic question, to leave it in intelligent abeyance, and concentrate on what, after all, is the relevance of 'status,' namely meaning and message. For some, doubtless, this will be too compromising an activity. In which case, let their conscience be respected. But let them not proscribe a different, and a positive, will in others to venture at least an experimental sympathy towards the Book.

Habits and attitudes of centuries, of course, dog us in these pursuits. There is a long history of a literature of ill-will, into which we need not delve here. Some of its concerns arose from legitimate questions allowed to lapse into animosity and distortion. Others have arisen from the sheer perversity of collective religious self-interest and rivalry. Even the 'orientalism' that set itself objectively to academic tasks has drawn down upon itself suspicions and enmities and accusations, inspired in part at least by inbuilt distrust or personal antipathy.[3] All such hostility, justified or unjustified, given or received, must be taken, not as conducing to dismay but alerting to difficulty, and as a paradoxical stimulus to better things. For it is these, in the end, which alone can draw its sting or break its entail.

When that is said, however, there persists, for the Christian a peculiarly taxing question, namely the Quranic supercession of the Jesus of the Gospels – an issue complicated by the Islamic conviction that the ʿĪsā (Jesus) of the Qurʾān, duly preparatory to Muḥammad's ultimacy, is the proper version, displacing the Gospels.

Here is a sharp veto on the most cherished dimensions of Christian faith. 'Finality' ceases to be a proper term for Christians to use. Jesus, as the faith from Galilee to the present has

[3] Inhospitality to Western 'orientalism' on the part of many Muslim scholars can be attributed to several factors. Among them certainly is resentment over political imperialism and bitterness about its legacy, in particular, in the creation of Israel and the tragic Palestinian displacement and frustration. There is also legitimate displeasure when Western academicists take insensitive liberties with Islamic themes, in a failure or an unwillingness to appreciate that they are handling deep religious meanings. Traditions of Islamic scholarship are very different from those of Western assumption. One sharp example of the tensions involved is Edward W. Said, *Orientalism* (New York, 1979), and some of the writings of A. L. Tibawi might also be cited in this vein.

understood him, suffers a strange reductionism, all the more tragic in that Muslims, with their sincere veneration for Jesus the Prophet, by his name ʿĪsā, are contentedly oblivious to its desolating quality.

'Desolating' because it means that the Gospel is radically altered, and is, indeed, no longer extant within the New Testament. Instead the teacher Jesus is simply as the Qurʾān insists he was. But there his teaching is minimal. It means, too, that the Cross is eliminated and, with it, the New Testament experience of the Resurrection and, with these again, the significance of the Holy Spirit and the Church, of the Eucharist and ministry. To be sure, the 'Cross' is there, importantly, in the Qurʾān in the shape of an evil will to crucify Jesus. But this hostile rejection of his word by his time and place and people is countered by divine 'rescue.' Thus what we may call the implicit 'Cross' achieves no historical redemption of the evil. This exclusion, by Islam, of the divine meaning of the Cross and the Resurrection as God's 'reconciling of the world' involves a disavowal, within the divine reality *per se*, of the ultimacies of love by which the Gospel lives. A sharply disparate theology follows from this Quranic elimination of what Paul describes as 'God in Christ' – if it does not also precede it. The name ʿĪsā itself, which the Qurʾān unaccountably substitutes for the Hebrew Yashūʿa, the Arabic Yasūʿa and the Greek Iesous, serves in a haunting way to symbolize the depth of this disparity.

Such harsh disallowance of Jesus as the Christ raises quite crucial questions for faith and loyalty. Christians find it an insuperable veto on their sense of God. It is well that Muslims should know this, in the hope that some may come to wrestle with its burden in the good faith of relationship.[4] All that this issue entails on both communities can better be dealt with in a separate book: *Jesus and the Muslim*. We have surer hope of escaping polemic if Christian 'complaint' about what Christians see as Quranic reductionism about Jesus can be handled in a positive interpretation of the New Testament faith, sensitive to Muslim preoccupations, rather than in a negative rebuttal. The latter would necessarily blunt our own sensitivity to the impact of the Qurʾān in other areas and predispose our mutual relationships to prejudice and conflict. For, in the last resort, the issue belongs with witness not with debate.

[4] Some indeed are already doing so, notably among English-using writers Ḥasan al-ʿAskarī, lately of Osmania University, Hyderabad, India, and Maḥmūd Ayyūb of the University of Toronto.

In the present context the point is to appreciate how the situation deters the sort of Christian readiness for the Qur'ān which these chapters have in mind. Many will be compelled to ask: How is the Christian to contemplate positive acknowledgement of Muḥammad when his prophetic significance involves such crucial disavowal of truths Christian? Is God the author of confusion? Can authentic revelation contradict itself? Does God deny Himself? How is divine intention to be attributed to that which negates the central confidence of the New Testament? If those Scriptures be the divine word, can others be so also, thus confounded by disharmony?

These are in no way mere fastidious scruples. Rather they are deeply authentic troubles both of mind and heart. Reasons, both historical and spiritual, inseparable from the givens of Christian faith seem to exclude any Christian acceptance of the Qur'ān, or any Christian reception of the Prophet within whose mission and message came these radical negations of the Christian's *raison d'être* in God. Such will be the continuing conclusion of many present-day Christians, just as it has been through the long centuries. It would be sanguine to imagine that anything here could give that rejection pause.

These, and others, are the questions that have to be faced in chapter 8, in order to pave the way for: 'Ready for Response' in chapter 9. It will need a very deliberate effort after what some writers call an *epoché*, a suspension of judgement, where we neither forgo our loyalties nor impose them, but, living with our misgivings, aim simply to understand and know. This means a will to relate and not to antagonize, to hold claims in abeyance in order to be open to meanings. It means being truly ready for the questions and *not* being too ready with the answers as if they were all foreordained.

That such openness of heart goes often against the grain of religious conviction, other men's and ours, is all too obvious. Religion deals in absolutes, requires to believe its beliefs and, therefore, disbelieve its disbeliefs. This is true even of those systems which see themselves as undogmatic and propose a path rather than a doctrine. It is certainly true of those faith communities of Semitic order with which we are concerned. It may help us, then, in either faith, to remember that the final 'absolute' of all, commanding our ultimate commitment, is not, and cannot be, the institutional form or the doctrinal structure but the divine Lordship. The posture which allows form and structure only 'servant status' will be the surest pattern of loyalty to truth.

In thus attempting to see Islam with the insider's eyes as a condition of being ready for the question of Muḥammad, there is one important aspect requiring deliberate care. The Christian must beware of subjecting the autonomy of Islamic faith and Muslim integrity to criteria from Christianity which Islam's own premises explicitly or implicitly exclude. He must be ready to realize that in many of the areas of his concern – the nature of revelation, the sanctions of prophethood, the role of power in the securing of faith, and much else theological and ethical – Islam has its own frame of reference and decision. Otherwise he may be accused of seeking to 'Christianize' Islam, reading into it intentions or obligations it does not accept.

I myself have been accused – unjustly, I believe – of just such a fault, 'doing violence' as Dr Charles Adams puts it, 'to the historical reality of the Islamic tradition . . . forcing it into categories of interpretation and meaning drawn from a different historical stream of piety and experience'. This critic even charges that my 'deliberately seeking and finding Christian meanings in Islamic experiences and doctrines' amounts to culpable failure to allow the *sui generis* quality which these experiences and doctrines possess in their own entire autonomy both of history and life.[5]

Dr Marshall Hodgson made a similar charge in his three-volume work, *The Venture of Islam*. He first distinguishes with fine perception the characteristic ethos of the two faiths.

> For Christians, being based on revelation means being in response to redemptive love as it is confronted through the presence of a divine human life and the sacramental fellowship of which that is the source. For Muslims, being based on revelation means being in response to a total moral challenge as it is confronted in an explicit divine message handed on through a loyal human community.

Then he insists: 'These two senses of revelation not only contrast to one another: they exclude each other categorically.'[6]

While the warnings in these strictures are salutary, need we accept the wholly isolationist conclusion? It is one thing – a necessary one – to avoid 'Christianizing' what is properly and vigorously distinctive in Islam. It is another to conclude that, therefore, the disparate faiths are incommunicado. If there is a

[5] Charles Adams on 'Islamic Religious Tradition' in L. Binder (ed.), *The Study of the Middle East: Research and Scholarship in the Humanities and Social Sciences*, New York, 1971.

[6] Marshall Hodgson, *The Venture of Islam* (Chicago, 1976), vol. i, p. 29.

‘venture of Islam’, may there not duly be a venture *into* it and *with* it? To be sure, the autonomy of faiths must be fully acknowledged. Those who belong to them have their own intellectual and emotional convictions. Islam, like any other faith, has the right to its own theology, its own assurance about revelation, its own possession of and by Muḥammad. The caves of Mount Hirā’ where he found vocation were not the hillsides of Galilee. Mecca was the idol Hubal’s world, not Herod’s kingdom. The Quraish of the Kaʿbah were not the Sadducees. The particularity of Muḥammad’s story must be appreciated in its own right and as it was.

Yet it is necessary, at the same time, to believe that there are liabilities to mutual reckoning in every religion. Otherwise, we legitimatize all religious decisions simply because they have been historically taken. Doing so would effectively terminate all relationship. Each would then be left in impenetrable self-congratulation or delusion.

To hold this balance between due recognition of genuine religious identity, and an authentic concern for criteria that might belong to all, is no easy enterprise. But it is one that must be undertaken. The specifics of any one religion cannot well ignore the significance of yearnings and meanings arising from human sources which it has not shared. Least of all can this be so when the particular faith believes itself to be the quintessence of all religion, with a universal mandate as a ‘mercy to the worlds’. An Islam that has no mind to privatize its relevance has no warrant to immunize its claims. On the contrary, it offers itself as that which can assuredly interpret and discipline the human whole. It can have, then, no legitimate exemption from considerations belonging to Christian humanity, providing these are rightly pressed.

Whatever response we can reach to Muslims’ inquiry: ‘What is your view of Muḥammad?’ will leave many open questions. All a single writer can do is to undertake a personal venture, doing what justice he can to issues that others may see as insoluble. It could just be that it is only our own mutual attitudes that have made them so. But any consensus to change those attitudes will be hard to seek.

Without anticipating here the course of a Christian response to the question of Muḥammad, it seems likely that the theme which will emerge as being the vital core of his mission, and the very crux of the Qur’ān, will be that of the divine imperative to man. If so, the demands of that imperative today must be the ruling concern of any conclusion. It cannot fail to be a common, and in that sense a unifying, obligation. If, as again seems likely, a confident combativeness on behalf of God emerges as the primary lesson of the Prophet's whole career, then it will be fair to ask at the end whether the divine imperative and the Muhammadan militancy are well conjoined. As founded by the Prophet and found in Islam, faith in the unity of God is historically united with the structure of religious community politically expressed and enforced. The vital issue, therefore, is the question of that union.

It presents to a Christian an urgent invitation into effective confession of the divine unity and, for that very reason, an inescapable reservation of heart about the power dimension with which, in Muḥammad's story, it was incongruously tied. But there remains very much ground to be explored before that conclusion can be justified. If justified it proves to be, the case must stand only in the nature of the divine Lordship. Faiths that are jealous for the Lord may need to be so against themselves. From that necessity there is no exemption.

2

THE PROPHET IN HIS HISTORY

'Truly you have the very stamp of greatness.' So we might translate the four words of an arresting Arabic statement about Muḥammad in Surah 68.4.[1] With their context they provide a fascinating point of departure for a directly historical study of the personality and work of the Prophet of Islam. Surah 68 comes early in the Meccan period and its title, significantly, is 'The Pen', in reference to that sense of the written Scripture (cf. 96.4: ' . . . taught man with the pen') by which Islam lives. Its opening verses offer a rare glimpse into the intimate experience of prophetic self-awareness. They are certainly reassuring. 'By the pen and what the lines set down, you are not deluded. The grace of your Lord sees to that. Yours is an unstinted reward to come.' Then comes the phrase guaranteeing 'the stamp of greatness' followed by a promise that it will soon be clear who are the ones under delusion, Muḥammad or his taunting critics.

All the elements of the prophetic story, as Islam receives it, are here – vocation, Scripture, preaching, hostility, encouragement, conflict, anticipation, vindication – and through them all divine

[1] A very literal rendering of the verse would be: 'You are indeed upon a great nature.' It certainly takes us into the fascinating field of Muḥammad's self-awareness. Translators vary widely in their English of the words. Some examples are:
'Thou art upon a might morality.' (Arberry)
'Yours is a sublime nature.' (Dawood)
'Thou dost possess an eminently exalted character.' (Abdul Latif)
'Thou standest on an exalted standard of character.' (Yusuf Ali)
'Thou art engaged upon a might task.' (Bell)
'Thou art of a tremendous nature.' 'Pickthall)
'Verily thou art of a great religion.' (Lane)
'Verily thou art a grand character.' (Abul Fazl)
'Most surely you conform [yourself] to sublime morality.' (Muhammad Ali)
If hardly felicitous, these certainly suggest the difficulty of Arabic/English translation in respect of Quranic idiom and meaning.

grace and the enabling mandate of divine authentication responding to the situation of human obduracy which wilfully refuses to acknowledge it.

'Stamp of greatness' seems a right form of English. The noun *khuluq* means the inner moral character, the quality of disposition sometimes caught in the English phrase: 'second nature', meaning the instinctive behaviour that indicates the essential fashion of the self within. But since the passage has to do with the task of speaking prophethood, some have understood the reference to be the 'morality' within the Scripture, or, again, the lofty religion that Scripture tells, or even again, the actual recital and the burdens it imposed both of fidelity to the Word and fortitude in face of opposition. There is a tradition of 'A'ishah, the Prophet's favourite wife, that the *khuluq* was the Qur'ān itself.

It is right to bring all these meanings into one, in that the stamp of greatness belongs indistinguishably with the *persona* of Muḥammad, the nature and text of the Qur'ān, and the instrumental *Sīrah*, or biography, within which, in loyalty and courage, the partnership of message and messenger ensued. Surah 68.4 has in view a great task greatly matched in the fulfilment or, conversely, a great personality summoned to, and achieved in, the destiny of the Qur'ān. All subsequent Islam resoundingly confirms its verdict – the historians in their proud narration, the traditionalists in their treasured memories for imitation, the moralists in their enjoining of example, the mystics in their invocation of his benediction. All, to vary the metaphor, stand under the superlative dimensions of the Prophet as they are understood and received through all the diversity of Muslim religious experience. The outsider's first duty is to give himself to the discovery of the historical setting where all began and to which all returns, to a Scripture via a biography and a biography with a Scripture.

This first duty does well to take immediate stock of the historical setting as 'encounter', deepening into confrontation over issues sharply joined. The reader of the *Bhagavad Gita* is at once introduced to drawn-up armies 'on the field of truth, on the battle-ground of life'. By contrast the first words of the Qur'ān (though not, of course, the first page) have to do with: 'Recite in the Name of thy Lord who created' (96.1). But utterance in the Lord's Name quickly leads into a situation where rejection grows and fidelity with utterance grows with it into gathering intensity and 'the field of truth' becomes 'the battleground of life'.

There is nothing strange about such emerging confrontation.

It is, we might say, the occupational hazard of faithful prophecy. All the patriarchal precedents the Qur'ān recalls demonstrate the human unwillingness for truth, for challenge to tradition, which prophets painfully incur. Abraham is vilified and threatened by the idolaters he reproves, by the caretakers of the images he shatters. Moses comes to his victory by heroic antagonism to Pharaoh of 'the great house'. Establishments are always wary of disturbers, as Jeremiah discovered to his pain. Most prophets only learn in the sequel the personal cost of the missions they undertake. 'You took advantage of my simplicity,' was the way Jeremiah accused the Lord, when, in a bitter moment of anguish, he pondered the years of travail in which God's commission had involved him – all unsuspected at the outset (Jer. 20.7).[2] Was it not said of Jesus that 'there was a division among them because of him? (John 7.43 and 9.16). Jesus, as 'Īsā in the Qur'ān, though finally uncrucified, needs 'rescue' from the clutches of those who sought his death.[3]

So the antipathy Muḥammad encountered within his native city was no unusual event. It was, indeed, as in earlier histories, a tribute to the thrust of his message and the tenacity of his witness. To be radically at issue with the time and place is both the vocation and the vindication of prophethood. All loyal prophets have, in some sense, known the need to disown and to challenge, to differ and to defy, saying to the heedless or the obdurate: 'You non-believers, I do not worship what you worship, nor is your worship the same as mine' (Surah 109). That mutual repudiation is the steady note of the Qur'ān and constitutes the dominant feature of both the Prophet's *Sīrah* and the Book's atmosphere. What the Christian reader-student has to do is to take its quality, to explore the range of the truth

2 This translation is in debt to a German version. The original Hebrew is more forceful still, in line with the intensity of Jeremiah's protest (to God) about the consequences of a vocation to which he responded, all unawares, in youth. 'You ravished, you [almost] raped, me.' The task of prophecy fulfilled itself, had its way, against the grain of the prophet's own desires and happiness.

3 It is important here to realize that the prevailing view of the meaning of Surah 4.158, i.e. the rapture of Jesus to heaven uncrucified, does not imply that there was no will to crucify among his hearers. Quite the contrary. 'Rescue' would be pointless, without that danger to necessitate it. Jesus, emphatically, was one whom people of his time and place willed to crucify. See Muḥammad Kāmil Ḥusain, *City of Wrong* (Amsterdam 1958), for a perceptive study of the implications of the rejection of Jesus from within a Muslim assumption that crucifixion did not in fact occur in the end.

which occasioned the 'battleground' and ponder the military factors in the outcome. These are the concerns of this chapter.

I hope that, by coming to them promptly and with emphasis in this way, I have done justice to the inevitability of strife. The question about prophetic conflict is not Whether, but How? It is not about militancy, but its resources: not about encounter but the bearing of it on the message which excites it. If we were studying a compromise of acquiescence we would not be facing the compromises of resistance. The problem for the historian only begins because, in the oddly teasing phrase, the prophet 'sticks to his guns'. It is there that the burden of an outsider's 'acknowledgement' today must lie.

There is a tradition about Waraqah ibn Naufal, the cousin of Muḥammad's wife, Khadījah, that he greeted the Prophet, after his first experience of the call to recite, with the words: 'Would that I could live to the day when your fellow countrymen will expel you from this land. For you are God's envoy to this people.' Waraqah's words surprised Muḥammad, who replied: 'What do you mean? They will expel me?' 'Assuredly,' said Waraqah. 'No one has ever brought what you bring and escaped being the object of hostility and persecution. But if God let's me survive till then, I will give you every possible aid.'[4]

Waraqah did not survive. It is interesting to conjecture what kind of aid he would have given. Of all Muḥammad's entourage he was the most conversant with Christian precedent and became a Christian before his death. That may well explain the foresight in his salutation. His anticipation of expulsion from Mecca was correct, even though, in the event, Muḥammad's exodus was a deliberate decision taken in a situation where bitter and sustained rejection had made it an urgent necessity.

As the most cursory reader of the Qur'ān knows, that Hijrah, or emigration, was the pivot of the Prophet's story. It also originates the Islamic calendar, all of whose centuries are 'years of the Hijrah'. One might have thought that Muḥammad's year of birth would have had this honour or, still more fittingly, the year of the beginning of the Qur'ān. But A.D. 622 stands, not 590 or 609, as the inauguration of the Muslim era. It divides the Qur'ān also into Meccan and Medinan Surahs, into chapters that belong before and chapters that belong after the Hijrah. It is thus the watershed both of the Book and the biography: it is where prophethood culminates and rulership begins.

This means that before the historian can come intelligently to

[4] Quoted from A. Draz, *Initiation au Koran* (Paris, 1951), p. 13.

the militancy he must review the message for whose sake the confrontation was joined. Only so will he be able to measure the quality of the one in the conduct of the other, and decide whether the casualties feared from hostility were incurred by countering it. Only so can he assess what resources of temper and restraint the faith could command in the vital business of ensuring its hearing and its future.

Any such historical concern for truth and battleground as the Qur'ān presents them, faces a daunting complex. But to shoulder it is the deepest tribute to the original word, by taking it in its own seriousness as a prophethood resolute with its cause.

A study of the factors in the Meccan scene which explain the antagonism to Muḥammad is deferred to chapter 3. Those factors were communal, commercial, traditional and religious. They belonged with the 'establishment' of the Quraish in the city and its surrounding 'clients', and with their vested interests of trade, prestige and pride. They conduced inevitably to the politicization of Islam. It will here be simpler to narrate first and analyse later, so allowing ourselves to come directly to grips with what Muḥammad preached and how he organized its victory. In doing so, we will also postpone, to chapter 6, a necessary study of his prophetic experience *per se* on its inward side.

There is one feature of the whole which is obvious enough but often goes without adequate remark, namely the emphatic concentration of the Qur'ān, its singular focus on Muḥammad and the twenty-three years of his vocation, its exclusive involvement with the Quraishī situation. Readers of other Scriptures possess a far wider canvas. Biblical perspectives cover long centuries. The rigours of Elijah can be balanced by the tenderness of Hosea, the belligerence of Joshua by the sorrows of Jeremiah. There is a panoramic quality about the Old Testament where Persian pathos and Greek 'wisdom' find place at length within Hebraic experience, where exile is heir to exodus, and definitive experience, covering a vast range of time, is often reviewed, relived, revised, by chronicler and psalmist. In the New Testament the personality and work of Jesus pass into literature through the evangelical lens of corporate and personal discipleship tested by decades of mission and openness to a world outside the incidence of origin.

The Qur'ān has no such literary character. Its maturity as revelation, if we may so speak, is immediate. It does not incorporate into its nature the public reception of its message, except in the very narrow sense that controversy within the preaching years is mirrored in its pages. It begins only with the Prophet's call and ends forthwith at the Prophet's death. God, as one writer observed, was never heard addressing other than Muḥammad. To be sure, the Qur'ān is confident that it encloses and confirms all that is authentic in earlier Scriptures, and that it finalizes all religious meaning. But that confidence is not corroborated by explicit partnership with other literatures of faith or engagement with their deepest themes. Biblical citation within the Qur'ān is minimal. Concern for such rapport with other revelatory literature is, for the most part, precluded by the conviction that the Qur'ān's inclusiveness renders it unnecessary or identifies it as misguided by the mere fact that it fails to tally.

The severe particularity, in this way, of the 'front' on which the Qur'ān requires to be accepted is no small part of the student's difficulty. Its claim to finality discourages him from seeing it as contributory in a wider context. He is obliged by its imperatives to assess the essential 'encounter' of truth with the world, of prophet with humanity, within the terms contained in twenty-three years of one biography, in one context, and in one locale. If the facts of those terms are as chapter 3 explores them, do they not present a setting of 'encounter' which seriously delimits the sort of options by which religion could be tested and its sanctions determined? Yet will the Islamic status of Muḥammad allow them to be widened, varied, or set in any other context, so that the actual one need not monopolize our judgements? Those questions appear certainly, though also reverently, to belong to that monopoly by which Muḥammad serves the Qur'ān and the Qur'ān belongs with Muḥammad.

Orthodoxy and tradition answer them in the negative. We are required to study the Qur'ān as possessing a historical incidence entirely sufficient for the embodiment of the issues of religion and the exemplification of their solution. The 'encounter' the Qur'ān enshrines suffices all issues in its there-and-then.

The firm confidence of this institutional concentration of meaning in historical Islam can only be explained as the impact of the dynamism with which Muḥammad gave it voice. 'Recite in the Name of thy Lord who created . . .' That dynamic sense of commission, it is true, had to pass through early phases of disquiet and misgiving, especially when the interludes of awareness seemed to fail. But as they became more sustained, and the conviction of 'sentness' possessed his personality wholly, Muḥammad's preaching made transcendence vivid and demanding for all who had ears to hear. By the same token it kindled enmity from those who had not. Its chief notes were the unity of

God, the folly, therefore, of idolatry, and the reality of impending judgement. Confrontation was implicit from the beginning by virtue of the prophetic energies they necessitated and the obdurate interests with which they collided.

Much has been written about the excesses and crimes of the *Jāhiliyyah*, the times of wild uncouthness which piety ascribes to the pre-Islamic situation. Such utter darkness is hardly consistent with the evidences of incipient monotheism to which the *Ḥanīfs* bear witness, nor with the wistfulness for escape from bloodlust found in *Jāhiliyyah* poetry. But nowhere before Muḥammad had such yearnings found the thrust that could attain them. The Prophet possessed it in the experience of which the Qur'ān was both the inward and the outward side, corroborating each other. *Rasūl* and *Risālah*, messenger and message, were a mutual reality. 'Recite!' was no private command; it enjoined a public task. But it created a personal identity. As the text of what became the Arabic Qur'ān to his hearers was steadily accumulated so the commission, that had received in serial sequence the heavenly Book, grew steadily into the focal point of crisis. The *persona* of Muḥammad, as the Islamic confession of faith avows, became inseparable from the proclamation of the oneness of God.

It seems fair to conclude that the Prophet's sense of that destiny, to be pondered more closely in chapter 6, belonged with Semitic antecedents *and* with the sense that these needed Arab and Arabic fulfilment. Book-possession, or the status of scriptured people, characterized those earlier communities of faith in God as One. Prophets, undoubtedly, were the instruments whereby Scriptures arrived in their communities and communities, in turn, were furnished with them. Should not a 'native' Book of God be the proper privilege, the accrediting 'sign', of the Arab people? How might this be, without the mediation of a prophethood belonging with that people, born to their precious speech and master of their story? Were not these the latent, perhaps unconscious, aspirations, which, for Muḥammad, the strange external visitations of Quranic *Waḥy* might be taken to satisfy?[5]

External they certainly were in their spontaneous form. But they did not break dramatically into a situation of indifference. On the contrary, they occurred within the searchings, perhaps even the mystical discipline, which many historians associate

[5] On this issue see K. Cragg, *The Event of the Qur'ān* (London, 1971) ch. 3, especially pp. 56–62.

with Mount Ḥirā' and Muḥammad's withdrawal from the Meccan world. Though a withdrawal, it took with it, none the less, the burdens, the queries, the intimations, of a traveller's world and of a merchant's experience of life.

However we conjecture those beginnings, they had emphatic issue in the sharply Arab rejections they encountered. Muḥammad's witness to God and His unity, crucially involved as prophethood made it with his person, met with firm resistance. His audience countered his words and threatened his person with a variety of charges, finding him crazy (81.22), dubbing him a soothsayer (52.29) or a mere poet (37.35: 52.30), accusing him of copying old stories (68.15), or cribbing from a stranger (16.106). Why was not some great man chosen (43.30), the better to command a credibility? they asked. Inspired by Satan (81.25), he was a disturber of old tradition, a disparager of ancestors whom Mecca would continue to follow (43.19, 21). These hostile reactions oscillated through ridicule, calumny, conspiracy and denunciation during the entire decade before the deaths of Khadījah and of Abū Ṭālib in 619, when Muḥammad's personal position became still more perilous. The emigrations of some of his persecuted following to sanctuary in Ethiopia relieved their tribulation but did nothing to establish his mission in the Meccan heartland.

The gathering impasse is reflected in the texture of the Qur'ān. Its stamp is on the patriarchal narratives and the double role they fill of exemplifying faithful endurance under adversity, on the one hand, and the condign retribution that ultimately overtakes the heedless and the rejectors. On both counts Muḥammad stood to draw solace and stamina from these precedents. The stories are a clear example of the way in which Quranic content and prophetic biography illuminate each other.

The other interior consequence of the encounter between the Prophet and his native city was the strong antithesis in which the Qur'ān is involved between guided and misguided, *muslimīn* and *kāfirīn* the heedful and the heedless, the gainers and the losers. The former, sadly, are the fewer. The Islamic Scripture has many sombre accents of reproof and rebuke in face of human hardness of heart and resistance to truth, both ancient and immediate. Warning and appeal run through its pages and the burden of strong controversy is always present in its pleadings. It is perhaps here that the necessities of its particular context bear most heavily upon its form and temper. The outside reader often finds himself wishing he might savour the message of divine transcendence in a constituency more congenial to its wonder, less stubborn in its waywardness, than the one Muḥammad had to face in Mecca, so that his quality might be known in a joyful availing of his word.

But it was not to be so. The Qur'ān, and with it its resolute spokesman, headed towards Hijrah out of obduracy and from verbal mission into the test of physical power. After thirteen years of sustained and patient witness by word alone, and of relatively scant response within a community proudly resistant and incorrigible, Muḥammad determined on emigration. The divine word could not be allowed to fail of 'manifest victory'. If this was manifestly *not* attained by preaching, then the very loyalty that preached must pass beyond its verbal task into an active accomplishment of 'victory'. A Mecca that had rejected the warning word, the spoken summons, must be confronted in a new dimension, that of force.

Such, it clearly seems, was the decisive logic. The Hijrah is not rightly seen as a lapse away from prophethood, but as its due sequence of obedience. There was the impulse of dire necessity, if Prophet and prophethood were even to survive. There was the providential opportunity in the promise from the new locale, the city of Yathrib, soon to become Medina, and the pledge to 'defend' Muḥammad. There was the benefit of an allegiance, toughened by deliberate exile, from his emigrating followers and good hope of developing a base for action where still neutral, or hostile, Yathribites could be induced towards Islam. With all these there was the prospect that a Mecca which had refused persuasion and failed to forestall departure could prove vulnerable to returning exiles adequately mustered to her reduction. So ensued the post-Hijrah campaign of military combat 'in the way of God'.

Vulnerable Mecca certainly was, with its caravan routes stretched out from north to south along the Red Sea littoral, miles of which Yathrib threatened from the flank. Vulnerable, too, to any adversary ready to violate the months of truce by which pilgrimage and commerce alike were intermittently ensured, by the Meccan shrine's prestige, against the marauding disorder which might otherwise have hindered them. Vulnerability, one might say, is always a temptation. Arab society, emphatically, was no exception.

But it was not mere opportunism which tempted Muḥammad into armed action, once settled in Medina. Those monthly truces themselves, affording violaters the advantage of surprise, were symbols of the old order. They depended on the authority of the shrine-holders and so, in turn, on the idol worship these approved. They were also palliatives by which a chronic feuding was made tolerable in uneasy compromise with commercial interests. Faith in divine unity had every practical reason for calling them in question, however outrageous this might seem to traditional minds. The 'manifest victory', as the Qur'ān repeatedly calls it, proper to the sole Lord of the worlds, could not stay for the institutions of the old pagan order or deny itself the tactical benefit of defying them. On the contrary, acting outside them and against them would be both a sign of their repudiation and a means to their defeat, pagan as they were and creatures of the *Jāhiliyyah*, or 'years of ignorance.'

It is from this angle, not that of adventurism or bare aggression, that the 'battles' of Badr and Uḥud and of the Ditch must be seen in the years that immediately followed the Hijrah to Medina. Muḥammad was simply following the logic of his essential challenge to Quraishī power as custodian of the pagan faith. The first was a signal victory, which the Qurān describes as '*yaum al-furqān*' (8:41) 'the day of the criterion', when Muslims measured themselves against the Meccan caravans and gained not only the booty but the new standing which their success achieved. The issue had been joined and the Quraish stung into retaliatory action in order to reassert their authority and recover their prestige. When the inconclusive fight at Uḥud and the desultory engagement of the Ditch checked somewhat the thrill that Badr had occasioned, Muḥammad's cause was able to contain them and to draw from them lessons of tenacity and discipline.

The way through and beyond the period of indecisiveness – once the decisive issue had been joined – lay in a steady, partly military, partly political, consolidation of Medinan resources. The city itself was increasingly implicated in and with Islam simply by being the base of Muḥammad's campaign. With the growth of his assurance and his people's identity in the Medinan years, that involvement became irreversible. What was never thought of as irreversible was the exile. The *Muhājirūn*, or emigrants, were Meccan, with a trickle of later emigrants to reinforce them. The new direction of prayer, the *Qiblah*, away from Jerusalem and towards the still pagan centre, underlined the unbroken significance of the shrine that awaited cleansing and recovery – recovery not merely of its physical locale, but of its Abrahamic role. Muḥammad's purpose turned on a vigorous marriage of Medina's occasions with Mecca's ultimacy.

Among the occasions were the building of prestige, the recruitment, or the confiscation, of resources, the enlistment, or if need be the intimidation, of the tribes. Inevitably the conflict with Mecca meant suspicion, or accusation, of connivance or conspiracy with the parties. It is painful to sort out the truth in the welter of charge and counter-charge that embittered the combatants and bedevilled their neighbours. Even neutrality is suspect where strife intensifies. The Jews particularly were in the cross-fire of partisanship if only because the Prophet's earlier anticipations of their acceptance of him had been more evidently denied and because, in Medina, the separate autonomy of Islam was more totally affirmed.

In the forcible expulsions of this period, the seizures of property and the dispersal of tribes, the history of the *Sīrah* comes to its most desolating chapter. The Banū Nadīr, the Qaynuqāʿ and the Qurayẓah, were the most notable victims, the last named suffering a complete massacre of their males and the selling into slavery of their women and children. 'Not fearing the reproach which any one reproaching may bring' is set down in Surah 5:54, as one of the characteristics of a people whom God loves and who love Him. It is a feature of the early historians that they register no compunction about these dark areas of the Medinan story and of the sanctions of Muḥammad's success. Perhaps one should look beyond episodes, however tragic, to the entire complex of tribal custom, cultural psychology and legal obligation – not to mention communal strategy in a war situation – by which atrocity might be legitimatized or 'reproach' assessed. No doubt such perspective of judgement is right and to deny it to the history would be itself unfair. But the more this plea is pressed the more urgent becomes the problem involved in the fact that here is a claim to religious ultimacy situated so starkly in a context that denies it, indeed utterly disfigures it.

In practical terms Muḥammad's energies and strategy and Medina's potential prevailed. His later marriages served to strengthen his alliances and his political wisdom enabled him, via the Treaty of al-Ḥudaibiyyah, to negotiate a return pilgrimage to Mecca and to consolidate his tactical position. He demonstrated his foresight and his staying power where his own more fervid followers found his timing frustrating and his tactics too moderate. When, eight years after the Hijrah, Mecca was finally repossessed, the magnanimity which had been denied the hapless Qurayẓah and their like came memorably into its own. The capitulation of the city appropriately symbolized the mutual dissolution of the bond that bound the Quraish to their deities. Worshippers abandoned their worships as those who now knew themselves deceived by their rites and superstitions. They had no stomach for tenacity on behalf of gods by whom they had been deserted and betrayed.

This is not to say that the eradication of paganism was complete in Mecca by the fact of conquest. On the contrary, the *Risālah* of Islam still had much to do to discipline and reorientate the pagan mind. But it is to say that, in sequel as in prospect, Muḥammad's armed *Jihād* made faith and campaign a single victory. In the two years of his life that remained, the pattern of the Medinan tenure was renewed with accrued impetus, in Mecca. The city's interests, as in the expedition to Ḥunayn, were recruited into Islam's cause, with the objective of unifying tribes into one allegiance and ensuring that the sovereignty was God's. It was only a measure of the incipient conflicts and tensions of Arab society throughout Muḥammad's life that at his death Islamic authority, though resoundingly virile, was still precariously poised. The future owed much to the vigour and resource which the first two Caliphs, Abū Bakr and ʿUmar, brought to their inheritance of power and crisis.

The salutation of the faithful, hallowed by long usage, at the Tomb of Muḥammad in Medina runs:

> Peace be upon thee, O Apostle. We witness that thou hast truly delivered the message, that thou hast striven in the way of God until God glorified His religion and perfected it.

The greeting echoes the final words of the Qur'ān:

> This day I [God] have perfected for you [pl.] your religion and completed My grace upon you. I have made my will and pleasure clear – Islam is to be your religion. (Surah 5.3)

It also echoes the vital unity of witness and endeavour in Muḥammad's prophethood. There is no doubt as to the final priority of the witness. The *Jihād* of his post-Hijrah career would have had no ground or cause but for the pre-Hijrah vocation. There are several traditions which attest his life-long concern for integrity of a mission discharged. On his death-bed he is said to have asked of his companions whether he had faithfully delivered his message and fulfilled his mission. 'God is my witness that you cannot reproach me.' Deep within this desire to be reassured there breathes a sense of the divine mercy over all. His dying anxiety was that the purity of faith should be effectively preserved.

It is, therefore, in the last analysis, by the content of his witness that the external historian must assess Muḥammad, insofar as he may aspire to do so from outside the ethos which only the faithful possess in cherishing the story. Any due reckoning with Muḥammad must become a reckoning with the Qur'ān. Yet, for that very reason, the messenger persists in the message, the *Rasūl* in the *Risālah*, the personality within the witness. The very fabric, and certainly the feel, of the Scripture are bound up with the vicissitudes, the values and the decisions, of the *Sīrah*. The text of the one, and the texture of the other, interact and cannot well be disentangled. The conduct of the Prophet's *Jihād* becomes part of the revelation.

So in acknowledgement, such as Muslims seek, of Muḥammad, we have no escape from the burden of the actual events. Some appeal to benevolent oversight, or tactful goodwill, would be disloyal both to Islamic criteria and to religious integrity. The more eagerly we press the immediate circumstances (to be discussed in the next chapter) the more directly we incur its implicit denial of an ultimate or universal standing. Perhaps there may be relief in pleading that all revelation has to transcend, as well as occupy, particular occasions and that, even where compromising, these need not obviate or impede the significance which is both within and yet beyond them. This, *pace* the historicists, is what both the mystics and the idealizers in their various ways have done. Even so, the claims of historicity will not abdicate and a dilemma remains in holding together a significance which transcends a context and the context that disserves it. Some, sensing this paradox, will opt for a forthright admiration which either scouts misgivings or allows them no relevance.

The dilemma here is particularly pressing in the sphere of education and the inculcation of faith. All religions, in some measure, have inward reason to discriminate in how they commend themselves, in their developing apologia as the generations pass. But the tension between embarrassment and confidence will often be far easier for the insider concerned with nurture than for the outsider faced with radical decision.

It may be that the issue in all this is finally insoluble. The purpose here was simply to narrate its elements as they stand in the history. The chapter to follow will deal with politicization in more detail. How Muslim historians have handled 'the Prophet in his History' in the last century, as heirs of the tradition-makers, will come in chapter 5. It remains here to conclude with two final reflections, significant for the over-all response we are invited to make.

The first is the fact that the Muslim sense of God is so closely associated with the prophetic story. This is properly so and happens wherever there is belief in historical revelation. That Islam is strongly non-incarnational does not at all mean that thoughts of God are not intimately bound up with events and attitudes He is believed to have willed, enjoined, succoured and prospered. The militancy, therefore, within the Qur'ān, belongs dynamically with what we may call the Book's 'predication' of God. The reader senses how the ardour of the Prophet's campaigns rides with the strictures against unbelief and even with the harshness of the anticipations of eternal destiny. What the story lacks, we have to say the Scripture lacks, in respect of dimensions of pathos, tragedy, tenderness, healing, or solicitude for enemies.[6] These emotions occur, in part, in the Meccan period, and in marital and personal context.[7] But when the exigencies of the *Jihād*, as historically pursued, take over, they are overborne by the need to pursue it with vigour and venom.

The situation can, perhaps, be illustrated by a semantic study around the term *ṣabr*. Both verb and noun are a frequent usage. In the setting of prolonged verbal and physical encounter it is easy to understand why. 'Patience' – the broad meaning of the term – was evidently vital to Muḥammad's fidelity when confronted with ridicule and rejection, and to his determination when facing antagonism in the field. 'Suffering' as that which demands 'patience' (to put the matter the other way round) was incurred in either case, suffering from hostile hearers and their hardness of heart, suffering from hostile warriors and their sharpness of steel. Both are deep in the Quranic story.

Ṣabr, by the same token, may be either 'long-suffering',[8] or

[6] The late Dr Muḥammad al-Nuwaihy, of Cairo, in an unpublished lecture, stressed that these dimensions were, indeed, present in the Qur'ān and must be understood in Muḥammad's yearning over the heedlessness that rejected his appeals. He cited Surah 36.30 in evidence of his conviction, *Yā-ḥasratan ʿalā-l-ʿibād* ('O the pity of it about My servants'), and saw in God's *ḥasrah* ('sorrow, sigh') a pathos, with and about, the travail of His messenger. *Ḥasrah* is used elsewhere about the remorse of the unbelievers, and some translators have 'Woe to . . .' rather than 'pity for . . .' as its meaning. However this may be, Dr Nuwaihy's reading of the text deserves to be noted as close to prophetic experience elsewhere. But it does not of itself reverse the broad perspective we are considering.

[7] For example, 43.89: 'Pardon them and say, "Peace" '; 15.85: 'Forgive them with a generous forgiveness', *et al.* (directives to Muḥammad about the unbelievers); 2.230: 'Dismiss them with kindness . . .'; and 65.1: '. . . perhaps God may bring about a [new] situation' (to those divorcing wives).

[8] An odd English usage! – as if length of suffering could somehow ensure its quality. But forgiving, long-suffering certainly is, and implies, as in 'Love suffereth long' (1 Cor. 13.4).

'tenacity', a gentle forbearance or a bold persistence. There is, as a proverb had it, the 'patience' of the tent-peg under blows and of the mallet inflicting them. There is Surah 70.5, *faṣbir ṣabran jamīlan* ('Be gracefully patient'), or Surah 2.177, commending the *ṣabr* which faces adversity, hardship and danger, or Surah 3.142 and 146, where the *ṣābirūn* are those who endure manfully in the *Jihād*. That God is with them is reiterated in 8.46 and 66, in the context of the battle of Badr, where the phrase about 'weakening' or 'losing heart' is linked with *ṣabr*, very much in the sense of 3.139 and 47.35 where 'suing for peace' would be a gesture of defeat preventing the clear success which is pledged to those who 'endure'. In such usage the virtue of *ṣabr* is a resolute 'No surrender'.

It would be fair to say that the word *ṣabr*, by its very ambiguity, epitomizes the issue between the 'patience' which redeems and transmutes an evil situation by so bearing it as to bear it away, and the 'endurance' which defies an adversary until he is defeated. Whether one allows that sort of contrast depends, no doubt, on how one reads the nature of the situation and the 'evil' of the adversary. The simple, present, point is to indicate the Quranic instinct as it is evident within the range of a single term and to note how that instinct characterizes theology too. For the campaign which required the tenacity was 'in the way of God' and so provides a referent for God in His willing, and rewarding of it.

Being so constituted, the Qur'ān does not afford its readers a theology operative, for example, in the pastoral care of communities lately won from idolatry, or in mental encounter with a world of sophisticated philosophy sceptical of worship. Nor does its ethos take definition from a ministry around which the poor and sick and troubled gather, drawn by its charisma. To ask for these, it will be said, is to be looking for the New Testament. Religious origins, we should be warned, are simply different.

Yet these 'referents' for God that are certainly present in actual histories – however elaborated by the theologians[9] – have to do with what a faith sees as finally worshippable. Our sense of God is the shape of our wonder, the yardstick of our values, the spur of our devotion and the criterion of our adoration. That is why it matters so intensely. Any 'prophet in his history' is in

[9] That they are so elaborated in the direction of absolute, even arbitrary, divine transcendence is familiar enough in Islamic theology. It is a matter of hope that the potential that is surely to be found in the Qur'ān to moderate that tradition may be more fully realized in contemporary thinking within Islam.

a vital way the clue to God in His heaven. What the word spoken authorizes, employs, develops, vindicates and bequeaths, becomes thereby an index to its great commissioning. All evaluation of Muḥammad must be a theological decision. We cannot reach it in the history alone. Nor can we reach it, the history apart.

We can be encouraged by the second of our final reflections. It is that, as Islam insists, the whole story was, is, 'on behalf of God' and tributary to Him. Islam has properly no institutional autonomy *mini dūni-Llāh*, as the Qur'ān's phrase has it, 'to the exclusion of God'. 'God's is the sovereignty of the heavens and earth' (2.107 *et al.*). Whatever may be the temptations of dogmatists, scribes, rulers, fanatics, interpreters, custodians of every order, they cannot rightly claim the custody of God, 'exalted be He'. The obligation to 'let God be God' is paramount. What matters, then, is that we should be sensitive to the deceptiveness of idolatry and how in devious ways it can penetrate our defences and beset us in disguise. The Qur'ān has an admirable vigilance in this behalf and it was never more needed than amid the pretensions and the delusions of contemporary man. Chapter 7 will explore this more fully. Meanwhile we shall be right in concluding that 'the stamp of greatness' on Muḥammad (68.4), with which we began, consists in that witness to the greatness of God of which *Allāhu akbar* is the confession: 'Greater is God'.

There is a nativity narrative about the son of 'Abdallāh and Āminah that, as a new-born babe emerging from his mother's womb, 'he fell confidently with two hands on to the ground, picked up a piece of earth and turned his face toward heaven'.[10]

[10] Quoted in Emil Esin, *Mecca the Blessed and Madinah the Radiant* (London, 1963), p. 66.

3

THE POLITICAL EQUATION

'No intelligent ruler arises to take me as his master. My time has come to die.' Regret and resignation in this saying of the old Confucius pointedly illustrate what, by this yearning, must be seen as the very virtue of Islam. The origins of the Muslim religion themselves brought to pass the intelligent rulership which took the faith as its master and when Muḥammad's time came to die the promise of the partnership was complete. Prophet and ruler were one personality. The alliance between the legacy of the one and the precedent of the other carried the unified enterprise of Islam, religious and political, to one of the most phenomenal expansions of recorded history, for range, speed and finality. Having summarized the historical narrative of the Prophet's Islam with the Hijrah as its fulcrum, we must turn to explore more reflectively the whole issue of power and religion. For it is there that vexing questions belong, whether for religious estimates in general or for the Christian conscience in particular.

The military dimensions of original Islam and its uninhibited embrace of the political arm are certainly crucial factors in deterring the Christian from a positive response to Muḥammad. For they are so sharply, and in some apologists, so confidently, alien to New Testament criteria, as to seem to warrant unreserved rejection by any thinking that has even remotely understood Gethsemane. Yet all such insistent quarrel with the politicization of Islam from the very beginning – a faith that has no catacombs – must be honestly alert both to the realities of the Meccan situation and the power dimension as everywhere inescapable.

Was it with such awareness in mind that Marshall Hodgson in his *The Venture of Islam* invoked the words of William Blake: 'I was then persuaded and remained confirmed that the voice of honest indignation is the voice of God'?[1] Blake, to be sure,

[1] Marshall Hodgson, *The Venture of Islam*, Chicago (1974). Words quoted are the heading of Book 1, vol. i.

went on: 'I cared not for consequences, but wrote' – which would tally with the Qur'ān's steady celebration of the pen (e.g. Surah 68 and 96.4). But, with Muḥammad, what was 'taught by the pen' was established by power, by power as 'the voice of indignation', indignation against idolatry with its counter-establishment, against recalcitrance and heedlessness, against sedition and treachery. Such indignation, it may be claimed, is only the other side of genuine conviction. The problem, however, in linking it with God, always assuming it to be 'honest', is that when it recruits the weapons of power it forfeits the very quality of truth and mercy which justified it in the first place. Do we then have to conclude, logically, with one Jewish observer of Christianity, that the 'only genuine answer to the powerful wicked forces of this world is . . . martyrdom'?[2] 'Martyrdom,' on the Muslim count, if martyrdom there had to be, would be faced, not in passive acceptance of the pains of hostility but in the active pursuit of counter hostility. There is here a wholly different understanding of *confessio fidei*, explicit in the very word *shahīd*, a martyr-witness.

Clearly here are very searching themes of concern between us and we must beware of stating them crudely or with polemic. They take us far too deeply into perplexity and paradox for trivial, dismissive or vituperative verdicts. It would be easy, as for some it is tempting, to reject Islam out of hand on this score. This would only be to superficialize an ultimate disavowal (if such it had to be) by ignoring the real essence of the issue and so facilitating from within Islam the sort of unfeeling and unprobing rejoinders that have been all too frequent in controversy. If we are really to invite others to face and know themselves, we cannot do so by ourselves ignoring the factors in their making. The narrative we have set down in chapter 2, from the Islamic historians themselves. Our task now is to estimate the elements in that situation objectively, to appreciate the logic those factors seem to teach and – only then – to assess the underlying dilemma. We shall perceive it to be a dilemma Islam believes itself confidently to have resolved. That resolution emerges, in our view, as only faintly and fitfully sensitive to its one-sidedness. For to study Islam, both in its history and its theology, is to encounter the most resolute and unperturbed of all faiths in placing trust, and finding pride, in political religion.

The most justly famous of Muslim analysts of faith and society, Ibn Khaldūn, in his *Prolegomena* to history, observes: 'If the

[2] David Flusser in the *Harvard Theological Review*, vol. 61 (1968), p. 127.

power of wrathfulness were no longer to exist in man, he would lose the ability to help the truth become victorious. Then there would no longer be *Jihād*, or glorification (i.e. acknowledged establishment) of the word of God.'[3] His discussion is a useful place of departure for our study. His controlling idea is that of *'aṣabiyyah*, or group solidarity. 'God sent no prophet except that he should be obeyed' (Surah 4.64). This 'obedience' cannot be merely a mental assent or even an ethical discipleship. It must constitute a bond of reciprocal prestige and protection, whereby believers and 'believed' (i.e. adherents and leader) are bound in one active and organized 'interest'. This communal 'protection' enables the prophet to 'succeed' and his 'success', in turn, 'assures' his 'people'. 'Peoplehood' itself – witness the Hijrah – stands in that adherence even, if need be, against the birth-or-tribe-peoplehoods it may have to challenge. Ibn Khaldūn quotes Surah 8.63: 'God brought them into organic unity' (a thing the Prophet alone could never have done) where the verse adds: 'O Prophet, your adequacy is God and those who follow you being believers' (8.64).

This organic, communal 'shape' which the prophetic message necessarily acquires by leave of God cannot be indifferent to the power and prestige necessary to its survival in a hostile world which is itself based on a tribal, commercial and/or 'municipal' establishment of interest and pride. Thus the 'wrathfulness that is one in God and in the service of God deserves praise'. Later, Ibn Khaldūn makes an interesting contrast with Christianity which, though it sends apostles to carry a message, does not, in his view, constitute a 'missionary religion' precisely because it had no *Jihād*.[4] For him, to be seriously 'a faith' religion must enjoy benefit of power as proof both of its own sincerity and of its competence to be effectively sincere. Verbal propagation is not only incomplete: it compromises, if not corroborated by the power-form of group solidarity politically operative. It is in this sense that Ibn Khaldūn is able to quote a tradition of Al-Bukhārī: 'There is no emigration after the conquest.' Naturally not. For Hijrah takes place out of a lack of 'establishment' but with a view to it. Once attained, the search for it ends in the advantage it bestows.

This instinct, it can be justly said, is implicit in the very term *islām* with its dual meaning of faith-espousal and power-

[3] Ibn Khaldūn, *Al Muqaddimah*, trans. by Franz Rosenthal (New York, 1958). vol i, p. 415.

[4] *Ibid.*, vol. i, p. 187 f. (repeated in vol. i, p. 322), p. 416, p. 256.

submission. It is also explicit in a transition of meaning and import within a single term *fitnah* as the Quranic story progresses. While the early Muslim believers are under duress and oppression *fitnah* means 'persecution'. When they become the dominant power *fitnah* means 'sedition'. This shift in the sense of the word indicates the whole logic of the developing situation. The term *fitnah* has both senses of the English word 'trial', meaning a 'tribulation' and so a 'test'. That which 'tries' one's mettle or loyalty is, thereby, an examination of one's worth. Thus the bitter Zaqqūm tree is a trying grief to the wrongdoers (33.14), and wealth and children, tempting the faithful away from costly commitment, are, likewise, *fitnah* to believers (64.15 etc); prosperity similarly (39:49). The faithful should not expect exemption from adversity (29.3) such as the persecution from which the emigrants escaped by their Hijrah (16.110, where the verb *futinū*, 'were persecuted' is used).

Clearly, 'persecution' is not a term that can be said of dominant majorities. Accordingly, when the term belongs to post-Hijrah success it denotes 'subversion' practised by a continuing opposition, now no longer able to oppress but still minded to harm and required, by Islamic power gains, to do so conspiratorially. Thus, in the famous rubric, 'subverting is a greater [evil] than *qatl*' ('slaying') (2.217). Surah 2.191 makes the same point and enjoins the duty to do battle (*qātilū*) 'until there is no more subversion'. That goal of victory achieved, the justification of force ceases, precisely in being demonstrated. It must not pass over into vindictiveness or excess. For its purpose is pacificatory in eliminating and disarming opposition. The politically submissive society vindicates both the message and the policy of the successful faith.

It is this forthright logic of the Qur'ān which makes it strictly inaccurate to say with Aḥmad Shawqī, one of the foremost men of letters in modern Egypt:

> They [detractors] say you [Muḥammad] have raided and God's apostles were never sent to destroy souls, they never came to shed blood. This is but ignorance, falsification and sophistry. For you conquered by the word before conquering by the sword.'[5]

[5] Aḥmad Shawqī, *Al-Shawqiyyāt* (Cairo, 1948), vol i. p. 242. Shawqī (1868–1932) was a prolific writer. The passage here cited is an example of how polemic obscures or distorts what is essentially at issue. Shawqī's proper concern is to rebut calumny (because post-Hijrah violence was, in his view, legitimate). This causes him to miss the fact that 'conquering

Had the verbal 'conquest' sufficed would there have been need for Hijrah and its sequel? Muḥammad did, indeed, conquer by the word, but only a limited number of devoted followers whom an entrenched Quraishī prestige-complex in Mecca sharply persecuted. Hence, in turn, as Muḥammad saw it, the urgent need to ensure the survival and then the triumph of his prophetic word-following by the more final and complete conquest of the structure that had resisted his word. In rightly making the two a temporal sequence, Aḥmad Shawqī cannot properly imply that the preaching dimension of the prophetic *Sīrah* had no mind for the power dimension. On the contrary, it allowed and sought it as the appropriate development from its own experience of enmity and rejection. One cannot well make the mere fact of sequence an apologia. It is the very nub of the problem. Can 'word' and 'sword' co-operate? That the one is prior, in time, in Islam is not at all in doubt, or that the other is justified in sequence. The underlying burden, for the observer from outside, is whether they *can* belong together.

That question cannot be honestly broached if we do not reckon realistically with what Muḥammad faced. 'Equation', as we used it in this chapter heading, might be defined as the relation between variables. The 'variables' of pre-Islamic Mecca and the Hijāz are in strong contrast, say, with those of Jesus in Roman Palestine. It is easy to take the point Malachi Martin makes in *The Encounter*: 'No religion relying purely and simply on spiritual principles, eschewing force of arms, and refusing to be inserted in a living political structure could have succeeded in the 7th century A.D.'[6] One should add: '. . . in western Arabia'.

There are several factors that need to be carefully explored here – the patterns of Arab society, the power-structure at Mecca, the traditions of violent feud and family 'honour', the growth of camel nomadism, the commercial interests, and the violent precedents of contemporary memory. Many of these are reflected, for the perceptive reader, in the Qur'ān itself. To review them even briefly is a large task. But it is one we must shoulder if the Islamic case for the true legitimacy of power is to be fully taken. Short of so taking it, we cannot formulate effectively or honestly the Christian, or any other, critique.

The point of departure for any such review must be the fact

by the word' was numerically partial and, therefore, required the implementation which the Hijrah inaugurated, in political and military form. No other conclusion is possible from the historical development itself as given in the Qur'ān.

[6] Malachi Martin, *The Encounter* (London, 1969), p. 152.

that the precincts of the Kaʿbah at Mecca were a *ḥaram* sanctuary, a sacred shrine protected by a 'truce-territory' which ensured safe access for the vital purpose of pilgrimage. The area of ground, or the span of time, in which strife was taboo, varied in scope from the immediate setting where sanctity was inviolate to whatever length of place or time the custodial authority could enforce and secure. This depended, in turn, on the prestige of the shrine, while the prestige served to buttress the protection which guarded it. Clearly, as we have seen in chapter 2, Muḥammad's message posed an immediate threat to this *ḥaram* status and to the pilgrimage tradition and immunity which it enjoyed and on which it verbally relied.

Given the attitudes of tribal conflict and competition, such guardianship was crucial. It had to be alert and vigilant for any threat, verbal or material, which might weaken or destroy it. The *ḥaram*, in Mecca's case, was bound up with the veneration, or worship perhaps, of the sacred stone the Kaʿbah housed, and with circumambulation as the form of veneration. Aspects of the ritual custody were shared among the Quraish, such as the veiling of the shrine, the watering of pilgrims and their feeding, the keeping of banners and the rest.[7]

Seen against this background the Hijrah emerges as the first step towards the establishment, in Yathrib, of an alternative *ḥaram*, or focal point of religious allegiance, with the first 'mosque', and a similar, if still potential, capacity to 'ensure' its 'believers'. To be sure the new 'base' was not itself to be a shrine for pilgrimage nor, of course, was its significance grounded in idolatrous tradition. Rather, it served to enable, in the event, the recovery for monotheistic worship and Muslim pilgrimage of the original Meccan *ḥaram*. By holding in steady view after the Hijrah the ultimate possession of Mecca, Muḥammad in effect joined together the two *ḥaramain*. Thus the whole meaning of the Hijrah and its sequel becomes evident by the light of the *ḥaram* theme.

This *ḥaram* power-based situation, religiously sanctioned and religiously necessitated, was made all the more crucial by commercial considerations. Shrines are also markets. It may

[7] See R. B. Serjeant, 'The Sacred Enclave in Arabia', in *Mélanges Taha Hussein* (Cairo, 1962), pp. 41–58. Serjeant is arguing from examples of the *Ḥuṭah*, or sacred enclosure, of the kind he investigated in the Ḥaḍramaut. He is confident, where others might not be, that the example can be taken as dependable for Mecca in Muḥammad's day. His discussion is purely academic, with an insistence that it 'has to do with patterns of action and not with questions of revelation and inspiration' (p. 47).

even be that Friday was the day of congregational prayer because Thursday was the customary day of trading fairs.[8] Such conjecture apart, markets could certainly profit by, and profit in, sacred months and sacred territory. A trading understanding in the tribal world could even promote a sort of worship pluralism by having tribal deities co-operate in the protection, with their symbols sharing a common shrine. At all events, the 'convoying', or 'composing' of the Quraish, referred to in Surah 106, the organizing of their caravans, can well be seen as an extension, in commercial form, of the guaranteed passage enjoyed in pilgrimage, only that it was 'secured' by pledge and promise. Plainly the cult and commerce of Quraishī Mecca interacted, and since both were grounded in power-interest a preacher's threat to either could hardly avoid being power involved, later if not earlier.

There is ample evidence of the increasing commercial prowess of Mecca in the period immediately before Muḥammad's mission. Their defeat of Abraha, attacking from the south in A.D. 570, enhanced the position of the Quraish. Hāshim, the Prophet's great-grandfather, had been the moving spirit in a wide extension of Mecca's access to Syrian and other markets, by safe conducts he was able to negotiate from Byzantium, Ethiopia and Persia. Within the Hijāz and among the tribes he seems to have been successful also in developing a popular stake in the trade encouraged by security pacts (the *īlāf* of Surah 106) which 'bought off' marauders but also 'interested' them in the profits that might accrue from non-molestation. There is a revealing hint in Surah 9:28 that loss of trade might be involved in the denial of access, by Islam, to the sacred house. Though the passage belongs to a late date in the evolution of events after the Hijrah, it seems fair indication of how mercantile factors married with cultic ones in the Meccan situation prior to Islam. In its success, of course, Islamic power came to provide the same trading 'umbrella' with vastly more reach and authority. Surah 2.198 makes it clear that Muslim pilgrimage would not preclude trade at the accompanying fairs. *Allāhu akbar* spells a far more resounding guarantee of pilgrim/merchant immunity for worship/trade than any antecedent system of pagan *ḥaram* prestige. But, in the confrontation we are studying, this was in no way yet

[8] The suggestion is developed by S. D. Goitein in *The Muslim World*, vol. 49, no. 3 (July, 1959), pp. 183–95; 'The Origin and Nature of Muslim Friday Worship'.

apparent. Nor, as Islam would insist, could it have been so without Muslim energies physically asserted.

What must not be overlooked in this analysis is the vital role of wells and oases and other natural items of well-being. Security both for cult and market belonged with these larger elements in social viability in a generally precarious context. The very prosperity of Mecca, and of other 'town' communities, fed the security issue on which it turned. There is evidence that after the time of Hāshim, inheriting but not emulating his 'common interest' approach to tribal/commercial matters, the ruling group in Mecca became more monopolistic in their policy and rapacious in their ideas. This may explain the economic threat, as well as the religious challenge, which they sensed in Muḥammad's mission with its protest against excessive wealth and usurious exploitation of the poor. If, subsequent to his success, Islamic ties and *Zakāt*, or alms, came to replace the sort of tribal and cash-nexus by which the Quraish flourished in their hegemony, that would only confirm, in retrospect, the sense of corporate risk which establishment hearers feared in and from his preaching. What cannot be in doubt, in broad perspective if not in precise detail, is that the confrontation could hardly have been confined to the realm of ideas, assent to belief, or merely cultic loyalties as such. Some would question whether it was substantially in these realms at all. There are always historians in modern times who want to put all things under the feet of economic forces.

There are some social historians who suggest that what was happening in Mecca in the period of Muḥammad's youth constituted a slow but perceptible change from a society based on clan relationship to one in which urban organization tended towards a sort of embryonic statehood. By the *īlāf* or 'client adhesion' (if we may so speak) the Quraish were consolidating a nucleus of identity in which 'interest' and 'covenant' infiltrated, or even superseded, blood relation. This may have tended to a certain unification of worships and deities insofar as tribalism had meant plurality of gods and the new forms of obligation implied a unified 'divine' protection. If so, Islam was certainly to provide the stimulus and the vital secret for such *Tauḥīd*. That fact is in no way diminished but becomes more intelligible *if* we can understand the urge to monotheism in the context of the earlier search. It is impossible to say whether, or how far, these trends help to explain the *Ḥanīf* tradition which has so long intrigued and puzzled historians. But certainly when Islam became 'established' it afforded just that quality of authority – political, judicial, and fiscal – for which the situation had been preparing, despite its cultic habits. As Eric R. Wolf observes: 'Muḥammad accomplished for the Meccan traders that which they could not accomplish themselves – the organization of state-power.'[9]

To appreciate this claim a glance is necessary at the instincts of tribal feud and blood relationship by which Arab society understood itself, and the concept of 'manliness' (*murū'ah*) with which it served them. It was very much a case of 'the strong man armed keeping his palace', or, more likely, his tent and his water. Pre-Islamic poetry is full of this praise, sometimes reluctant, sometimes exuberant, of the virtue of manly self-defence and blood-revenge. Zuhair, for example, in one of the *Mu'allaqāt* declares:

> Who holds not his foe away from his cistern with sword and spear
> It is broken and spoiled.
> Who uses not roughness, him shall men wrong.

The same singer conveys the vigilance of suspicion:

> He climbs the sandy hillock of Thalbut and searches its deserted top, fearing that an enemy may be lurking behind the guide-stones.

while another warns:

> Too kind a man may be with fools
> And move them but to flout him more.
> Mischief oft may bring thee peace
> Where mildness works not folly's cure.[10]

Such fighting strength was not only prudent; it was noble. *Murū'ah* requires it not simply as protection but as glory. The term has kinship with the Latin *virtus* as that quality of 'manliness' (the root derivation is parallel) by which the self is proved. Refusal to retaliate and avenge is not only craven but disloyal. Family bonds must be honoured, beyond a death incurred, by a death inflicted and one's own death risked. Otherwise responsibility itself is compromised and betrayed. It seems clear that this readiness for life-sacrifice, whether meted out or undertaken, passes over into Islam. The usage *aslama nafsahu* 'he gave up himself in surrender', taking his life in his hands, occurs in pre-

[9] Eric R. Wolf, 'The Social Organisation of Mecca and the Origins of Islam', in *Southwestern Journal of Anthropology*, vii (1951), p. 356.

[10] In C. J. Lyall, *Translations of Ancient Arabian Poetry* (London, 1930), Couplets 53, 27 and (Zuhair) and *Al-Ḥamāsah*, Lyall, p. 5.

Islamic poetry, and it is possible to argue that this *islām* within *murū'ah* is closely akin to that sacrifice of self and defiance of death which characterized Muslim allegiance from the start and which lay behind the notion of *Jihād*.[11]

The vital difference, wrought by Islam, was that the *murū'ah* of the days of the *Jāhiliyyah*, or 'Ignorance', as the Muslim historians call them, passed from blood- and kin-relationship into the *élan* of faith-based unity within a single worship and under a single command. Blood revenge gave way to faith-militancy *fī Sabīli Llāh*, 'in the way of God', without losing the concepts of sacrificial 'honour' long tested in the old order. The death-defiance of the old pagan order was now consecrated to the service of God, and Muslim history gives ample evidence of its quality.

It was not merely that a tradition inherently combative was inherited. It was radically transformed by the heir. The new community of faith overrode the blood-claims, reduced their incidence by its unification of worship, and tempered the old *murū'ah* esteem by the new criterion of *taqwā* and piety. 'The noblest of you with God (in God's reckoning] are the most devout' (49.13). Thus Islam had the best of both worlds in that it conserved the will to sacrifice and to scorn death but enlisted it for a cause that could curb its excesses and discipline its ways. Some would claim that human belligerence is better handled in these terms than by visionary ideals of meekness and non-resistance – ideals which, anyway, could have had no purchase on seventh-century Arab society.

Moreover, this Islamic pattern of taming by recruitment had the further advantage of taking up and extending existing trends towards the control of blood revenge which arose from the commercial factors we have reviewed. These were leading to a preference for money payment and arbitration wherever kinship enmities threatened the network of trade interests and the 'client' relationships which sustained them. Muḥammad's mission certainly set faith above kin – witness the Hijrah, and his authority, when 'established', overcame blood-claims by the common reality of community and cut off their entail down the generations by the new fact of corporate *Jihād* both within and beyond Arabia. According to Surah 2.178–9, private retaliation, the *lex talionis*, is still legitimate, forgiveness or compounding for money are better, and revenge, if exacted, must be strictly

[11] See Bravmann, 'Spiritual Background of Early Islam and the History of Its Principal Concepts', in *Muséon*, lxiv (1951), pp. 318–56.

limited. There follows the enigmatic comment: 'In retaliation there is life for you,' which *may* mean that there is security because it obtains, deters aggression, and prohibits wild vengeance, but *may* also mean that, for 'men of understanding', the saving of life will always be paramount by the forgoing of an admitted right, whereas an absolute veto would be an impossible ideal and a poor tactic.

These observations on the context of Muḥammad's career as Prophet and ruler, brief and tentative as some of them must be, underline the need to relate our categories of judgement to the actual circumstances within which he was born and through which he had to act. Realism may not be pleaded to elude issues. But issues are not well broached unrealistically. The evident context of force and power and polity in which Islam originated cannot be gainsaid. All that we have noted in the Meccan scene, the *ḥaram* tradition, and the Arab psychology, received further accentuation from the precedents of the surrounding world. In one of its rare notices of external history the Qur'ān comments (in Surah 30.2–3) on the continuing conflict between Persia and the Greeks. The years 603 to 628 saw the last great war between the two empires, both of them critically weakened by their hostilities, and in 629 the restoration of the true Cross (as it was believed) to Jerusalem was taken to symbolize the triumph of the 'Christian' over the Zoroastrian power.

The rivalry of Persia and Byzantium contributed, indirectly, to the commercial opportunities of Mecca. But it also involved Arab mercenaries recruited from the time of Justinian (A.D. 527–565) who created the client state of the Ghassānids north of the Hijāz, to be countered by the Persians in the client state of the Lakhmids in the north-east of the peninsula. These military buffer 'states' made war conditions familiar on the adjacent 'nomad' areas. To the south were the struggles and vendettas of Ethiopians, Himyarites and the Jewish leader Abū Nuwās, whose wars and atrocities echoed through the Hijāz while Mecca itself stayed profitably immune from Ethiopian occupation and Byzantine political control. There is little doubt that contemporary history played a formative role in the Prophet's mind.

The year of his birth traditionally coincides with Abraha's expedition against Mecca which is the theme of Surah 105. Abraha's prestige and resources were such that the Meccans could hardly fail to celebrate his confusion as 'a famous victory'. In Surah 85.4: 'Slain were the men of the *ukhdūd* [trench], the fire of fiery fuel' is generally taken to refer to the massacre of Christians in Najrān by the Jewish ruler, Abū Nuwās – surely unique in history as a Jewish holocaust-maker. It is recorded that a friend of Muḥammad's grandfather, 'Abd al-Muṭṭalib, took part in an expedition to avenge the massacre. It may be that the event helped to generate a repudiation of a unilaterally Jewish orientation of the supreme deity, since his 'protégés' had behaved so 'normally'. At all events the memory horizon of the youthful Muḥammad had much cause to be aware of Christian disunity, of Jewish 'questionability' and of religious strife in general. Furthermore, Mecca, his birthplace, and the Quraish, his community, had contrived to stay secure from these depredations and even to prosper despite them.[12]

Did Muḥammad himself ever play a soldier's part in the pre-inspiration period? It is hard to say. There is a tradition, revived by recent historians, of his sharing in a local Arab conflict known as the Fijār war. 'I remember being present with my uncles . . . I discharged arrows at the enemy.' Zakaria Bashier, who cites the passage, observes: 'These varied experiences [in travel] provided material for the ponderings of his nature-loving heart and supplied musings for his active mind.'[13] Among them may well have been the memorable storm in 605, when the Prophet was fifteen, which battered the Ka'bah itself and brought shipwrecked Byzantine sailors into Jiddah where they were allowed to sell what, Crusoe-like, they had salvaged from their wreck.[14] Muḥammad's mentors were certainly far travellers. According to the historian, Al-Ya'qūbī, Hāshim died in Gaza where, to this day, a mosque bears his name. 'Abd al-Muṭṭalib died in the Yemen and Naufal, a great uncle, died in Iraq. The journeys and trade negotiations in which the mature Muḥammad was certainly involved must have widened his awareness of the world and its warfares, while the Qur'ān bears ample witness to his acute, and often wistful, sad, consciousness of remoter history, traced in ruins and decay.

On every count, then, it seems fair to conclude that Muḥammad's *Sitz im Leben* was such as to teach and require a lively sense of the power-equation in human affairs and scarcely to generate the sort of power-repudiation by which faith inauguration proceeded elsewhere. This is not at all to mean that the

[12] See Ibrahim Amin Ghali in *L'Orient et Les Juifs* (70 632) (Paris, 1970), p. 229. Cf. C. V. Gheorgiou, *La Vie de Mahomet* (Paris, 1962), p. 53.

[13] Zakaria Bashier, *The Meccan Crucible* (London, 1978), p. 53. The author is a Sudanese Muslim.

[14] See Muhammad Hamidullah, 'Les Rapports Economico Diplomatiques de la Mecque Pre Islamique', in *Mélanges Louis Massignon* (Damascus, 1957), pp. 293–311.

original message of the Prophet was not, essentially, a religious call and a faith about peace. On the contrary, there were those thirteen years of steady, even heroic, reliance upon the word alone. It *is* to say that as and when that venture of, and for, faith, seemed demonstrably to have failed to achieve adequate success in *that* dimension, the criteria of action then ripe for decision would be those instinctive to the historical and social context that obtained. If we quote here the verdict of Fazlur Rahman, it is to listen also to the consensus of the time and place of Muslim genesis as we have now reviewed it.

> Muḥammad never lost the hope of success nor, indeed, the dire and stark realization that he was duty-bound to succeed. . . . It is part of the Quranic doctrine that simply to deliver the message, to suffer frustration, and not to succeed, is immature spirituality.[15]

There is, of course, a deep issue here as to the understanding of 'immature' and 'spiritual'. Decision may well turn upon prophetic precedent, and precedent itself is subject for selection and debate. We cannot assess the political equation in Muḥammad's faith without considering this larger 'quarrel' within prophecy before him. It is evident that the Qur'ān uncomplicatedly assumes the activist 'patriarchs' to be the true exponents of prophetic action. Moses, David, Abraham the iconoclast, Noah the flood-rider – these are the precedent-makers as paragons of success and vindication. The Muslim Scripture is completely silent about the patient servants of the Word, about Amos, Hosea, Isaiah and, supremely, Jeremiah who, for the sake of the integrity of the Word itself abjure power and believe with passionate devotion that it is truer to 'fail' worthily than to succeed unworthily. It has always been a mystery – and to Christians a pain – that the Qur'ān should be so oblivious of the greatest levels of Hebraic prophecy as the Bible knows them. But at least that silence is congruent with Islamic norms. To have involved the Jeremiahs and the suffering servants of the Biblical tradition would have been to entertain an intolerable interrogation of Muslim assumption and assurance.

It is important to understand the powerlessness of these ultimate 'prophets' for what it was and means. Perhaps it can be explored by reference to a Quranic passage itself:

> It is not right for a mortal man to whom God gives the Book and the authority and the prophethood then to say to people:

[15] Fazlur Rahman, *Islam* (London, 1961), p. 15.

> 'Be my servants instead of God's servants.' Rather: 'Be spiritually the Lord's [*kūnū rabbāniyyīn*], you who have studied and taught the Book.' He [God] would not order you to take angels and prophets as lords. (3.79–80)

Islam is categorical that the final loyalty is to God alone. Here in this passage is a clear hint that prophetic ministry itself, precisely because it is 'on behalf of God', can, for that very reason, be tempted to usurp what is God's. Such temptation can hardly attach to faithful deliverance of the message, to what the Qur'ān calls *al-balāgh*, 'communication'. It *can* attach very sharply to the message that undertakes politicization, inasmuch as the power-equation both requires and justifies self-interest and enmity, by which the message incurs potential compromise, being sullied and obscured.

It was for this reason that in the Biblical tradition of Amos, Hosea, Isaiah and Jeremiah, the divine *balāgh* neither invokes nor covets political sanction. It prefers, if need be, to suffer consequences rather than repel them. It may well address and rebuke the state and stand loyally in courts of power with the Word, but it does not ally with them so that its meaning is blunted and its claim subjected to negotiation. Of course it has business with the political order. How could it fail to have? It may even be accused of treason to it, as was Jeremiah. But to retain liberty of witness or of accusation it must keep its spiritual independence.

Hence the quality of patience and suffering which inevitably emerges from the mission of the greatest of the prophets, the travail so tellingly embodied in the figure of 'the suffering servant', by whose fidelity through pain, society is 'healed'. Just because prophecy must preserve its freedom of utterance to, and against, society and the state, in a way that, identified with either's vested interests, it could never do, its experience must be hazardous and, by necessary vocation, insecure. So long as the prophet stays only a preacher and a warner, his personal fortunes will be no better than the fortune of his words, and, being only and always their servant, he wills to have it so. Adversity, then, must be incurred. We have seen this dimension plainly in the pre-Hijrah experience of Muḥammad himself. What the Biblical precedents, at their deepest, seem to say to that situation is that there are no short-cuts to ease the calling.

So at least it was with Jeremiah, confronted with an establishment which rejected his warnings. Prophecy with him, we may say, becomes autobiographical, in the sense that everything is bound up with his personal endurance. The message brings him nothing but pain and antagonism. 'The word of the Lord is made a reproach unto me,' he cries (Jer. 20.8). But the seed of 'the new covenant' is sown in that experience, in that an individual's fidelity is divinely valued within a nation's apostacy. Further, the precedent emerges from which the New Testament proceeds in its awareness of Messianic redemption. For ultimately the costly patience of such prophets is there understood to be one with the gentle uncompulsiveness of God Himself. Were God to arm the prophets with force or save them by arbitrary vindication, He would have changed the ground of truth's approach. Thus prophetic defencelessness is the corollary of the divine will to have from humanity a response to righteousness grounded only in men's love of it, and not in sanctions or consequences they may incur at the Prophet's own hand if they reject it. The suffering of the prophets in that cause is no more, no less, than their partnership with divine grace in its *lā ikrāha* (Surah 2.256) or non-compulsion.

It is by such criteria that the Christian is minded to ponder the Quranic situation and Muḥammad's power-involvement – instinctively so minded. Whether the instinct is appropriate and the criteria apposite we have still to ask. Our earlier review could be said to have called them into question for their impracticality. But it is certainly right and necessary to outline them honestly if consideration is to be radical. No evasion of the contrast here could be loyal either to Christian conscience or Islamic realism. Before moving to this final matter, it is well to show how the Islamic view of Jesus is caught up in the issue.

For 'Īsā (Jesus), in the Qur'ān, while a faithful teacher and witness and warner to his people, is not externally 'successful'. Antagonism to him culminates in a direct threat to his life. Accordingly, God 'rescues' him by rapture into heaven, thus denying his foes their purpose and vindicating His faithful servant from their calumny and their schemes. Some modern, indeed also medieval, Muslim writers see in this 'rescue' a symbol of Jesus' lesser status, in that, given Roman imperial power in the way, it was not his destiny to achieve Muḥammadan success in political terms. Muḥammad's more 'effective' destiny is further seen as indicating his 'finality' as 'the seal of the prophets'. Jesus' lesser – albeit highly honoured – standing is explained by his not enjoying the sanction of external vindication, making no triumphal entry into a capitulating Mecca.

But, by the same token, his fidelity with the *balāgh* must not be left inconclusively unrecognized, nor his adversaries, for all their political immunity, essentially on top. Jesus' divine rapture to heaven 'disconcerts' and frustrates them totally and fittingly rewards the faithful servant of the Word. This Quranic vindication of Jesus is thus of one piece with the general picture of prophetic 'ideology' dear to Islam. The 'power and wisdom' of God – just the very terms Paul uses to celebrate the Cross itself – are identified in Quranic rescue from it. The fact that, by this strategy, the evil that wills to crucify is not redeemed but only thwarted, does not weigh in Quranic criteria. The immediate point, however, is simply the manner in which the Qur'ān's view of the climax, in rescue, of Jesus' mission conforms with, and so confirms, the pattern of prophetic vocation which Muḥammad completes and perfects. For Muslim thinkers, Jesus' being non-political is a privation necessitated by Roman power not the ultimate form of prophetic destiny. For the same reason, we may note in passing, it is no part of a divine sonship or identity with the mind of God.

Islam, then, has this characteristic and assured reliance on the inter-dependence of word and arms, of faith and power. It has a clear sense of the indispensability of political and military means to religious ends. Thus Surah 22.40, in reference to the wrongs the faithful suffer, legitimatizes *qatl*, 'killing', and adds, further, that '. . . had not God defended people through their self-defence, cloisters and churches, synagogues and mosques, where the Name of God is cherished in recital, would have been destroyed.'

That logic seems obvious to the Muslim mind. For, as Aḥmad Shawqī, earlier quoted, observes about the 'rescue' of Jesus, 'evil will stop at nothing,' and 'had it not been for the subsequent use of the sword Christianity too would have remained the religion of the oppressed and the persecuted'.[16] Islam is naturally concerned – and with much historical justice – to associate others with its own realism about force.

But, in turn, we cannot exempt Islam from others when we reverse the picture and ponder what the force-factor does to the faith it 'secures'. For here, too, the involvements are reciprocal. Nor is the Qur'ān unalert to them. Force, when successful, will not only ensure survival: it will generate hypocrisy. The 'security' it may physically provide, it may spiritually undermine. Successful enterprises attract time-servers. The power that sanctions truth inspires deception. The force that dispels the fears of disciples arouses the fears of outsiders and may indirectly

[16] Aḥmad Shawqī, *Al-Shawqiyyāt* (see note 5 above').

dispose them to conform. Then something irreparable goes out of the quality of religious allegiance. The *munāfiqūn* emerge or, rather, lurk behind their façade of insincere conformity. These are the 'hypocrites'. Their *nifāq*, 'hypocrisy,' figures prominently in the post-Hijrah Qur'ān. The root verb is quite frequent. A whole Surah, 63, is named after them. It is hard to know how far they were an organized political opposition and how far a hidden moral menace. But it is clear that theirs was a response of subterfuge to the external progress of Muḥammad's cause. That cause, in reaction, had to become increasingly vigilant about their dissembling and bad faith. Increasing vigilance only generated a keener countering subtlety. Such is the descending spiral of unworthiness to which religion with the power-equation is prone. The fact of it is not to say that, therefore, only perpetual minority status and persecution make for sincerity or that faith is only wholesome in catacombs. But the paradox of such an impossible conclusion must be allowed to curb the blithe assurance that all is well when the sanction-makers flourish.

It is salutary here to recall the basic distinction the Qur'ān itself makes between the two meanings of *islām*. The hope is that they can be properly combined. But they *are* distinct. The one is a personal, religious, 'submission' to God: the other is a visible, political 'submission' to Islam. In the great century of Islamic expansion after the Prophet's death what the world accepted was not only a faith but a rule, not simply a creed but an empire. This, of course, is the right correction of the false formulation, so long current in the West, that 'Islam was spread by the sword'. The fact was a deep amalgam of faith and conquest, within which it was always proper to apply the Qur'ān's concern at an earlier point, as recorded in a fascinating passage in Surah 49.14. Certain bedouin came to Muḥammad and said: 'We have believed [*āmannā*]. He was directed to tell them: 'You have not believed. Say rather: "We have submitted" [*aslamnā* – the verb that yields the noun *islām*]. For faith has not entered your hearts.' Clearly there could be a form of outward *islām* which was not *īmān*, or faith. Given sincerity and docility, faith could well be taught and enter the heart. But only then would a mere outward *islām* be righted. In v. 17 of the same Surah is a pointed reference to the idea of these new *muslimūn* 'surrenderers' that they have conferred a favour on Muḥammad by doing so.

It can, of course, be claimed that detecting such prudential adherence is more than half the battle. But the problem remains. To please the power-wielders is no small factor in human affairs. The question is how we see it in the things of God. Islam at least has the realism of meeting the issue head-on. It may be that the non-Muslim serves it better by actually withholding an assent, lest Muslim confidence should mean that 'the question not be put'.

But there is something else, also within Islamic experience, which needs to be noted before we can conclude this area of our response to what Muslims ask of us. The question of power and religion soon involves controversy over the forms the ordering takes where its legitimacy has been assumed. Indeed, all the more so for the assumption. Thus the theme we are studying is not confined to Muḥammad's own career. Islamic history very soon became entangled in contention over the inheritors of power. The Shīʿah divergence belongs here, and with it the nature of Caliphate and Imamate, and the problem of how ongoing religious truth and ongoing political authority were to keep the original Muḥammadan 'harmony'. The Ummayyads, for example, were said to have divorced government from true religion. Dr Muḥsin Mahdi, of Harvard University, argues that the Damascus régime after ʿAlī, 'secularised' the true 'city-state' of Medina and disfigured the idealism and consensus of pristine Islam, while the ʿAbbasids in Baghdad went even further by creating an oriental theocracy.[17]

Such deplorings – Shīʿah, Khārijite, Wahhābī, or other – of actual Muslim governance, in the name of true Islamic statehood are familiar enough throughout the history. In modern times, they have been disturbingly in the conflict of political debate, of state-making, as in Pakistan, and of constitution writing. The necessity of the Islamic state is one thing, its definition is another. In this sense the power-sanction is a 'solution' which requires solution, an answer which proliferates with questions. The questions lead us again into criteria which an original confidence had ignored or assumed. The power dimension is then seen to be no answer in itself but something beset with disqualifications which, in the end, take us back into scepticism about what we may perhaps awkwardly call the political perfectibility of man. It is to the credit, as also to the discomfiture, of Islam at the turn of its new, fifteenth century, that it has been in such travail about nationality and nationalism, independence and liberty, power and justice, statehood and revolution – in a word, about 'Islamicity.' Perhaps it is precisely in this travail that the limits of the politicization of religion can best be explored and any

[17] Muḥsin Mahdī, in J. Kitagawa (ed.), *Modern Trends in World Religions* (Chicago, 1959), pp. 11–13.

Christian response about Muḥammad saved from abstraction or polemic or controversy.

In that connection it is important not to overlook Muslim minorities in the contemporary world who are without benefit of statehood. Indian Islam has for several decades shown a considerable resilience, though also in other quarters a profound disquiet, at the forfeiture of status and political security that has resulted from partition. The very existence of Pakistan seemed to set a grim interrogation mark over the very survival of a true Islam in conditions other than those which Pakistani Islam had virtually ensured within frontiers of Islamic dominance. It could be that this very fact will generate new criteria of Islamicity which will abandon, even confidently dismiss, the power reliance. One such mind is Ḥasan al 'Askarī, who wrote in 1971:

> My deep conviction is that the Prophet of Islam did not create a state. Consequently, the controversy between Sunnī and Shī'ah over the question of knowing who should succeed the Prophet is without foundation. It follows, too, that the principles having to do with the Caliphate and the Imamate are not Quranic. I believe that Islam can survive without political power, without a state.

After grounding his case in eschatology he continues:

> What I am suggesting is strictly a personal view. It emerges from the sad testing ground of the conflict between faith and history. Perhaps Islam will have to disappear as a historical and political institution, as a communal structure. Only then will the true Muslim be able to appear.[18]

A personal view indeed! And a brave one, too, in that in the context he speaks of 'occasion for Christians to come to the help of their Muslim brothers'.

Outside the minority communities, and the Indian ethos, there are, however, few Muslims ready to contemplate such abnegation of the past and the long confidence about the legitimacy, the authenticity, in some form, of the power dimension in faith, creed and cult. The Hijrah and its sequel would seem to leave us little room to doubt that this was the confidence and decision of Muḥammad, his unquestioned legacy to his people. So how we should conclude the issue?

Could it be that Islam stands among religions as the most

[18] Hasan al–'Askarī in *Verse et Controverse: Les Musulmans* (Paris, 1971), pp. 132–3 (my translation).

forthright witness to the reality of power as a 'friend' that cannot be dismissed, but that the Christian must never forsake the contrasted witness of Gethsemane and the New Testament that it is an 'enemy' who must always be distrusted?

As we have seen in chapter 2, it will not do to formulate the issue of Muḥammad as ruler in terms of 'sincerity', as Christian, or secular, assessments have often done, alleging a declension in prophetic integrity, a lapse into temptation. It is truer to see the whole pre- and post-Hijrah story as a single unity of commitment to a mission, received as from God, the means to which developed from word to action, from preaching to power, by an inner logic that the 'divine' must necessarily 'succeed' – a logic which was always there, if only latent. It was circumstances, as we have argued, rather than deterioration, which brought it out into the open.

But not to question 'sincerity' is to be left squarely with the issue. To disallow a contrary verdict about 'character' is to incur more heavily a verdict about decision. This is the reason why Margoliouth-style denigration is in the end diversionary.[19] We have to take account of the actual Meccan situation with its inevitable power/prestige complex, its built-in competitiveness, once a monotheist of Muḥammad's calibre arose within it. This, in the foregoing, we have honestly sought to do. There can be no doubt that the Prophet's militancy ensured his cause, and ensured its compromise.

In the first phase of the *Riddah*, or reversion to pagan loyalties, which critically followed Muḥammad's death, Qurra ibn Hubayrah al-Qushayrī wrote to Amr ibn al-'Āṣ, Abū Bakr's envoy:

> You people of Quraish lived securely in your *Ḥaram* and people [i.e. the tribes] were in security with you. Then there appeared a man from among you and announced what you heard [i.e. the call to Islam]. When these tidings reached us we did not dislike them. We said 'A man from Muḍar is to lead the people.' This man has now died . . . Therefore, go back to your *Ḥaram* and live there in security. If you do not do as I say I am ready to meet you [in fight] wherever you fix the place.[20]

[19] David S. Margoliouth, *Mohammed and the Rise of Islam* (London, 1906), is often cited as exemplifying an animus against Islam which has sharply provoked the susceptibilities of Muslims.

[20] Quoted from M. L. Kister, 'Some Reports concerning Mecca from Jāhiliyyah to Islam', in *Journal of the Economic and Social History of the Orient* (London, 1972), pp. 66–67.

An obscure text – but how revealing. A *de facto islām* quickly and readily reverting to the *status quo ante*. The need for submission was at an end with the demise of this 'man from Muḍar'. Mecca should revert to its previous relationships. All the zeal and vigour of Abū Bakr were necessary to cut off this incipient non-*islām* and secure the future of the faith, by the imposition of his power. Islam survived the crisis. There were endless instances of the same situation in the earlier sequences of Muḥammad's *Sīrah* and the later history of Islam. Had it not been for what Ibn Khaldūn calls 'praiseworthy wrathfulness' the faith would have succumbed. Surah 22.40 is approved.

But Al-Qushayrī's message, in its simple frankness, houses the counterparting problem. The man is a pragmatist not a believer, a conformist while it serves. Power-wielders may reply that, regrettable as this is, the preachers and pundits can always care for it and resolve it, behind the shield the wielders hold, whereas prophets or evangelists only could hardly avail if left defenceless. Power, even if an 'enemy', must still be loved. We must opt for a both/and, not an either/or.

Even so, there is a further question. Faiths may well discover this compromising necessity in their entail. Is it well that it should be hallowed in their origin? For, if the friend/enemy of power has to be conceded, it will always need most urgently the disqualifying disavowal, the *lā ikrāha* ('let there be no compulsion') of the Qur'ān (2.256), the 'put up thy sword' of Gethsemane. To the Christian mind, nurtured by Jesus and the Gospels, it will always be a burden and a tragedy that force has been so uncomplicatedly enshrined in the very canons of Islam via the pattern of the *Sīrah*. For that sufficient reason, any appreciation of Muḥammad *in situ* must resolutely retain the contrasted meaning of the love that suffers as the Christ. Christianity in history has so far and so readily besmirched its own originating nature as to make that resolve paramount in all its external relationships, lest its own temptations should be mistaken by others for its – or their – proper norms.

So, in their origins in Jesus and Muḥammad an abiding, and irreducible, disparity persists. It must be allowed to stand without compromise and without concealment. For the rest, the realism which is the Prophet of Islam's most obvious plea, as we have generously seen, may perhaps invite the two faiths to a closer perception of the due limits of the political order *vis-à-vis* the things of faith. At best the state can only achieve a modicum of justice, holding the ring for spiritual forces which it cannot itself embody or absorb into its order. Such possible achievement will always be dogged, and perhaps destroyed, by the perennial temptations, the compulsiveness, besetting statehood in the actual world. To be sanguine here is to be deceived. To be an easy 'realist' is to be unrealistic.

The whole issue merges into what we can believe about God and what we mean by *Allāhu akbar* – to this we will come in a later chapter. For prophecy, after all, is instrumental and even when final is penultimate. The last word belongs to God. It is at the end of the day the accountability of prophethood to God alone which matters. Islam has been confident that the Hijrah contains the pattern of being effectively accountable. With Jesus the pattern of accountability was 'the cup My Father has given me'. There will always be a profound if reverent contention between the two. So let us leave 'recognition' of Muḥammad on this score where, surely, Muslims, too, would wish to leave it, namely within the sovereignty of God – the right focus both for the reverence and the contention. To 'recognize' Muḥammad is to identify an issue. But then the same is true in the Christian's 'recognition' of Jesus. In neither case can the 'recognition' and the issue be separated. Nor have they been, in the discipleships since Good Friday and 'the year of the Hijrah'. For the Christian the pattern of Muḥammad's *Sīrah* will always be in conflict with the power and perspective of the Cross.[21]

[21] An Indian Muslim writer, Barakat Ahmad, in his *Muhammad and the Jews: A Re-Examination* (New Delhi, 1982), has suggested a radical revision of the traditionalist accounts of the massacre of the Banū Qurayẓah and other forceful dealings of Muḥammad with the Jewish tribes. He argues that several details of the massacre are highly improbable and believes that less than twenty of the leading combatants were beheaded and that executions took place on the battlefield and not in Medina. Hygienic grounds would argue against the city location. He also queries the more sanguinary aspects of the judgement of Sa'd which led to the deaths.

This concern for an arguable review of what the Tradition records is welcome. But Barakat Ahmad's account oscillates somewhat and leaves the essential militancy unaffected. On the battle preceding the executions, he quotes the poet, Ḥasan Ibn Thābit:

We left them with blood upon them like a pool,
They having accomplished nothing,
They lay prostrate with vultures circling round them (ibid, p. 90).

A. J. Wensinck, the most famous of scholars in *Ḥadīth* in Islamics this century, accepts the story in its horrendous form. See his *Muhammad and the Jews of Medina* (Leiden, 1908), trans. by W. Behn, re-issued 1975.

4

MUḤAMMAD IN THE SOUL

> A hundred thousand graces, blessings and perfect salutations be upon the soul of the leader of lovers and the foremost of all mystics, the Prophet Muḥammad . . . If he had not existed, who would have existed? . . . He was such a prophet that God had ordained for him an abode without roof in the very proximity of Himself, as well as a hundred thousand miracles, and a hundred thousand signs of intimacy completely unknown to any angel, prophet, or saint. He pitched the tent of His glory in the desert of the existence of this world.[1]

So writes Zain Badr ʻArabī in the preface to his compilation of *The Hundred Letters* of Sharafuddīn Maneri, spiritual master of Bihari Islam in the thirteenth century (1283–1381) – letters which are replete with the same loving exultation of the Prophet of Islam.

Both writers are in excellent company. They exemplify the deep personal devotion to Muḥammad which is so central an element in the whole religion of Islam. It must, therefore, be a central concern for the Christian in his readiness for the theme it celebrates in sustained chorus of mystical discipleship across the centuries. In treating of Muḥammad, he must know that he is moving within a sanctuary of soul-wonder, and not simply within a sequence of historical event. He is handling hearts' love.

It is because of this that we cannot be content with the two previous chapters and their estimate of the Prophet in his Quranic career and the prose of historians. Chroniclers and biographers do not suffice. The picture is three-dimensional. Within the historical and the political there is the mystical. It is the intense, Sufi, form of that cult of Muḥammad which, in prosaic guise, provides a major realm of Muslim ethical guidance *via* the canonical Tradition, or Ḥadīth, in which there is a will

[1] Shaikh Sharafuddīn Maneri, *The Hundred Letters*, trans. by Paul Jackson (London, 1980 – Classics of Western Spirituality), p. 9.

to the imitation of the Prophet in the minutiae of personal behaviour and the patterns of social conduct. That aspect of the aura of Muḥammad will occupy us in chapter 5. His mystical significance, which concerns us here, is the ardent, spiritual poetry of relationship as it obtains between the lowliest of disciples and the master of masters. It is a manifestation of religious meaning which presents the Christian with fascinating areas of thought and awareness.

Take another lyrical 'praise' of the Prophet, from the *Tawāsīn* of the famous mystic martyr of Islam, Ḥusain ibn Manṣūr al-Ḥallāj (858–929).

> What is more manifest, more visible, greater, more famous, more luminous, more powerful or more discerning than he? He is and was, and was known before created things and existences and beings. He was and still is remembered before 'before' and after 'after', and before substances and qualities. His substance is altogether light, his speech is prophecy, his knowledge heavenly, his form of expression Arabic, his tribe is 'neither of the East nor of the West' (Surah 24.35), his genealogy is from the patriarchs, his mission is conciliation and his title is 'the unlettered one.'
>
> Eyes were opened by his signs, . . . God made him to speak His Word, and confirmed him as being the 'Proof'. God it was who sent him forth. He is the 'Proof' and the proven. He it is who quenches the thirst of the intensely thirsty heart. He it is who brings the uncreated Word, untouched by what touches it. . . .[2]

Such ecstatic writing, sustained and renewed through the whole of Muslim history, presents an Islam in which the divine grace is mediated through the prophetic personality so that the human lover may thereby cherish the divine. Surah 3.31 is often cited, with comparable passages, as the warrant for this devotion. For the Prophet is there directed to 'Say: "If you love God, then follow me, and God will love you and forgive you your sins." ' Thus a personal discipleship to Muḥammad is set within the soul's love *to* God Himself as being the context where the love *of* God, and His forgiveness, are to be had by the soul. Though rigorous interpretations of the Qur'ān deny all 'mediation' on the part of the Prophet, religious wistfulness and yearning have long responded to this life-line and the loving cult of Muḥammad has

[2] *The Tawāsīn of Mansūr al-Hallāj*; trans. by Aisha 'Abd al-Raḥmān al-Tarjumāna (London, 1974), p. 21.

been, for the devotee, the always precious, often lyrical, haven of divine refuge.

Hail to thee, of soul of souls most tender, hail!
Hail to thee, cupbearer of God's mysteries, hail!
Hail to thee, O pleader for the fallen, hail!
Hail to thee, O refuge of all sinners, hail!
Hail to thee, O mine of lore, all hail to thee!
Hail to thee, O secret of the Scriptures, hail!
Hail to thee, epiphany of mercy, hail![3]

The *Maulid*, or birthday, festivals of Muḥammad, on which such poems are recited, are deeply popular occasions despite the strictures against them that come from Wahhābī-style reproach. That Islam, with its strong insistence in the Opening Surah: 'Thee it is, O God, we worship, Thee it is to whom we come for aid,' should neverthless possess so large and long a refuge in Muḥammad is a fascinating thing and deserves a lively Christian understanding.

It is wise to trace it back to Surah 33.56 and the *Taṣliyah* there enjoined. The verse reads: 'God and His angels call down blessing [*yuṣallūn*] upon the Prophet. O you who have believed, call down blessing upon him and salute him with salutation.'

The word translated 'call down blessing' is the verb normally used for ritual prayer to God. Yet in 33.56 it denotes an activity of God himself, which however (the same verb) believers are to emulate. The usage *Ṣallā 'alā* (lit. 'pray upon . . .') is taken to mean a divine 'satisfaction' in the Prophet whereby God approves and takes joy in His messenger. This may come to mean, further, an inward divine pleasure in which divine initiative to reveal the Scripture rejoices in the agent of the Scripture revealed. In mystical terms it means the amity between will and fulfilment in the divine counsel. Believers, therefore, in their turn must likewise rejoice and, failing to do so, would lack not only a due recognition of Muḥammad but a proper submission to God.

In that way, *Taṣliyah* or the saying of the phrase: *Ṣallā Allāhu 'alaihi wa sallam* ('God celebrate and salute him') only gives devotional expression to the form of the *Shahādah* itself, linking in one conviction the Lordship and the prophethood. Some, it is true, would qualify this interpretation by pointing out that the

3 Quoted from Emil Esin, *Mecca the Sacred, and Madinah the Radiant* (London, 1963), p. 66, being a slightly amended version of a *Maulid* attributed to Sulayman Chelebi of Bursa. See E. W. J. Gibb, *History of Ottoman Poetry* (London, 1958), vol. i, pp. 246–7.

immediate context of Surah 33 has to do with Muḥammad's vindication against calumnies directed against his domestic life and, that therefore, the 'calling down of blessing' means simply the divine approval of his integrity as something which believers, too, should acknowledge. But *Taṣliyah* in Islamic piety goes far beyond such simple rehabilitation against malice and innuendo from a hostile source. It is the ground of relation to God through the celebration of the 'virtue' of the Prophet and of that 'virtue' as the mystery of his prophetic status availing for his community. It is the way of placing oneself reciprocally within the divine favour. For God calls down blessing to reward the salutation of His messenger.

Taṣliyah has often taken its place in the *Adhān*, or call to prayer from the minaret and has been likened to the *miḥrāb*, or niche, towards which the Muslim prays in the mosque 'orienting' him towards Mecca. Muḥammad is then the *Qiblah* of the soul, the focal point of divine experience for the faithful, just as the physical Mecca is the focus of the liturgy of *Ṣalāt* itself. He thus becomes in turn the *imām* through whom one 'faces the face of God'. This *tawajjuh*, or seeking the light of the divine countenance, comes to pass by virtue of setting one's sight on the merit of the Prophet. Thereby, as in a *miḥrāb*, the desire to appear before God is made good. Responsively, the divine face is believed to be lifted up upon the believer through and by the soul's esteem of Muḥammad.

The great exegete Al-Baiḍāwī, commenting on 33.56, says quite simply: 'They are concerned to manifest his honour and to magnify his dignity. You too care likewise for that is even more appropriate for you, and say: "O God, call down blessing upon Muḥammad . . ." '

In *Taṣliyah* both the angelic world and the human world are united in the exaltation of Muḥammad. The angels of the divine presence were called upon to prostrate before Adam at the creation. Muḥammad has the even greater honour in that God, in 33.56, joins with the angels in heaven's tribute. It is significant that, though human believers are enjoined to 'call down blessings', their customary form is, rather, to say: 'May *God* send down blessings upon him . . .' The human response to the command cannot presume to 'duplicate' that in which God Himself engages but fulfils itself in petitionary association with the divine benediction that Muḥammad receives.

In many of the Sufi liturgies for *Taṣliyah* the Prophet's family (*āl*) are also included, meaning in the Shī'ah world the house of 'Alī and the Imāms and, in the Sunnī world, the earlier prophets and patriarchs. Most notable among the latter is Abraham, 'the friend of God'. The association of others with Muḥammad in the invocation of divine blessing is the way of celebrating their varied characteristics in the divine economy of prophethood and at the same time extolling the finality of the Prophet in whom, as it were by anticipation, those predecessors had their standing before God and their ultimate realization. Thus in *Ṭahārat al-Qulūb*, 'Abd al-'Azīz al-Dīrīnī, says:

> Adam knew him [Muḥammad] and made petition through him, and Muḥammad took a covenant from all the prophets to himself. He took the purity of Adam, the lamentation of Noah. A part of his teaching contains the knowledge of Idris. Included in his ecstatic experiences is the grief of Jacob. Within the mystery of his ecstasy is the endurance of Job. Enfolded in his bosom is the weeping of David. A part only of the riches of his soul exceeds the wealth of Solomon. He gathered into himself Abraham's friendship with God. He attained the converse of Moses, God's interlocutor, and was more exalted than the highest kings. He excels the prophets as the sun excels the moon or the ocean the drop.[4]

The observer from without may wonder how this supreme standing of Muḥammad and devotion in his name square with the doctrine of the divine unity in Islam and with the believer's *islām* to God alone. It seems a clear instance of the familiar tension known to every faith between dogma and devotion. God's Messenger may be strictly a spokesman according to the doctrine of *Waḥy*. But, for that very reason, devotion needs him for a mediatorial significance. In this sense he is clearly 'more than a prophet', though rigorous orthodoxy denies that there is ever more than prophethood, in God's education of mankind. That it should be so within the faith most strenuously committed to the utter 'otherness' of God and man is remarkable. We discover that something of what we thought to be quite at odds *between* Islam and Christianity about God-with-man is there *within* Islam, only it belongs to the person of Muḥammad not to the person of Jesus. Purely doctrinal contrasts between Christian faith in the Incarnate Word and the Islamic doctrine of the prophetic as final plainly do not fit the situation as *Taṣliyah* reveals it. To exclude what the New Testament holds about the person of Jesus is not to escape the questions to which it is the

[4] Constance E. Padwick, *Muslim Devotions: A Study of Prayer Manuals in Common Use* (London, 1961), pp. 170–1.

Christian answer. Sufi Islam has, with long fidelity to its instincts, found in Muḥammad the human axis of divine grace both received and celebrated.

Reproached for their temerity by the custodians of pure theology, the Sufi masters have not themselves ignored the seeming contradiction. Questioned as to how the *Taṣliyah* could be said at the end of the prayer rite when, presumably, the soul is absorbed with God alone in His unity, they have conceded that '. . . the awe of God's presence may so strongly dominate the heart that the worshipper may be unable to turn from the greatness of the divine interview to thought of anyone else.'[5], but claimed, too, that such preoccupation with God need not exclude the vision of a created being. The salutation of the Prophet only means that he is the *Imām*, or 'leader', of their worship of God. If one is asked whether the two loves might not be rivals, there is the story of one master who responded to a night vision of Muḥammad with the words: 'Pardon me! Loving God makes me forget to love thee.' To which came the Prophet's reply: 'Blessed one, he who loves God loves me also.'[6]

Approval in those terms 'frees all faults', in satisfying all scruples. It represents a theological judgement responding to a religious instinct. The sort of 'associationism' of the human with the divine which *Taṣliyah* involves is justified here by a decision about God Himself. He allows, even welcomes and enjoins, a love from mankind which history combines with transcendence to generate, rather than a love which can only rightly be God's in utter dissociation from all else. The implications here for Christian thinking are plain. They bring us close to what we have always believed to be the significance of Jesus in his person and his ministry, only that the idiom is different by the difference between Mecca/Medina and Galilee/Jerusalem. But there can be no doubt that the Muḥammad of Islamic mysticism and devotion indicates how close, in that area, Islam comes to the instincts, though not to the content, of Christian theology.

And just as, for Christians, the faith of the Incarnation means the expression of the perfectly human (Incarnation being a doctrine about man as well as about God), so also does the *Taṣliyah*. Muḥammad is celebrated as the perfection of humanity, not merely in the sense of moral example which we survey in chapter 5, but in the metaphysical sense as the divine 'idea' immanent in the whole creation.

[5] *Ibid.*, p. 154.
[6] *Ibid*, p. 154.

This perspective requires, in some quarters, a doctrine of the perfection of Muḥammad's immediate parents, 'Abdallah and Aminah, and their parents beyond, so that the culmination of the mystery in Muḥammad himself may be appropriately reached. Many *Maulid* eulogies include his ancestry, both close and distant, in their range of celebration. That of Shaikh Yūsuf al-Nabahānī of Damascus, who died in 1932, runs as follows after rejoicing in Adam and Shith (ie. Seth) in the first Paradise:

> At length, there came the best of mankind, purest in lineage and esteem, from the finest of all the diversity of peoples, noblest in breeding, his grandfather, his mother, his father, alike the worthiest. His glory spreads its splendour everywhere. The light of the most perfect of prophets passed unfailing from master to master, like a torch before the brow, a light which the thoughtful and thoughtless alike can see, like a star riding in its blessed sky.
>
> At length, the light rested on the brow of 'Abdallāh, to the chosen one the best of fathers. There is nothing opprobrious attaching to 'Abdallāh's glorious name, and his mother, too, is exempt from all things mean . . . Alas! alas! it was decreed in his orphanhood that his father died before his mother bore him. The very angels of heaven grieved with his grief and cried unto their Lord at His decree. And He said: 'Leave to Me my pure one and my servant.'[7]

The eulogist goes on to note that no other children shared this parenthood that the solitary inheritance of purity might be the Prophet's alone.

Ascribing immaculate physical genesis to Muḥammad in this way is, of course, deplored by many writers on several counts. There is the basic historical question whether we can say that his parents were 'believers', having lived and died entirely within the *Jāhiliyyah* and before the revelation. Further, the traditional view holds, in the words of Katib Chelebi in his *Balance of Truth* that '. . . prophecy is simply a gift from God: there is no possible shadow of doubt that birth and pedigree have no part in it. It is a mighty boon, in comparison of which the boon imagined by those who take the contrary view is of no consequence.' He adds:

7 Yūsuf Ibn-Ismā'īl al-Nabahānī, *Al-Natm al-Badī' fī Maulid al-Nabī al-Shafī'* ('Sweet Order for the Birth Feast of the Prophet Intercessor'), Damascus 1941 (my translation).

'The best course . . . is not to meddle in this controversy but to hold aloof from it.'[8]

The concept of immaculate parentage, however, is only instrumental to the larger theme of Muḥammad's cosmic significance as some Sufi philosophers regard it. What, by some, is called *Ḥaqīqat Muḥammadī*, 'the "Reality" of Muḥammad', is the animating principle of the whole creation. In him is embodied that pre-existent 'intention' which lies behind all things and is fulfilled within them. There is something analogous here to the *Logos* doctrine in the New Testament. The human is taken as the clue to the divine but, as such, the human finds its essential expression in the perfect humanity of Muḥammad. What was divinely breathed into Adam at the creation, namely the 'breath' of the Creator's purpose, is incarnate in the Prophet in whom the human essence finds perfected form.

This doctrine is often housed within the metaphor of 'light'. The *Nūr Muḥammadī*, or 'Light of Muḥammad', is the sun of creation whence all life and illumination derive. By its indwelling in him, he is *al-Insān al-Kāmil* 'the perfect Man', in whom the divine Names and attributes were perfectly expressed. In that sense, 'the perfect Man' can be described as 'a copy of God'. It is as if, of necessity, the 'human' has to be abstracted out of the 'ordinary' and elevated to immunity from human frailty so that the divine, otherwise inaccessible and incomprehensible, can be humanly discerned and loved.

The Quranic theme of Adam as the *Khalīfah* of God, the 'deputy' or 'vice-regent' (2.30), which normally means mankind's 'technological' trust of external nature as a realm of legitimate 'empire', is developed by some Sufi metaphysicians as applying instead to Muḥammad, in the loins of Adam, as the 'trustee' celestially of that divine glory which originated the universe. Absolute being is thus linked with the world of nature and of history in the 'idea' of Muḥammad – 'idea' in the sense of the identifiable clue by which the divine may be 'read' and the human defined.

The prophetic vocation of Muḥammad – seen in non-mystical Islam in the strictly didactic, verbal and historical terms we have already studied in chapters 2 and 3 – becomes here a theosophic reality in which he is much more than a messenger and a warner and emerges as 'the confidant' of God, the sharer of the divine secrets. There is no mistaking the radical transform-

[8] Katib Chelebi, *The Balance of Truth*, trans. from the Turkish by G. I. Lewis (London, 1957), pp. 67 and 72.

ation of Muḥammad's significance by such speculative formulations which, whatever their arguable grounds from enigmatic Quranic texts invoked to sustain them, seem so antithetical to the general view of the role and status of Muḥammad.[9]

Ibn al-'Arabī in his *Fuṣuṣ al-Ḥikam* and other works was perhaps the most abstruse and elusive of all the thinkers developing the metaphysics of prophethood in treatise form. But its most endearing expositors are the poets, and foremost among them the great Jalāl al-Dīn Rūmī, whose exaltation of the Prophet hails him as the elemental source of creation, existence, and all the virtues. He delights in the traditional saying ascribed to God Himself addressing Muḥammad: 'Had it not been for you, I would not have created the spheres.' This *Lau lā ka* ('but for you . . .') can be read in mysterious ways. Prophecy, as directive and guidance, holds the key to the explanation of why all things are, namely for their due subjection to the divine will. Had that 'will' been otherwise, nothing would have been. But, further, prophecy finalized in Muḥammad means that the divine desire contemplates the perfect satisfaction of its realization. In both his famous *Mathnawi* and in the prose work *Fīhi Mā Fīhi*, Rūmī cherished the Prophet's personality in a wealth of anecdote, *dicta* and legend, all impregnated with mystical light and meaning. Muḥammad's physical body 'cast no shadow' being purified and transparent with the divine light. 'From the ocean of absolute certainty he grants pearls to the inhabitants of this world.' He is the goblet full of wine which God Himself, as cupbearer, proffers to the faithful.[10]

Mystical delight in Muḥammad after the manner of Rūmī's verse and prose sometimes makes its own version of the 'illiteracy' of the Prophet. The general question here is followed up in chapter 6. The term *ummī* used of him in Surah 7.155 and 157, is generally taken to indicate a complete incapacity in Muḥammad to read or write, so that his recipience of the Qur'ān

9 See R. A. Nicholson, *The Idea of Personality in Sufism* (Cambridge, 1923), pp. 80–101.

10 See Annemarie Schimmel, *The Triumphal Sun, A Study of the Works of Jalāl al-Dīn Rūmī* (London and the Hague, 1978), pp. 283 and 287. See also the same author's 'The Prophet Muḥammad as a Center of Muslim Life and Thought', in A. M. Schimmel and A. Falaturi (eds), *We Believe in One God: The Experience of God in Christianity and Islam*, trans. from the German by G. Blaczszak and A. M. Schimmel (London, 1979), pp. 35–61.

Also Annemarie Schimmel, *As Through a Veil: Mystical Poetry in Islam* (New York, 1982), ch. 4: 'God's Beloved Intercessor for Man: Poetry in Honor of the Prophet'.

is the more evidently a divine 'miracle'. With many mystical writers, however, it means a transcendence of ordinary means of learning and wisdom by virtue of a celestial intimacy with God. Language and letters belong to the mundane realm of partial knowledge and natural enquiry. What truck with these has the possessor of heavenly lore through intimacy with the absolute truth?

It is fascinating for the historian of religions to trace, if he can, or otherwise to speculate about, the affinities of these doctrines of Muḥammad's 'Light' and 'Perfection', as Sufis have received them through many centuries. Our purpose, however, is only to register their presence in the devotion, and the philosophy, of the most warm and fervent areas of Islamic religious experience. All the discouragements to esoteric ideas 'orthodox' Islam was urgent to enforce were here defied or disregarded in a sustained and resourceful piety inspired to bold and often soaring flights of a theosophic mind. It was not simply that scruples, taught by the pundits, were cast aside; it was that authentic participation in the mystique of Muḥammad demanded to be stated in these terms.

In the light of the range and continuity of this dimension in Islam of speculative devotion, it is a half-truth to say, as many do, that Islam is an essentially simple religion, free from subtlety. That is true of orthodox theology and of the *Shahādah* at its face value. It is also true that there is a persistent warning in the 'official' world of Islam against theological 'ambition' to understand. That 'God knows' is the characteristic instinct of Muslim faith and the right believer is ready simply to believe without pressing inquiry tediously. Revelation is not for the curious but for the obedient. Yet, even so, the impulse to ponder and explore has proved irresistible for some of the finest minds and poets. There are two factors to note in reading this situation.

One is the external fact of contact across cultures involved in the expansion of Islam. The formative centuries were spent in sustained inter-action with faiths and systems which were partially recruited into Islam while being also diminished or submerged as minorities. These were often more articulate and sophisticated than their Islamic masters, by virtue of their different history and temperament. Some of their deepest features, intellectually or spiritually, struggled for survival in Islamic form. The dominant mastery became, in some measure, an absorbent school. The results of this situation are plain to see in the story of Islamic arts and architecture, where the borrowings in styles, skills and techniques, were large and rewarding. It could hardly be otherwise in thought and theology where questions about God and man, quiescent in Muslim origins and attitudes, were irrepressible. It was, in fact, Islamic experience of their pressure which at length induced the will to hold the issues on a very tight rein of dogma and authority. But if Muslim thinkers, by and large, were so minded, their caution and reticence could not prevent speculative interests around them from venturing where reverent believers feared to tread. Nor could such interests be successfully excluded from the thoughts of bolder or more hospitable spirits within Islam. Whether Hindu, Christian, Jewish, Mandean or Manichean, the influences were present and, in alliance with factors domestic to Islam itself, they generated these fascinating ideas of the hypostasis of the eternal Muḥammad, his pre-existence and his mediatorship as the secret of the cosmic mystery. Research, as well as being seriously incomplete in this field, is of no common mind as to the course of these inter-cultural contacts and there is still a sharp debate as to where the major indebtedness lies. Our concern here is with the fact, not with the data, of this interpenetration, and with the significance that, by way of *Taṣliyah* and the role of the Prophet in *Waḥy* and *Tanzīl* it went so far, and so ambitiously, in the direction of theosophic speculation in approximation to systems of faith and philosophy so sharply contrasted with Islam in its Arabian genesis.

This historical situation as Sufism, and kindred accents within Islam, underline it must surely be relevant to contemporary relations between faiths. It leads us to ask whether any faith can successfully insulate itself from the interior concerns of other patterns of belief and allegiance. It prompts the realization that many of the areas of controversy or of issue *between* faiths are in some degree also issues inside each of them. Muslims can hardly lay a simple anathema on Christian belief about Jesus as 'the Word made flesh' when within their own tradition, and despite their vehement dissuasives, there exists a comparable accent in their own heritage. The formal question whether 'revelation' is rightly confined to 'words about will' or can be expressed in 'personality disclosing nature' lies squarely *between* Islam and Christianity, broadly seen. Yet it belongs *within* them both in their own 'privacy' of tradition and worship, with minority verdicts in either case betraying sympathies beyond their borders, whether in a purely human Jesus or a 'supernatural' Muḥammad.

Due realization of this should save us from hasty or rigorous attitudes and give pause to the simplistic verdicts to which timorous or assertive dogmatists are liable. Religions, in their established form, acquire an identity consciousness which then defines and defends itself in terms of otherness, and we become sharply partisan. Montagues are not Capulets; Guelphs are not Ghibellines; Muslims are not Christians. We sound and often feel like opposing teams, divided by a *versus*. In the contrast of loyalties, it is easy to forget that the competitors' are 'united' by the game. The name of the mortal 'game' is the same. We are all living, dying, mating, yearning, hoping, fearing, striving, wondering, doubting, believing humans. It would be strange if all those common denominators of time, flux, life, death, infinity, reason, passion, mystery, and the rest, did not involve even our belligerent postures in kindred frailties and formulas.

Any 'name of the game' parable must not, of course, be pressed too far, or it might take us into folly. But it does hold in the simple sense that faiths as guidance and interpretation have at least in common what needs guiding and interpreting, namely the human manifold. And much of their rivalry has to do with the custody rather than with the substance of their faith, with its collective prestige on behalf of its meaning rather than its meaning in full control of its prestige. Much in the burden of our relationships has to do with the psychology of loyalty as an end in itself.

So much, it would seem, we learn from the significance of the whole mystical strain in Islamic life and devotion. But if, in these ways, Islam is less 'simple', more subtle, than classical exponents claim and has its own form of issues that recur elsewhere, that fact alone does not terminate the Christian's puzzles in understanding his relationships. It may be instructive to realize that some in Islam have been impelled to wonder about how the simple creed 'There is no god but God, and Muḥammad is the apostle of God' is to be linked, in its terseness, with the mystery of God and His business with the world, thus so singularly and prosaically joined with a single human name out of all the myriad legions of humanity and the immense range of history. It may be well to appreciate that the very brevity of creeds may merely conceal the complexities they seem to avoid, that simplicity can only be a right criterion if it suffices, and that it may not 'suffice' even for *all* proven adherents, not to say external learners at the door. In the soul dimension of Islam the confession 'Muḥammad is the messenger of God' is much more than a statement and has become, through long centuries, both mystery and ecstasy. This is no more, no less, than a deep religious sense of what those large, round, equal discs convey to the believer – in their Arabic script: *Allāh, Muḥammad* – as they adorn the mosque. To divest them of their Sufi subtlety might leave them merely placards.

How should the Christian relate in both thought and community to this Muslim 'possession' of and by Muḥammad in the soul? The question is the most searching of all those we have to face. There must be careful note of the fact that Islam, even in spite of itself, finds place for categories of relationship between divine ends and human means, between the eternal and the historical, unlike and yet akin to those that are at the heart of Christian experience in Jesus as the Christ. That may spell hope for the mutual theology we seek. It may help Christians to see beyond the exigencies of propositional controversy to the inward experience. It may enable Muslims to discover within themselves the sanctions which explain and warrant the New Testament faith in Jesus as the point and place of divine self-giving to reveal and to redeem. Both developments would greatly serve the future of relationships by excluding what was arid and polemical and fostering a more reverent openness of spirit.

But, gain as this would be, there remains the Christian anxiety about a pattern of religious awareness which follows, in part, the Christian elements of divine/human 'association' and historical 'mediation' of the eternal, but joins them to a personality so far different from the central figure of the Gospel and from that Gospel's categories of suffering and grace in which God's reconciliation of the world consists. This brings us back to issues already faced in the two preceding chapters. It has to be taken forward into the discussion of the Qur'ān which still awaits us. In respect of both there is hope that the very celebration of Muḥammad may suggest a clue to the New Testament recognition of Jesus. For what but a *Taṣliyah*, 'a divine salutation', is the familiar New Testament cry: 'This is My Son, my Beloved, hear him'? Sonship, there, is the unity of wills, the harmony of ends, the point of the divine satisfaction in the human means of its translation into fact. *Taṣliyah*, evidently, is a kindred term, a Muslim and a Christian theme. Only the living translation differs.

5

MUḤAMMAD THE DEFINITIVE MUSLIM

A contemporary Egyptian author, Yūsuf Idrīs, has written a play, *Al-Farāfīr*, in which he pictures the world as the work of a dramatist who has left his characters with a half-finished story. He himself has disappeared and the actors have to go on, improvising their parts. An intriguing fantasy, but by no means an Islamic view of the world. The human drama is fully 'directed' in and by Islam. Religion is firmly politicized[1] and human character is set in a framework of rite and law by the Qur'ān.

Situations, however, are always in the making when it comes to life itself, and for these, as well as for areas of decision on which the Qur'ān itself was silent, guidance needed to be found in the explicit terms that their sense of Scripture had led Muslims to expect. For these the example of Muḥammad was ready to hand. Though his death, in 632, was a traumatic experience for the believing community, they were not abandoned. If we have to think of them as 'improvising', it was under the tuition, and by the imitation, of the Prophet. There is a real sense by which Muḥammad continued to direct Islam from the grave.

So our theme in this chapter is the Tradition of Muḥammad in the inclusive meaning of the term. Such had been the eminence and the indispensability of Muḥammad to believing Islam that when death removed his hand from the helm of its destinies and the Caliphs took over the political leadership his personality continued to dominate. His authority and stature as the sole recipient of the Qur'ān and as the successful 'establisher' of Islam meant that his words and actions, outside Quranic *Waḥy*, were understood as a sure source of *hudā*. Moreover, the knowledge that by the fact of his demise no more Qur'ān could be awaited, made the supplementary role of Tradition all the more necessary.

Muḥammad's death had not meant any incompleteness in the

[1] Yusuf Idris, *Al Farāfīr*, Cairo, 1964.

Qur'ān. It had not been allowed to happen until the Book was complete. His death and the sealing of the work of *Waḥy* were one event. But in both its aspects, that one event, as the closure of Scripture and the passing of its human voice, necessitated his perpetuation by memory so that, from his aura, even in the most ordinary details, Muslims might draw continual direction. His *Sīrah*, or life-story, we might say, took over the script where the Qur'ān left off, but always in subservience and conformity to it.

The English word 'Tradition' covers two distinct Arabic terms, the one *Ḥadīth*, the other *Sunnah*. *Ḥadīth* is material in currency, reportage, what is 'said' to have been thus-and-thus, while *Sunnah* is the 'path' to be followed because of *Ḥadīth*, the 'way' it enjoins or exemplifies. Islam found its 'way', from Muḥammad's. The Qur'ān is always prior, Tradition broadly complementary. By *Ḥadīth* and *Sunnah*, Muslims were enabled to enlarge *Sharī'ah*, or sacred law, and so direct themselves with a confidence that, through their discipleship, Muḥammad was still directing them.

No intelligent observer outside Islam can appreciate Muḥammad without reference to the meaning of this his posthumous authority. It has few parallels in the whole of religious history. Though the Canonical traditionalists finalized their task by the third Muslim century the instinct within their piety and scholarship has persisted in varying ways all through the centuries since. In this last, the fourteenth, Muslim century there have been more biographies and interpretations of the Prophet than in any previous time. These are not, of course, verbal collections of sayings, or records of actions, habits, and judgements; the feasible time for those passed with the decades that could arguably have recalled them. But modern historians and apologists follow the same broad instinct to 'validate' their own views or solutions by attributing them, or arguable anticipations of them, to the mind and the policy of Muḥammad. He thus emerges as bestowing, even if diversely, the necessary *Imprimatur*, or at least the *Nihil Obstat*, by which Muslim advocacies should properly hope to prosper today.

The variety and resourcefulness of these sponsorships sought from, and attributed to, Muḥammad in recent decades by Muslims make a fascinating study and reach all the way from spiritual quietism to ardent revolution, from Marxist socialism to utopian internationalism. Nor have outsiders been exempt from the pattern. Even the English poet Shelley wrote a passionate piece, mainly in praise of the French Revolution but entitled it, without warrant of content, *The Revolt of Islam*. We have ‘Muḥammads’ of some enthusiasms that other loyalties would regard as criminally secularized.

A few examples we may note later. The immediate point is to realize that the Muḥammad with whom the Christian mind has to reckon is, from this angle, the paragon of ideals, of ideologies, of ‘interests’ philosophical and economic, which invoke him as their champion or symbol. He cannot be confined to historical retrospect away from debates and causes which currently claim him. He is caught up in the flux of arguments that are more than Islamic in a private sense. His image both shaped, and is shaped by, these tensions. He is the mirror of Muslim self-understanding, the crucible of the contemporary value judgements of Islam. It is important to reckon with the movement of the interpretation of Muḥammad as well as with the historical actualities, as far as we may be able to ascertain these from the Qur᾽ān and the Tradition. The concerns of the two or so centuries of Tradition formation and creation certainly determined the material. It continues to be so with the portraiture of Muḥammad in the current time.

There are, in particular, two passages in the Qur᾽ān from which the impulse to Tradition can be derived. Both begin with the singular imperative to Muḥammad: *Qul* and, in verbal form, the *Amr* of divine directive. Surah 6. 161–3 reads:

> Say: ‘As for me, my Lord has guided me to a straight path, to a right religion – that of the community of Abraham, a man of single faith, who had no part with idolaters.’ Say: ‘My prayer and my ritual acts, my living and my dying, are all in and for God, who is the Lord of all being. There is none like to Him. Accordingly I am so commanded. And I am the first of the *muslims*.’

And 39.11–12:

> Say: ‘I have been commanded to worship God in sincerity of religion before Him. I have been commanded to be the first of the *muslims*.’

‘First’ among the Muslims Muḥammad was, within the *Sīrah*, followed early by Khadījah, his wife, and ‘Alī, his cousin. That may be one sense of the two verses, though Muḥammad was not the first of the *Muslims* historically, given the fact that Adam, Noah and Abraham were *muslim* to God, prior to Qur᾽ān, *Ramaḍān* and *Ḥajj*, as the final institutions of ‘Muhammadan’ Islam. The other, and perhaps likelier, sense is that Muḥammad is ‘the first of Muslims’ in a primacy of character and example.

That ruling conviction was the matrix of Tradition. To enter its fertile wealth of personal detail about the Prophet is to meet a thousand bewildering facets of his reputation and of the first two Muslim centuries of discipleship, all held together by the total assurance of an admiration due and an obligation known. It is to sense law finding its precedents and society its norms. It is to trace an umbilical cord nourishing the embryonic Muslim ethos in the womb of the *Sīrah*. Even the controversies of the community, whether in matters of ritual or of economics and precedence, are formulated in competitive traditions, so that even inconclusiveness, if such it has to be, may be Muḥammad's too.

Thus, for example, the question of women and their attendance at the mosque. There are traditions that they are not to be prevented when they ask permission to do so. There are others in which they are definitely discouraged and told that for them prayer at home is more meritorious. Commentators suggest that when Muḥammad yielded to his wives' request to go with him to the mosque this should not be taken as a precedent, because, sad to say, the moral atmosphere of that pristine time was not sustained later. So the enviable privilege of those first *Muslimāt* does not extend beyond them. 'A'ishah, who survived Muḥammad many years, recalled that had the Prophet seen what new things women have brought into their lives he would definitely have prevented them from going to the mosque.[2]

It was, of course, precisely to cope with 'new things', whether deplorable or necessary, that Tradition was meant, tying back innovative necessities, required by evolving circumstance, to appropriate principles. Finality and flux make for this kind of paradox in every religion. What cannot be static because it is alive must, nevertheless, be under authority because it is religious. Tradition mediates between the two and, ironically, makes of one time the source to guide all times. But the 'one time', being a period, has 'time' within itself. So the traditionalists agreed that, for the most part, a later tradition abrogated an earlier one. It was, however, often a matter of uncertainty as to which traditions were later, and which earlier, within Muḥammad's lifetime. Then issues of content could easily become conflicts of chronology.

In appreciating Tradition in Islam it is well to note the

2 *Saḥiḥ Muslim*, rendered into English by 'Abdul-Ḥamīd Ṣiddiqī (New Delhi, 1978), vol. i, pp. 240–1. The traditions here add the note that as and when women do attend the mosques they should not apply perfume.

complete commitment with which the Companions refer their questions and the way these cover the entire range of their affairs with an implicit trust in the Prophet's word as a full solution. Simple matters of personal hygiene; private ones about sexual behaviour, menstruation and intercourse; social ones about lavatories, baths, streets, houses, bedchambers, camps, tents and public places; economic ones about trading, bargains, debts, ownership of vital resources, water rights, landmarks and wardship; ritual ones about ablution, prostration, fasting, postures at prayer, response to the *Adhān* and the like; and legal ones about divorce, inheritance, paternity, dowry and status law – all were zealously referred to him without reservation either of confidence in his verdict or of frankness in their inquiry.

Something of the savour of Tradition may be had by choosing, at random, questions of the questioners and the answers of Muḥammad:

> Tell me that thing about Islam which will dispense with the necessity of my asking anybody else the question.
>
> Say: 'I affirm by faith in God' and then remain steadfast to it.
>
> Who is the best among Muslims?
> He from whose hand and tongue Muslims are secure.
>
> What are the evidences of *Īmān* [Faith]?
> There are three qualities by which any who has these characteristics will cherish the sweetness of faith: (1) he to whom God and His messenger are dearer than all else; (2) he who loves a man for God's sake alone; (3) he who has as great an abhorrence of falling back into his old unbelief as he has of being cast into Hell.
>
> Which sin is the gravest in the eyes of God?
> That you associate a partner with God.
> What next? That you kill your child out of fear to add another mouth to your family.
> What next? That you commit adultery with the wife of your neighbour.
>
> 'Ā'ishah reported: 'The Messenger of God loved to start from the right hand side in his every act, putting on shoes, combing the hair and performing ablution.'
>
> They asked. 'O Apostle of God, how should a virgin's permission be indicated by her when asked before her marriage?
> He replied: 'By her silence.'

I asked the Apostle of God: 'If a man should come and ask me to sell something which I do not have, may I purchase it and then later deliver it to him?
He replied: 'Do not sell that which you do not have.'

O Apostle of God, what words does God most like to hear?
The words which God chose for His angels to say: 'May the Lord be glorified and praised.'

The saying attributed to Muḥammad by Ibn Ḥanbal, 'My eyes sleep but not my heart,' was meant to explain his ability to awaken for night prayers. But it might figuratively be borrowed to express this bond of attraction for his community from within the sleep of death. When Muḥammad Iqbāl, the poet philosopher of Pakistan's genesis, considered Muḥammad from the angle of a distinction made, perhaps unfairly, between the prophetic and the mystical in religion, he wrote that, whereas

> the mystic does not wish to return from the . . . unitary experience . . . the prophet's return is creative. He returns to insert himself into the sweep of time with a view to control the forces of history, and thereby to create a fresh world of ideals. . . . The desire to see his religious experience transformed into a living world-force is supreme in the prophet.[3]

Here, as often elsewhere, Iqbāl was much too exuberant. 'Controlling the forces of history' and 'creating a fresh world of ideals' are poetic claims. But there is no doubt of Muḥammad's 'return', or perhaps, better, continuance as a living force in the 'reading' and re-reading of his religious experience. Invocation of Muḥammad, with very rare completely secular exceptions, continues to be the habit, and the hope, of contemporary Islamic ideology. The answers, as sometimes in the early days, may be willed upon him. But the questions are not thought at all to pass him by. In some cases, there may be a degree of prudence or calculation in this, a feeling that if change is to take hold it must plead this way. But even where that is so, it is secondary. The association of even competing ideas and prospects with the person of the Prophet means that he remains the touchstone of Islamic identity and loyalty. Even pioneers shelter in him.

'Abd al-Raḥmān al-Sharqāwī's *Muḥammad Rasūl al-Ḥurriyah* is

[3] Muḥammad Iqbāl, *The Reconstruction of Religious Thought in Islam* (Lahore, 1933; rev. edn, London, 1934), p. 124.

an interesting example.[4] Its very title is an adaptation of the *Shahādah* where Muḥammad is *Rasūl Allāh*, and for many such adaptation is little short of blasphemy. To be the 'Apostle of God' does not admit of being dubbed the 'Apostle of Liberty'. That might be the kind of atheism proposed in the French Revolution. Al-Sharqāwī, however, thinks the two titles compatible, or, if not, 'liberty' is the one that matters. He sees Muḥammad as essentially a human reformer whose prime concern was the lot of his people. When he cites the Qur'ān it is more for its argument than for its status. Quraishī opposition to Muḥammad was the ugly face of capitalism. The Prophet identified with the poor, whereas the gods of Mecca were patrons of the wealthy. He was burdened by the oppression of the slaves and militated against polytheism as the sanction of an economic system that exploited them. Islam means in its doctrine of *Tauḥīd* that 'man must be left solitary before what he worships . . . None should have spiritual authority over another. The idols must give way . . . together with those who in their name control the fate of others'. Economic and social emancipation through effective theism was Muḥammad's aim. He is seen by Al-Sharqāwī as exalting manual labour, spurring Arab 'nationalism' and advocating a free scientific spirit.

Muḥammad Rasūl al-Ḥurriyah has many precedents. In the late nineteenth century, for example, first in Aleppo and then in Cairo, 'Abd al-Raḥmān al-Kawākibī (1854–1902) developed a vigorous case for the 'socialism' of Muḥammad. He saw the Prophet as the champion of the principle that wealth, being derived from labour, should be communally owned and fairly distributed, not cornered and monopolized by the few as a means to exploitation. This could be adduced from *Zakāt*, and *'Ushr* (the tithe tax), from inheritance law, and from Muḥammad's insistence that vital commodities should be communally controlled.

Al-Kawākibī, who was also a vigorous pioneer of Arab nationalism, understood Muḥammad in terms that have become very influential since, and scholarly research into the background and

[4] 'Abd al-Raḥmān al-Sharqāwī, *Muḥammad Rasūl al-Ḥurriyyah* (Cairo, 1962), p. 55. This work was some nine years in composition, years which coincide with the Nasir regime in Egypt which began in 1952. Dr M. M. Badawi, a reviewer, said of it: 'I do not think it would be an exaggeration to say that the secularization of Muḥammad is here virtually complete.' See *Journal of Arabic Studies*, Cambridge, i, 2 (1972) p. 175.

social 'level' of the first Muslims sustains him.[5] The poet, Aḥmad Shawqī, described the Prophet as 'the Imām of the socialists', though he added, 'but for their claims and their exaggeration'. The song in which he did this became famous in the repertoire of the legendary Egyptian singer, Umm Kulthūm, and the lines were quoted by 'Abd al-Nāṣir in his speeches.[6]

Such fervent enlistment of Muḥammad's example was natural in the context of the strong pressures for social change and the ideological challenge of Marxism. Khālid Muḥammad Khālid (b. 1920) was another forceful advocate of the Prophet's 'socialism', in his passionate *Min Hunā Nabda'* ('Here We Start') and other works. He demanded that problems of poverty and exploitation should be tackled radically and argued that Muḥammad's assumption of political power was only because, in his time, he could achieve what was socially imperative in no other way. Similarly, today issues like birth control to curb the human misery flowing from over-population should be met by firm religious leadership repudiating *Taqlīd*, or blind conservatism, in fulfilment of the Prophet's dynamic example. Sayyid Quṭb (1906–1966), one of the martyrs of the Muslim Brotherhood and author of the Quranic commentary, *Fī Ẓilāl al-Qur'*ān ('In the Shade of the Qur'ān') was a powerful exponent of the Prophet's social principles, though he saw them in far more exclusively Islamic terms than Muḥammad Khālid.

These and scores of other writers, for whom their mention must do crude justice here, were responding to numerous pressures – Western influence, national aspiration, the collapse of the Caliphate, the decline of 'clerical' leadership, the growing dichotomy in education (traditional and scientific), the 'laicization' of life under the impact of technology, and the sheer complexity of change. It is significant that in this maelstrom of development it was the 'image' of the Prophet, rather than the Caliphate, or the *'Ulamā*, or the Azhar, or the Sufi Orders, which gave resilience to the response. The *Ijtihād*, or enterprise of mind and will, which is the organ of 'development' within Islam,

5 Researches carried through by W. Montgomery Watt and presented in his *Muḥammad at Mecca* (Oxford, 1953) and his *Muḥammad at Medina* (Oxford, 1956). These findings drew some Muslim reproach upon the author whom they suspected, without warrant, of a 'socialist' bias against 'orthodox' views.

6 According to *Al-Ahrām*, Cairo, 24 Dec. 1961 and 23 Feb. 1962. For Umm Qulthūm see J. Berque, *The Arabs, their History and Future* (London, 1964), pp. 227–8.

leading to *Ijmā'*, or 'consensus', could appeal more readily, and pliably, to the mind and personality of Muḥammad *via* the Qur'ān and Tradition, than to other arguable arbiters in the Schools of *Fiqh* and *Kalām*. There was much that was highly dubious in Thomas Carlyle's famous nineteenth-century 'rehabilitation' of Muḥammad against Western calumnies in 'The Prophet as Hero' among his *Heroes and Hero Worship*. But in an uncanny way Carlyle had a sound instinct which his welcome among Muslims seems to confirm. For, in an elastic sense of the term, and suitably subdued to celestial mandate, there is something of the 'hero' element in the steady, lively and resourceful reliance of Muslim thinking on the mind of Muḥammad, actual or attributable, in understanding its destiny today.

One great 'asset', beyond the 'socialism' we have noted, was the 'vitalism', if we may so speak, of Muḥammad's career in general. Undoubtedly the most celebrated exponent of this 'feature' of the Prophet was Muḥammad Iqbāl (1876–1938), whose *Reconstruction of Religious Thought in Islam* was earlier quoted. Iqbāl linked what he saw as the dynamism of Muḥammad's mission as prophet with a philosophy of creativity adapted from the French philosopher, Henri Bergson. Like the more sober pioneer before him, Muḥammad 'Abduh (1849–1905) of Cairo, Iqbāl saw *Taqlīd*, or obscurantist worship of the past and its authority in text and pundit, as the main factor in stagnation and immobility. It could best be countered and banished by a realization that Muḥammad, as seen by the Quraish, was the most determined innovator of all. Muslims in atrophy of will were no better than they. There were new, modern idols to be repudiated, not least within moribund Muslim societies. The *Jāhiliyyah*, or 'unruly ignorance' which the Prophet denounced and enlightened in pagan Arabia, was back again, Iqbāl alleged, in the decadence of a nominal Islam.[7] The popularity of his poems gave his ideas a wide currency and the daring, sometimes outrageous, terms in which he cast them had a galvanizing effect on attitudes and opinions. The 'image' of Muḥammad was his constant spur:

> The womb of the world never bore Muḥammad's like.
> We who know not the bounds of country

[7] A pagan, alert before his idol, Iqbāl said, was better than a Muslim asleep in the mosque. The accusation that decadent, conventional Islam is itself a *Jāhiliyyah*, odd as it may be, is not confined to Iqbāl. See, e.g. Muḥammad Quṭb, *Jāhiliyyat al-Qarn al-'Ashrīn* ('The *Jāhiliyyah* of the 20th Century'), Cairo, 1964.

Resemble sight, which is one, though it be the light of two eyes.
We belong to the Hijaz and China and Persia,
Yet we are the dew of one smiling morn.
We are all under the spell of the eye of the cupbearer from Mecca.

Of that Prophet leader, he wrote:

The song of love for him fills my silent reed,
A hundred notes throb in my bosom.
How shall I tell what devotion he inspires?

In both poems and treatises, Iqbāl understood the *Takbīr* of Islam, 'Greater is God', as a call to absolute desire, to a transcendence of compromised selfhood in the name of ultimate Self-realization. At the end of *Asrār-i-Khūdī*, he revelled in the famous fable about the old sheep who put himself across as an apostle of God to a group of tigers, whom he invited to embrace the sheep's religion, abjure their tigerness and accept a diet of hay. The tigers finally fell for the stratagem and adopted a placid existence. Whereupon their very souls died within them. The wily sheep even quoted Quranic precepts for his case. Unveiling the ruse in this rather Nietzschean tale Iqbāl summoned the Muslims of his time to their 'true' destiny of renewal and dynamism of soul, with Muḥammad as their proper mentor.[8] It was in these terms that he understood Surah 17.85: 'Say: "The soul proceeds from my Lord's *Amr* [command]" ' meaning that the divine energy is life's directing force imparted by God Himself. Spontaneity, vigour, initiative, venture – these are, therefore, its qualities. For lack of these Muslim society decays.

The doctrine of Muḥammad as *Khaṭm al-Nubūwwah*, 'the seal of prophecy', he read in these same terms. The culmination of prophecy is meant to throw men upon their own resources. The 'supernatural' sources of guidance having been consummated, their meanings are now internalized. This means the stimulation of critical judgement, the end of both *Taqlīd* and *Taqdīr*, hidebound authoritarianism and the idea of 'fatedness'.[9]

The boldness, sometimes even cavalier tone, of Iqbāl's thinking make him an unique figure. But such was his eminence in

[8] Muḥammad Iqbāl, *Asrār-i-Khūdī* ('Secrets of the Self'), trans. by R. A. Nicholson (London, 1920), lines 369, 388–392, 399–401. The tiger/sheep legend is in part vi. John Robinson published his study, *Truth is Two-Eyed* (London, 1979), though probably not consciously echoing Iqbāl.

[9] Iqbal, *The Reconstruction*, p. 126.

the antecedents of Pakistan and in the voluminous literature his ideas aroused, that it is not improper to see him as the expression of a search for Islamic renewal and assurance in the flux of twentieth-century history, the coming recession of Western imperialism and the emergence of new nationalism. Arab Muslim thinking, by and large, was more sober and circumspect.

Two pioneer figures among them, after Muḥammad ʿAbduh, and roughly of Iqbāl's generation were Muḥammad Ḥusain Haykal (1888–1956) and ʿAbbās al-ʿAqqād (1889–1964). The former produced, in 1935, the most substantial and influential of 'lives' of the Prophet in this century, and followed it with a moving study on the Pilgrimage with the title *Fī Manzil al-Waḥy* ('In the Abode of Revelation'). In *Ḥayāt Muḥammad*, he shows himself, in the prefaces, acutely aware of Western *animus* and anxious to proceed in due scholarly sophistication served by genuine religious devotion. But he aims also to prune away the accretions of piety in token of which he ceased the usage that repeats the formula of 'benediction' on the Prophet at every mention of his name – a decision which drew down upon him the wrath of many critics.

There was a patent sincerity about both his major works. His decision to base himself on the Qur'ān alone, and to exclude unreliable Tradition, he vigorously defended against the 'hagiologists'. Some would say that his critical 'liberalism' was extremely modest and left many basic issues unfaced. Much of his apologia at crucial points remained entirely traditional. It was as if he was genuinely concerned for a gesture of duty academically acknowledged and, at the same time, of caution for his orthodox fidelities. He presented his work as no more than a beginning.[10] His instinct to meditate in the Ḥijāz, despite the initial distaste he had for some aspects of the *Ḥajj*, was sound and imaginative. It was there, at the end of *Fī Manzil al-Waḥy*, that he commended, above all, meditation on Muḥammad's life as a single whole.

> His is a power which can lift mankind to the heights of the Spirit, where life will be brotherhood and love and care for the knowledge of all that is, in the world of existence, so that knowledge may illumine brotherly concord and love and that both may grow in human worth and excellence and bring us by their protection into the fullest peace.[11]

[10] Muḥammad Husain Haykal, *Ḥayāt Muḥammad* ('The Life of Muḥammad') (Cairo, 1935), pp. 21, 23, 63, 563.

[11] Muḥammad Ḥusain Haykal, *Fī-Manzil al-Waḥy* ('In the Abode of Revelation') (Cairo, 1937), p. 637.

The academic mind may read a cloudiness in this flowing Arabic conclusion. But the true realist must recognize it as the genuine pulse of Islam. It is parallel to Haykal's treatment in *Ḥayāt Muḥammad* of the Prophet's famous 'Night Journey' and 'Ascension' (Surah 17.1). Muḥammad, he avers, then stood face to face with reality, beyond the veil of time and place. Humanly all judgements are relative because of our finitude. But Muḥammad then saw it from eternity to eternity when the whole universe was gathered to his spirit.[12]

Al-'Aqqād's *'Abqariyyat Muḥammad* ('The Genius of Muḥammad') (1942) does not aim to be a biography. It is a presentation of Muḥammad as the universal example of the virtues after which all sincere folk strive. His greatness is a moral greatness recognizable in every aspect of his career, as prophet, husband, preacher, leader, ruler, administrator, and man. Al-'Aqqād sets out to emulate Carlyle and outdo him, as only a Muslim should. His work embodies, in simple popular form, the sort of possessive adulation which dismays the external scholar and yet speaks the sympathies of the masses. He has had numerous imitators across the Islamic world in every decade since.

To dismiss this phenomenon as sheer romanticism would be unwise. The student who may be so tempted needs the restraint he can learn from a very different disciple whose historical scholarship brought him into sharp confrontation with the obscurantists and whose literary qualities place him in the first rank of twentieth-century Arab Islam – Tāhā Ḥusain (1889–1973). He did notable service to the cause of academic freedom but when he turned from that encounter over pre-Islamic poetry to what he called 'the margin of the *Sīrah*', it was in order to distil for educational and edifying purposes the narratives, and even the legends, of the Prophet's biography. In *'Alā Hāmish al-Sīrah* (3 vols. 1933) he wrote: 'I was driven to write this book by an inner compulsion. As I read about the life of the Prophet, I found my soul swelling with it, my heart overflowing and my tongue set free.'[13] He wanted to set down the Muḥammad of the heart and the imagination from whom the unquestioning faith of simple souls could find incentive. Scholarship and historicism were not all. We must mediate the spiritual background of the Prophet. Men of a religious nature, he claimed, find themselves gravita-

12 Haykal, *Hayāt Muḥammad*, p. 189.

13 Tāhā Ḥusain, *'Alā Hāmish al-Sīrah* ('In the Margin of the Life-Story'), (Cairo, 1933), vol. i, p. 5.

ting in an uncanny way towards Mecca. Muḥammad is not rightly seen as a 'Hero'. He is 'God's Apostle' in that his spiritual experience brought about a new relationship between man and God.

It is this sort of *confessio fidei* with which the observant Christian has to reckon, the more so because it comes from one strenuously committed to the place of critical scholarship, but for whom it is not all. A comparable, yet slightly different, angle is to be found in the several works of Muḥammad Kāmil Ḥusain (1901–1977).[14] At points, he writes almost like a humanist, conceding 'supernatural' beliefs, such as the Prophet's 'Night Journey,' and the *Waḥy* of traditional faith with its 'miracle' of the 'illiterate' Prophet, *if* these are necessary to religious attainment and peace of spirit. If the state of 'hallowing' which Moses knew in 'the sacred valley' of true religious assurance avails for others without such 'miraculous' credence, then so much the better. Such souls are privileged. But let them not despise, still less denounce, the naturally 'religious' who need such certainties to be mediated from authority *lā raiba fīhi*, as the Qur'ān has it – 'in which there is nothing dubious'.

This kind of psychological validation of beliefs, which need not necessarily be held as dogma proposes, is rare indeed in Islam. But, in its sophisticated way, it commends the romanticism about Muḥammad which we have been at pains to explore. Our selection, out of the amplest of writing in several languages, is of course quite invidious. We have concentrated on the pace-setters, on the callers of the tunes. It serves to focus, if only in a cursory way, the fact we must recognize, that any adequate response to Muḥammad has to be a participation in the aspirations he fixes in the emotions of discipleship.

It must be remembered, too, that this 'possession' of Muḥammad takes added importance from the present crisis in

[14] Notably *Al-Wādī al-Muqaddas* ('The Hallowed Valley'), Cairo, 1968, trans. into English by the present writer (Cairo, 1977). Dr Ḥusain, a noted surgeon and a very erudite author, was concerned about the erosion of religious faith under the impact of scientific attitudes. He believed that religious faith was a deep psychic necessity in human life, that a sense of the transcendent was a vital sanction of human behaviour. He wanted religious faith, therefore, to be itself 'scienticized'. He was fond of medical metaphors and saw morality as a system of inhibitory mechanisms like those which check excessive energy and so safeguard the heart. Laws of spiritual life must be in line with the other laws of nature. To realize this was to be on the way to building universal religion, since both rational and dogmatic elements would be demoted when religion was properly seen as a function of the psyche.

Muslim education. Muslims are still very much only in the process of formulating a satisfying Islamic position of their own on the questions the West broadly characterizes as 'liberal'. Psychology and sociology are disconcerting factors in the picture with their queries about 'absolute' values, the bewilderment of their relativism. How, then, should contemporary education integrate the world and ensure the continuity of faith and cult? Do we educate merely for 'roles' and 'professions', as so much Westernism seems to say? Do we educate for the sort of value-free liberation from illusions of commitment, as current social sciences often imply? And what of the steady pressure of the physical sciences and the mentality they induce? If 'man' is the only measure for man, where are the external norms by which to 'measure' him?[15]

It is in the stress of these and kindred questions, which are questions of existence as well as of education, that Muslim search goes back instinctively to the person of Muḥammad, the human instrument of their revelation, the human axis of their religious identity and, in the case of Arab Muslims, the human 'hero' of their history. He is 'the definitive Muslim' in a sense which takes us beyond Tradition *per se*, beyond historians, beyond necessary scholarship, into the very being and becoming of Muslim experience as human.

Are we reaching, at this point, something like an ethical interchangeability between religions alongside a non-interchangeability in respect of their historical content and their spiritual personality? There are Christians who see their vocation, in respectofMuḥh10.5ammad,asoneofseekingtodispossessMuslims of his 'image', and its 'place' within them, and have the 'image' of Jesus there instead. Something like that is the witness to the meaning of their new allegiance as given by Muslims who have become Christians. Certainly the right to that 'option' must be both open and precious, if faiths are not to become closed shops. Such freedom of movement of belief is inseparable from any proper form of freedom of belief itself.

But can this be the whole relationship? What if something like a transposition of 'images' is already happening within a continuity of unbroken adherence? It is fair to say that some approximation to the likeness of Jesus, within the prescripts of the *Sīrah* in its broad and irreversible shape, has taken place in

15 An interesting example of this concern for education, and especially higher education, among Muslim thinkers as the critical arena of their intellectual problems is Fazlur Rahman's *Islam and Modernity: Transformation of an Intellectual Tradition*, Chicago, 1982.

recent interpretation of Muḥammad. The emphases of apologia change. The concerns of presentation respond, sometimes only half consciously, to the ideals of others. Features which were once maximized as glorious by the first chroniclers are minimized as only 'necessary' by the present interpreters. Evaluations stay with their historic focus but renew it in the staying. It is as if the self-awareness of Islam moves with the personality of Muḥammad and that they are mutually defining.

In this light, must we not conclude that an important aspect of Christian relationship to Muḥammad and his people will be the steady, yet sympathetic and honest, availability, to their sense of him, of those areas of reference to which Jesus has committed us?

6

THE PROPHETIC EXPERIENCE

'His words are not his own devising. The Qur'ān is revelation imparted' (Surah 53.3 and 4). But how imparted? And how do words and their revealing relate to personality speaking by receiving? These have always been vital questions in the understanding of Muḥammad and in the faith-structure of Islam. They are, therefore, central for any Christian, or other, concern for Muslim relationships. Critical aspects of religious security of mind as well as important decisions about commentary and interpretation turn upon them. We cannot hope for an honest adequacy in Christian acknowledgement of the Prophet of Islam without careful study of the 'imparting' to him of the Qur'ān. If we can attain a proper perspective at this point the way may be open for a welcome liberation of mind from inhibitions which, on both sides in differing ways, have too long persisted.

The term at the heart of the issue is *Waḥy*. Both noun and verb are used in 53.4. 'Revelation imparted' adopts the passive sense of the verb and could be translated: 'inbreathing inbreathed', or 'inspiration inspired'. For *Waḥy*, as 'revelation', is not only the content or the result: it is also the experience and the inward phenomenon. The word means *both* the utterance carrying meaning *and* the enabling that produced the utterance. Islamic orthodoxy has a very explicit account of the whole psychic and mental situation by which and in which the Qur'ān was received – an account which bears strongly on its whole approach to exegesis and underlies its visual cherishing of the Book in calligraphy and its reverent memorizing for recital. This means that the whole pattern of devotion by which Muslim religion is expressed reflects orthodox belief concerning how, by *Waḥy* from heaven, prophethood became Muḥammad's during the twenty-three years of his vocation. It is this account, with the religious attitudes of certitude and obedience it sustains, which we must explore.

It is well to say at once that any study in this area will be a concern to understand the Qur'ān, not to discount it. Muslim susceptibilities are naturally very sensitive at this point, suspecting that inquiry into *Waḥy*, in some subtle way, intends to decry it. Some even exclude altogether any consideration of the 'how' of the Qur'ān as being inappropriate to the nature of its authority. For most Muslims the status of the Qur'ān is, quite simply, indubitable and, as we must argue later, this fact of the situation is a truth with which we must reckon. That, however, does not make fears about honest study anything but unworthy and improper. It may well prove that the power of the Book emerges more strongly, not to say more religiously, from a careful review of all the factors within personality and environment by which its contents must be appreciated.

There are, indeed, many points at which the Qur'ān itself encourages intelligent investigation and calls upon hearers and readers for *tadabbur*, or mature reflection (4.82; 47.24). Even outright dogmatists tend to argue for their stance. So there is nothing improper in reverently inquiring into *Waḥy*. Nor is there any danger to essentials.

In his famous *Discourses*, the great Jalāl al-Dīn Rūmī cited the verses from Surah 53, already quoted, which deal with an early vision of Muḥammad's in fuller description than almost any other passage.

> By the star when it sets, your kinsman here [i.e. Muḥammad] was not astray nor was he deceived. His words are not his own devising. It [the Qur'ān] is nothing less than a revelation imparted. One of awesome might taught him, one endued with strength. Erect he stood, away on the far horizon. Then he drew near, hovering down, and came to within two bows' length, then nearer still, and he revealed to his servant what he revealed. His own heart [Muḥammad's] did not deny his vision. Are you [pl.] then to question what he sees?
>
> In another coming down he saw him by the sidrah tree on the far bound of Paradise, close by the garden of the refuge, and the sidrah tree was wrapped in mystery. His eye was transfixed, never turning from the sight. Truly he saw the great signs of his Lord. [53.1–18]

From that experience of vision and its sequels came the spoken word, the oral communication it inspired and empowered. Rūmī goes on to explain what he understands that speaking from the experience to entail in respect of both the words and syllables required and of the relation to these of the Prophet spokesman. In doing so Rūmī sets down, in terms unusually pedestrian for one so mystical and poetic, the concept which has broadly characterized Islamic reception of the Qur'ān. It is the concept of a celestial imparting of syntax, vocabulary and word sequence, so that the prophetic speech verbally iterates the divine speech and auditors to whom the Prophet dictates it thereby transcribe the sentences of a heavenly Book textually mediated to them, as to him.

> When the Prophet was transported out of himself he used to say: 'God says:' From the standpoint of form, it was his tongue that spoke. But he was not there at all. The speaker in reality was God. Having at first perceived himself ignorant and knowing nothing of such words, now that such words are being born in him he realizes that he is not now what he was at first. This is God controlling him . . . God is wholly free of forms and letters. His speech is beyond letters and voice. But He delivers His words by means of any letters and voice and tongue that He desires.

This 'humanizing' means the Arabic Scripture. Between its eternal source and its earthly presence stands the mystery of *Tanzīl* (lit. 'descending', 'causing to come down') which, like 'Incarnation' in the Christian faith, both denotes in concept and conceals in mystery the divine/human, the eternal/temporal, relationship. Within that concept and mystery, it has always been crucial for Muslims to insist that the will and personality of Muḥammad do not consciously participate. To hold so is, for them, the necessary guarantee that the Scripture is undeniably divine, and being thus undeniably divine, is literally indisputable. So, in turn, the reader and believer may be utterly secure.

Rūmī clinches the case with a startling metaphor.

> Men have fashioned upon the highways, in caravanserai, and on the banks of pools, men of stone or birds of stone, and out of their mouths the water comes and pours into the pool. All who are possessed of reason know that the water does not issue out of the mouth of a stone bird: it issues out of another place.[1]

It must surely be a vital part of any Christian scholarship with the Qur'ān, and of Christian engagements of mind and spirit with Muslims, to face the problems which this account involves. To do so will be positively for the sake of the Qur'ān and its authority, not for the contrary.

[1] *Discourses of Rumi*, trans. by A. J. Arberry (London, 1967), pp. 51–2.

There is, no doubt, great attraction in this version of 'Thus saith the Lord'. 'It is written', in the Biblical tradition, too, has the reassuring ring of finality ending all questions. Yet a confidence of this order incurs heavy liabilities. It means a diminution of the prophetic role and seems to do violence to prophetic experience in its actual incidence. It proceeds by the implication that the more an activity is divine the less it is human, that God's recruitment of personal powers requires an abeyance of their due exercise in reason, emotion and love. Agreed that the divine ways may be arbitrary. But is there not the likelier possibility – given the way creation is – that God's employment of human agency might in fact enhance, harness and fulfil the human potential so honoured, including the idiosyncrasies of thought and speech that are the mark of personal life and are evident enough in the Qur'ān itself? Is apostolate really to be understood by the analogy of stone figures devised by cunning plumbers and sculptors to impress the eye but which deceive none save the unwary? Does prophethood have no part but that of a mere channel otherwise uninvolved? The undoubted fact that the original source is beyond prophethood itself need not reduce the prophet to a pair of lips. The Qur'ān itself declares: 'The faithful Spirit descended with it upon thy heart . . .' (26.193–4, and 2.97), and the heart is the seat of cognitive and feeling life.

But what then, it will be asked, about those 'idiosyncrasies', those personal factors of hope and stress and action and interaction which so evidently belong with Quranic, as with all, revelatory situations? Will not these distort and distract the revelation itself unless they are excluded by deliberate 'dictation' to the Prophet of the words that can indubitably convey it? The Qur'ān is very conscious of this issue and records the danger that even Satanic deceit, as well as human fallibilities and slips of the tongue, may put the true message at risk. The critical occasions of prophetic deliverance attract these malign intentions (cf. 23.97). It is to obviate these perils that the revelatory initiative from heaven takes care not only of the meaning conveyed but also of the exact verbal sequences of its expression. The cargo of the word is too precious, and too precarious, in earthly conditions to have it otherwise.

Here, Islam in its view of the Qur'ān is close to a religious instinct which has many parallels elsewhere. There are other Scriptures believed to be 'God-breathed' in this literal sense. The issue merges into the even larger one of the ability of human language, in any way, to 'carry' divine truth, the more so if, as in Islam, one presupposes a theology of absolute transcendence. All one can finally say, Qur'ān-wise, is that God confers on language the capacity to speak truly for Him and from Him and that when such language is heard it is found to be Arabic. The question 'How?' must be absorbed into the dogma, and the mystery, of *Tanzīl* itself. God has caused it to be brought down, whether through Gabriel or 'the Spirit', or both, and done so syllabically without the intervention of the thought forms or the conscious composition of the Prophet.

Even so, those thought forms are emphatically present when the words are heard by the audience and become current in the hearing community. Otherwise revelation cannot obtain, for the simple reason that it has not arrived. If the Qur'ān, in public reception is not, and cannot be, exempt from popular concepts and current vocabulary, can it be thought exempt from these in its incidence within the prophetic mind? Preaching, whatever may be said of revelation, is intelligible exchange. When Muḥammad spoke of 'Allāh' the word was already current, had a connotation for his hearers, and signified a sense which belonged with their prejudices and his mission. Likewise with all the key-words of his communications: *raḥmah, īmān, ta'wīdh, tauḥīd, faḍl, fauz,* and scores of others. Such 'mercy', 'faith', 'refuge', 'unity', 'goodness', 'victory' were all significant, already, to his constituency. Even if a message is radically changing what words transact it must begin with them in their current value. Thus revelation cannot impinge upon a human community except within the mentality it possesses. If that is so when the message is prophetically conveyed to its public, can it be otherwise when it is prophetically received from its source? What is conscious and intelligible within the will to preach can hardly not be so with the coming into possession of what the preaching tells.

Deferring for a moment the Qur'ān's own evidence for this, the traditional case against it had better be set down. Apart from the yearning for religious certitude which underlies it, it stands in the belief in Muḥammad's 'illiteracy' and the consequent miracle of the Qur'ān as a surpassing eloquence on the lips of one who could not read. The resulting *i'jāz,* or matchlessness, of the Scripture as an Arabic marvel enables it to propose the unanswerable challenge: 'Bring a surah like it' (2.23; 10.38), 'Bring ten surahs like it' (11.13). Being arguably inimitable in its Arabic eloquence and allegedly coming through an unlettered man, the Qur'ān is the more indisputably divine in its origin and status. Once more we have the instinct to assume that proof of the divine stands in abeyance of the human. The divine quality of the text as God's word is not by means of a human capacity deepened and tempered, but by an incapacity not otherwise called upon.

There are many problems here. The non-Arab is, of course, unable to appreciate the proof. He has to take it on trust – a course which, in purely literary terms, he is well advised to follow. But will a pure linguistic consideration be appropriate to guarantee religious truth? Excellence of language may superbly serve relevatory content. Yet can it of itself commend it? For its universal constituency, as distinct from its Arabic immediacy, the Qur'ān's authority and appeal must turn upon spiritual impact rather than on literary form. We shall see in chapter 7 how well able it is to do so.

Meanwhile, uneasiness on the linguistic score is bound to continue. Not only is the *i'jāz* of the Scripture partial in its evidential range, it is also built on a doubtful foundation historically. Was the Prophet really 'illiterate'? What might the Quranic term *ummī* (7.157–8) really mean? It seems doubtful that an effective merchant could have been unable to read and handle bills of lading, ledgers and documents. References to Muḥammad's not having himself written down the Qur'ān may simply indicate the use of scribes or secretaries, rather than an inability of his own. More importantly, there are strong reasons for thinking that the vital phrase *al-rasūl al-nabī al-ummī* (the prophet-apostle who is 'unlettered') in Surah 7 has to do, not with any inability to read or write, but with the fact that he belongs with, and is sent to, a people who as yet possess no 'Book' of their own, who as yet have had no prophet of their own kin and kind. With this tallies the frequent emphasis that the Qur'ān is 'an Arabic Qur'ān' (e.g. 12.2; 20.113; 41.3; 42.7; 43.3). *Ummī* is very often in contradistinction to *al-Yahūd*, the Jews, when used in the plural *ummiyyūn*. Hence the translators suggested in some quarters, 'gentile', or 'of the common folk'. These have part of the idea without the clue. Arabs, unlike 'the people of the Book', were, as yet, 'unscriptured'. One of their own (a vital necessity – prophets and people are blood kin) is now sent to them, bearing a Book in their own language by which they become 'Scriptuaries'.

This more satisfactory understanding of Muḥammad's descriptive *ummī*, if approved, shifts the significance from bare 'illiteracy' to 'lack of native Scripture' (a lack which his vocation was steadily making good). It invites us to think of *i'jāz*, not as a merely linguistic wonder, but as a veritable Arabicizing of monotheistic faith, the genesis in Arab experience of the kind of significance which resided for Jews in Moses, Elijah and all the prophets.[2] It lay in revelation becoming an Arab possession in the Arab's tongue. This dimension gives a far more dynamic quality and authentic stature to the Prophet than does Rūmī's picture of the statue by the pools.

The mystery that *Waḥy* involves is there more deeply when seen in these terms. Muḥammad's being the unscriptured means to Scripture does not diminish the Quranic story. To question his actual 'illiteracy' (and so forfeit the traditional view of *iʿjāz*) is not to say that he was a scholarly researcher or that there was a fund of private knowledge or personal acumen to explain the resulting Scripture. On the contrary. While Jewish and Christian elements in his background have certainly to be reckoned with, there can be no doubt (unless of a tendentious kind) that the Qur'ān constitutes a massive document of religious meaning whose deepest sources lie beyond personal human factors. We may hope to explore them more adequately by having out of the way a mechanistic theory which, however persistent in Islam, does it so little justice. To say and believe, as with Muslims we surely must, that he did not 'have it from himself', nor of himself, is not to have to believe that Muḥammad was the recipient of a heavenly dictation which by-passed all his yearnings of heart or processes of mind and virtually ignored both the stress of his environment and the travail of his personality. Rather the sounder, worthier likeness to reality is ours, as we shall see, in being disembarrassed of the traditional view and the anxieties which fathered it.

Resuming, then, a positive argument, how does the Qur'ān itself sustain us? The clue is in the phrase already noted, '. . . upon your heart' (26.194 and 2.97). This ought to read '. . . upon your lips', if there is no active, positive role the heart, and so the personality, have to play. Of such a role the Qur'ān manifestly leaves us in no doubt. There is an evident inter-play between the events and decisions of the Prophet's task and the contents of the Book. Commentary itself has always been deeply concerned for what are known as *asbāb al-nuzūl* ('the occasions of the coming down') of the Scripture. That they are the 'occasions', not the 'causes', is clear enough. But that distinction, important to theologians wrestling with how the eternal and the temporal/temporary can converge as they do, does not affect the clear fact that the Quranic text relates intimately to personal

[2] See ch. 2, n. 2, and K. Cragg, *The Event of the Qur'ān* (London, 1971).

and communal situations where Muḥammad speaks and acts. It seems impossible to think that there can be a divorce between mind and word just at the moment of *Waḥy* when there is such an intimate juncture between event and word, when the import of *Waḥy* is uttered.

This is in no way to say that the content is self-induced, or that its revelatory quality is necessarily impugned. It *is* to say that revelatory content must have been in vital relation to the 'heart' and 'spirit' of Muḥammad. It is this that makes the chronology of the Qur'ān significant for its interpretation, as *Tafsīr* or exegesis, has rightly recognized. To be sure, some have sought to welcome the non-chronological arrangement of the Book, as we have it, thinking thereby to help detach it from time and place and so assert its timeless nature. But this is both a false and an impossible proceeding. If one is to believe in revelation, one must acknowledge its where and when. Not to have these is to be out of this world.

It is not a bare chronology that matters but rather the immediate setting and the unfolding of the whole, the process by which through twenty-three years the Book accumulated and the history developed. It is 'a Qur'ān. We have made a serial thing in order that you may recite it to the people at intervals', says 17.106. It was the unbelievers who wanted it 'all at once', a single whole (25.32). The gradualism of the Qur'ān, it is there explained, was in order to 'strengthen' Muḥammad's 'heart'. Throughout there is this emphasis, within the text, of the tenacity, the travail, the tempering, necessary to its incidence. They are all necessities within the personality and within the actualities of a developing situation which would both require and test them. It seems strange in the extreme that Muslim theory about *Waḥy* could so far diverge from the plain evidence of the Book itself.

The details of this are familiar enough. There is the basic classification of Surahs into Meccan and Medinan, before and after the Hijrah. There are the perceptible changes in style and vocabulary that result from the vicissitudes of preaching and militancy. Links are clearly present, for example, in the emergence of the patriarchal precedents into strong emphasis just at the time when Muḥammad's own experience of opposition called for the encouragement they afforded him and the warning they held for his detractors. Then there are the explicit references – though these are fewer than might be expected – to pivotal events in the unfolding story, the pledges, battles, treaties, declarations, which marked the Prophet's passage to victory in the post-Hijrah period. The case for the *asbāb al-nuzūl* may even be pressed – though problematically on other grounds – to include quite fleeting and unlikely situations, revelation-wise, of a private kind (33.37f. and 66.3f.). It seems on every count incontrovertible that the location of the Qur'ān in history means its active apprehension in prophethood. The *Waḥy* which bestows the one moves so evidently with the course of the other. One cannot intelligently suppose a momentary suspension of personal participation, while *Waḥy* supervenes, between the lively personal engagement of Muḥammad in the before and after. Mission, vocation, obedience, controversy, confrontation, leadership, decision, tactics, attainment, all seem to disallow any abeyance of 'the heart' while ears receive and lips declare.

A reverent realism here in no way undermines or calls in question what *Waḥy* means and conveys. Rather, we can turn to that positive study the more properly for having in view a personality *wholly* occupied in and with prophethood, rather than negated at its most critical.

Everything due from such a reverent realism is there in the command to Muḥammad, found only in two successive verses of Surah 96: 'Recite in the Name of your Lord . . . Recite. Your Lord is the most gracious.' *Waḥy* here is a commanding awareness of the reality of God, made vocal in language of which God Himself is the source – language to be spoken, commandingly, to the world. Nothing is here for private congratulation. All is for urgent public witness. The words are not for perusal but for utterance. The imperative about recital is on behalf of the imperative about Lordship. The awareness within *Waḥy* is 'commanding' on both counts as, essentially, is the whole Qur'ān. It makes a mission both for its content and its passion. These are inseparable. The resulting *islām*, we might say, is a theology of the words of God. Faith is for hearing and hearing is for faith. That is why verbal security is understood to attach to meaning, why the form must be communicated as well as the significance. Indeed, in the Quranic world they cannot be separated. All is in 'the Name of your Lord', the Lord who created and who taught the knowledge that is by and through the pen that writes.

The prophetic conviction here does not have to stay for 'justification' other than its own inherent mandate. The impulse it possesses comes from God's initiative. God's freedom in taking it takes care of all questions and makes the 'particular' that receives it (Muḥammad's person, the Arabic language, the Meccan scene) properly final and universal. This is the sense that describes the Qur'ān as *kitāb lā raiba fīhi*: 'A book in which there is nothing dubious' (2.2; 10.37; 32.2), because the prophetic experience which receives it receives it in these terms. Islam, in the Qur'ān, understands the mandate of Muḥammad to 'recite' and the making known of final truth as one, with the Arabic text as the point of evidence of both.

How are we to describe the personal element in this event.[3] Surah 53 makes it clear that there was an awesome visual factor in the authority to 'recite'. That there were antecedents of search and meditation seems to be evident from the address to Muḥammad in Surahs 73 and 74, both of which are early occasions of *Waḥy*. 'You who are enwrapped in your mantle . . . you who are enveloped in your cloak' are taken to refer to the Prophet's habit of withdrawal to the caves of Mount Ḥirā' for prayer and contemplation, and perhaps also to a 'mantle' that, Elijah-like, had already come to symbolize his status. Either way, these greetings require us to link his self-awareness, however we conceive it, with his commission. How could it be otherwise? One cannot be aware of the 'prophetic' only as a thing said and not of a self saying it.

Within that double awareness of self and statement there was certainly the presence of precedent. There were already 'people' with 'books'. We need not stay here to study the tangled questions of Jewish/Christian antecedents. 'Books' invariably came through 'prophets', who had their call mysteriously from above. When it came, they spoke loyally from their Lord. There might be poetry in their eloquence but they protested they were no mere poets, or 'professionals' with words. When their people closed their minds to them, the word was still a fire within and would not be gainsaid. Since all these features are evident in the Quranic scene, the parallels can hardly not have been operative, in some measure, within Muḥammad's person. Even nearer to hand was the significance of those incipient monotheists, the *Ḥanīfs*, whose contemporary thoughts, at issue with paganism, made them to be ostracized, as the name may imply.[4]

Whatever may be the detailed truth about these factors within Muḥammad's call, it is the central conviction of the divine Lordship which determines all. That conviction, it is fair to say, recruits the charisma which it creates, and there the secret of prophethood resides. In the sequences of the Qur'ān accumulation from 609 to 632, from Muḥammad's inaugural vision to

[3] K. Cragg, *The Event of the Qur'ān*, chs. 1 and 4.

[4] See W. Montgomery Watt, *Muḥammad at Mecca* (Oxford, 1953), Excursus, C, pp. 162–4.

his passing, the two proceed as one. Just as hostility tests the perseverance of the Prophet, so it sharpens by challenge the summons of the message. The tense encounters within the Qur'ān bring out both the fidelity of the messenger and the uncompromising nature of the message. *Waḥy* marches with occasion. The experience which begins in vision continues in contention, so that the theology it expresses carries the assurance of vision forward into the determination of conflict, with the consequences we have analysed in chapter 3.

In that double perspective all decision from outside Islam concerning Muḥammad at its centre does well to focus finally upon the sense of God by which his instrumentality was made. It cannot well be other than a response to the Qur'ān. Muslims, we may assume, will be glad to have it so, since, for them, the Book is the end where the Prophet is the means. Letting the issue turn squarely upon the Qur'ān is to be beyond all queries about sincerity concerning it within Muḥammad's person. It is to place all questions about prophetic status firmly within Quranic significance, accepting, with Muslims, his Quranic role as authentic and genuine, and on that ground, assessing the wide areas *and* the painful limits of a Christian kinship. In other words, we can properly take Muḥammad as 'the Prophet of the Qur'ān', and with many old cavils and polemics thus out of the way,[5] locate all critical acknowledgement within the actualities of the Book.

There is one strong deterrent to this which we must first surmount, and one powerful practical case which we can then develop. The deterrent, for Christians, is the fact that

[5] And certainly calumnies, too. One example out of many in medieval Christendom can be cited from William Langland's *Vision of Piers Plowman*, where with a dig at Christian hypocrites also, Muḥammad is described as a frustrated cardinal who, being denied the Papacy, went off to Syria.

> He took a dove and tamed it and taught it to take food,
> Having secretly slipped into either ear
> Such corn as the dove should peck from his shoulder.
> Whatever place he preached in, teaching the people,
> There the dove would come to this cleric's ear
> And make for her food. Thus Mahomet amazed them.
> When the dove came to nestle they all knelt in duty.
> For Mahomet maintained it was a messenger from heaven,
> And that dear God Himself in likeness of a dove
> Told him and taught him how to teach the people.
> So man by Mahomet was brought to misbelief . . .

Translation by Nevill Coghill (Oxford, 1959). p. 82.

Muḥammad, *qua* calendar, is after Jesus. The case, put tersely, is the argument from belief to truth, the sense in which faith makes its own content to be so. Of this the Islam of Muslims is a very powerful, though by no means unique, example.

Muḥammad and the Qur'ān belong to the seventh Christian century, Jesus and the Apostles to the first. What is later in temporal sequence claims to be final in truth. Muslims have often used this chronological circumstance to point up a religious superiority. 'Confirming what you already have . . .' (2.41 *et al.*) is the Quranic phrase about its perfecting of all previous Scriptures. Where these Scriptures, as now extant, seem to be other than confirmatory, they have to be accounted spurious or abrogated. Muḥammad is 'the seal of the prophets' – a belief which dating itself confirms.

Accordingly, it has long been a Christian difficulty to acknowledge the later when it is inconsistent with the earlier, given the conviction that the 'earlier' is itself 'final' and definitive. How can one ascribe authenticity to that which so confidently purports to displace, or otherwise improve upon, 'the Word made flesh'? One would seem to be attributing confusion, or worse, to the Holy Spirit, by any positive attitude to Muḥammad, and to be left with no Christian option but to regard the Qur'ān as imposture. So the Christian centuries since have too often and too crudely thought. This has been one of the main reasons for the sad closedness of the Qur'ān to generations of Christian minds or, if open at all, its polemical 'reception'.

But in more alert perspective, is this well concluded? It allows only the factor of time, when 'place' is no less relevant, even decisively so. One cannot assess the prophethood of Muḥammad merely by noting 'when' it is. 'Where' is critical. For places can be 'contemporary' in time and in no way 'contemporary' in character. The fourth century B.C. was one thing in Athens and another at Stonehenge. There was nineteenth-century cannibalism as well as nineteenth-century capitalism, depending on whether one was in Ecuador or Europe. In estimating Muḥammad's role in seventh-century (A.D.) Mecca/Medina one has to consider not only the years but the cities, not simply the date but the locale. In cultic terms the parallel would be closer with the Samaria of Elijah than with the Alexandria of Athanasius or the Jerusalem of Jesus. Prophetic meanings that might seem retrogressive by simple time criteria may be progressive by those of place and culture.

The issue is complicated, it is true, by the explicit controversy against crucial Christian understandings of Jesus in the Qur'ān. One cannot assess the latter only in terms of the preferability of monotheist faith to pagan idolatry, without regard to questions about Jesus and the Cross. But one can agree to 'contain' those questions within the predicates of theism and so acknowledge a positive mission in the place setting which the Qur'ān transforms. There are also reasons deriving from place, and having to do with Christian failure, which underlie Quranic attitudes to Jesus. These we cannot examine here.[6] We can say that, given a positive will, they need not oblige us to exclude the kind of prophetic achievement which is to be discerned in Muḥammad's place and time when both are taken together or 'times' are not distant centuries but immediate situations. This will not absolve us from matters of 'finality' in the abstract. It will save us from failing to take their measure in the actual.

This brings us on to what, perhaps, roundly, we called 'the argument from belief to truth'. What is meant here must be carefully stated lest the reader be appalled by the apparent suggestion that 'believing makes things so'. In one dimension that cannot be, and is not here intended. There is, however, a real sense in which religions live by convictions which do not admit of reference outside themselves. Outsiders may call this situation 'fide-ism', or a 'faith in faith', a kind of religious 'positivism'. The problem is what external categories of judgement could be competent to adjudicate against such faith and how, or by whom, they might be applied. Religions, of a certain temper, may concede an obligation to be referable beyond themselves, but others – or the same ones in different mood – will not do so, out of deference to their own authority, which, they will consider, must be total. Islam is no exception. Nor are Christians. Karl Barth, as a recent example, affirmed that Biblical revelation was the predication of God Himself. For him, there was no difficulty about the particularity involved, since God is free and chooses to exercise His freedom in these electing terms. If pressed for intellectual verification he disallowed the pre-supposition that would require it. In comparable terms, there are multitudes of Muslims for whom Muḥammad's prophethood, as noted in chapter 1, simply *is* final. Faith in the Qur'ān is self-warranting. The Book is documentation from God where a decision of faith finds, finally concentrated, the truth that justifies the decision. No historical, intellectual, or spiritual criticism legitimately concerns such decision.

6 See chapter 8.

Not all Muslims, of course, hold this position. But the fact of it is very real. If we may borrow a legal distinction, it is the *de facto* situation of Quranic authority for masses of our fellow men and women. Whether or not it is *de jure*, is a question that may be asked. But it will need no answer, if the distinction is not recognized.

It would seem to follow that the outsider, the Christian particularly, however anxious for external reference about Muḥammad, will need to reckon with the fact that, for so many on the inner side, there is no such referent, needed or existent. The fact of faith becomes a fact of the situation, a 'truth' of the matter. The Christian must continue to seek such a referent, believe that the seeking is right and hope to pursue it in partnership with those within. This will be our preoccupation in the chapters to follow. But the Christian cannot relate only in terms of that hope and search, for the simple reason that so many remain firmly outside it.

What other relation, then, may he have? He will have to relate to faith, rather than to creed, to people in their religion, rather than to religion in its dogma.[7] There will justifiably be for him a positive relation to Muḥammad precisely in the name and in the pursuit of a positive relation with Muslims. The theme of prophetic experience, as we are discussing it in this chapter, cannot be just an academic inquiry which historians monopolize. For such historicism is a company of limited liability. It will have to be a realm of spiritual study in which the Muḥammad of the faithful is always in view. Even on the historical level, the received consequences of events – whatever the receiving may have done to them – may be a right index to the events themselves.

To appreciate, in this way, the Muslim measure of the Prophet will not be a sentimental gesture. As such it could have no grounds. It will be a readiness to acknowledge in the continuity of Muslim experience an authentic clue to the experience of

[7] The need to relate primarily to the fact of belief rather than with debate about its 'credentials, belief apart', has especially marked the thinking of Professor Wilfred Cantwell Smith, of Harvard, in several works, notably: *The Faith of Other Men* (New York, 1962); *The Meaning and End of Religion* (revised edn, New York, 1978); and *Belief and History* (Charlottesville, 1977).

It may be argued that he carries his case too far in distinguishing 'faith' from 'dogma' and 'being-in-faith' from 'religion'. But the emphasis is salutary and points in the right direction, away from 'isms' and to 'believers'.

Muḥammad. It will be to take the Qur'ān in positive terms, both in its time and through the centuries as effectively revelatory.

It is interesting, if at first sight surprising, to note that *Tanzīl*, or God's causing revelation to come down, is a term also applied to a commodity like iron. Surah 57 is entitled 'Iron', and v.25 says, 'We have sent down iron which has such great strength and diverse uses for mankind.' Clearly the sense in which a mineral avails for man in the created order differs completely from the sense in which a Scripture does. But if the same verb *anzalnā*, used of God, can cover them both, perhaps a loose parallel may be made between the givenness, in the natural order, of iron and all its usages, and the Book in the spiritual order, with all its significance for the structure of Islam and of Muslim existence. If so, then the parallel may also suggest the sort of realism that is here in mind.

Before we let this formulation of a Christian position respecting Muḥammad take us forward into the content of the Qur'ān, there is one further consideration arising from the dynamic view of *Waḥy* for which we have argued. It is its bearing on the whole field of exegesis and commentary. The celestial 'dictation' view of the Scripture tends by its very logic to a less than lively approach to the sense of the text and to an excessive preoccupation with grammar, parsing and syntax. The Arabic itself becomes a thing of admiration and possessiveness as a literary phenomenon in which the believer participates by the simple act of recitation and the scribe of copying. There is nothing to deplore in this when it does not induce avoidance of genuine concern with meaning amd content. Such concern, indeed, it may well serve if it does not exclude the kind of *tadabbur*, or mental penetration the Qur'ān demands. All too often, however, it does hinder or displace an adequate encounter with the context.

The long-standing reluctance to translate the Qur'ān[8] works

[8] It was for this reason that Marmaduke Pickthall, as a good Muslim, entitled his English rendering, *The Meaning of the Glorious Koran* (London, 1930). A. J. Arberry used the title, *The Koran Interpreted* (London, 1955), not because, as some might suppose, he was issuing a commentary, but in deference to the fact that his English text was necessarily 'interpretative'. Editions which combine both Arabic and English, like that of Muḥammad 'Alī, escape the problem.

Any translator knows how the nuances and associations of original vocabulary elude satisfactory rendering into the second speech, or forfeit much in the transition. There are also latent ambiguities which the original happily holds within its secret but which a new tongue, lacking the common term, must opt to decide one way or another. Examples in the same way. It stands in the view that the Arabic form, i.e. the fact of being Arabic, is inseparable from its being 'the Qur'ān', so that translations can only be described as 'its meaning'. Admittedly the translator, where all great literature is concerned, has necessarily to be also an interpreter and take decisions about meaning which a great original enshrines, but a second language cannot, except with tantalizing options that impoverish. Yet the labour of decision here, which the Arabic-user escapes, may sometimes be salutary in that it compels a real wrestling with the sense.

Language veneration is not the only factor affecting commentary by a too slavish approach to the problems of meaning and form. Resistance to the relativities of time and place is another. We have seen how important to the Qur'ān is the matter of chronology which, in its own time-span, it recognizes by the division into Meccan and Medinan Surahs separated by the Hịjrah. Those Surahs are sometimes composite within themselves and datings are often approximate and marginal. But at least a time-span, with its episodes and sequences, is explicit in the Qur'ān. But what of the centuries since? How does the chronology operate beyond the years of incidence? In what way should the immediate time-span of less than a quarter-century relate to the time-span of Islam over fourteen centuries?

The instinct of the rigorous or timid mind is to answer that the significance is somehow locked into that initial time-span, that it is accessible there in absolute terms which admit of no radical 'translation' into the time-set of ongoing history. More flexible minds see that revelation in a there-and-then can only dynamically apply to a different here-and-now. It is of course just this interpretative obligation that the conservative temper suspects and fears. The fear is that any emphasis on the Qur'ān's having a timed context will lead to the notion that it has only a timed significance. Hence the desire to counter this danger by

---

from the Qur'ān are legion. Surah 30.30 may be cited: *Fiṭrat Allāh allati faṭara al nāsa 'alaiha*, 'The nature of God on which He natured people'. How should it 'go' into, and in, English? To start with, the frequent Arabic usage of verb and derivative together does not obtain. (We do not say, 'The nature he natured . . .') *Fiṭrah* may be either the created character that attaches to the human species or, in this context, it may be taken to be the proper religion intended for man by divine design and suited to human nature. Surah 30.30 for the Arab reader, chanter or calligrapher, does not have to say which; the English must, unless it resorts to a long sentence which then disserves the Arabic purity in another way.

assigning to the Scripture a static authority that has somehow escaped the factors of time and place or has made these factors somehow to be possessed of timeless quality.

Neither the fear nor the desire have any genuine ground. There is no necessary argument from 'in that time and place' to 'only for that time and place'. The 'only' need not be inserted. On the contrary, abiding relevance is ensured, but not by pretending that particular time did not historically condition the point, and points, of the relevance. Changing times and new situations must be responsibly within the view of right interpretation.

There is no need to argue this further. The bearing of it here is simply to observe how the view of the Prophet's experience for which we have pleaded coincides with it and sustains it. If we can understand the revelation as proceeding within a full engagement of mental and spiritual capacity, responsive to living situations, we can more readily require alert reception of it, from the text and in the present context of the reader's world. Only so will justice be done to the true dimensions of the Qur'ān – dimensions which are neglected by the narrow view of Muḥammad's part in them. To have the virility of living personality in the nature of the Book is to have from it a living perspective on the claims and encounters of every generation. Something of the 'translations' to be made from Quranic themes then, to their meaning now, will emerge in chapter 7. The menace of idolatry, for example, is a persisting crisis from the Quraish to the present but not in comparable form. To be concerned for 'a right estimation of God' (6.91; 22.74; 39.67), is surely a perennial necessity but one that has to reckon with the ever changing forms and moods of disesteem. So the constant tasks of Islamic abiding in the Qur'ān have to stay abreast of every shifting situation. To have its guidance rightly will be first to recognize in the great original an experience, not merely of loyal spokesmanship that had no other dimension, but of vivid personal commission known only through vision, by travail and in intensity of soul.

Perceptive Muslim thinking on the Qur'ān has known this well. Despite the prevailing orthodoxy which has dominated *Tafsīr*, or commentary, there has been a different tradition which has emphasized the personal endowments of the Prophet and accounted them significant of what *Waḥy* entailed on the inward side. Indeed, even the rigorists for a view of *Waḥy* that dispensed with active personal factors nevertheless attributed and hailed them despite their non-employment at the crucial moment of *Tanzīl*.

One modern example of the larger view was given by Muḥammad ʿAbduh. Writing in *Tafsīr al-Manār* he declared:

> God's preparation of him [Muḥammad] for his prophethood and his message is that He created him with a nature of rational humanity so as to send him forth with the religion that was for the original nature of man. He created him with a rational mind and a consummate intellectual ability, to send him forth with a religion of reason and scientific method.[9]

Others want to think more of 'genius' in spiritual terms, as evident from the survey in chapter 5. What matters is that, for all the strong belief in verbal inspiration guaranteeing from heaven an inviolate text, the prophethood within the Qur'ān be seen as a deep human experience under a directing sense of divine transcendence and, from it, deriving a compelling destiny to preach and to prevail.[10]

[9] Muḥammad 'Abduh, *Tafsīr al-Manār* (Cairo), vol. ii, p. 151.

[10] Some readers may have looked in this chapter for more attention to the whole phenomenon of prophetic ecstasy which transcends or eludes 'rational' analysis and in a quite inexplicable way 'explains' the psychic event of prophethood and all its consequences. The onset of 'inspiration' in these terms, as sheer psychic 'marvel', would (or could) coincide well with the concept of an arbitrary divine visitation 'out of the blue' and so, in turn, with traditional Muslim confidence that Muḥammad's destiny, being divinely willed, does not have to be 'explained' or made subject to investigative thought. We have not seriously developed here this line of understanding of the phenomenon of the Qur'ān for two reasons:

(a) Despite its arguable aptness for interpretation as arbitrary and evident divine bestowal, the psychic ecstasy view of Muḥammad's experience is in fact susceptible of relativizing theories no less than other views of inspiration. It *may* allow us to maximize the element of 'mystery' and 'awe' in the presence of the manifestly 'strange'. Or it may not. We become no less explainers by invoking the psychic than by investigating the historical. One can 'reduce' the Qur'ān to a mere phenomenon either way, whether by appeal to factors externally discernible, or by attribution to psychic causes. It would seem important to go beyond what may or may not be said about symptoms of the prophetic state, as Tradition records them, and centre all discussion on the actuality of the Qur'ān as Islam possesses it. It is the Qur'ān in its Islamic, religious stature that matters, rather than the 'how' of its genesis.

(b) That conclusion is reinforced by the fact that, whether *Waḥy* was 'this way' or 'that way', its incidence, at this distance of time, still has to be taken on trust. Psychic ecstasy of itself does not make it *sui generis*. Such phenomena are repeatable and absolute authority has been claimed for them historically before and since Islam. No faith in the finality of the Qur'ān can wisely base itself on accounts of the form of its incidence.

Short of that positive conclusion the Christian mind will not be able adequately to reckon with its Islamic duties. With it, despite all the persisting tensions and the necessary reservations, the Christian may hope to come to mature and honest terms with the Qur'ān, where all ultimate decisions must belong.

Nor does the Islamic concept of 'the seal of the prophets' do so. That Muḥammad was 'the seal of the prophets', i.e. prophet of the definitive and final revelation, is held to mean that ultimate truth has been authoritatively given and attested. It has now to be obeyed by loyal transcription into all subsequent and changing time. Change has to be cared for, not in its text but by its custodians.

However, readers concerned for an exploration of the psychic aspects of the Quranic state of *Waḥy* in which Muḥammad experienced the Qur'ān, especially in its early incidence, may turn to Tor Andrae; *Muḥammad, the Man and his Faith*, trans. from the German by T. Menzel (New York, 1936). For a wider background, see Alfred Guillaume, *Prophecy and Divination among the Hebrews and Other Semites* (London, 1938), and Abraham Heschel, *The Prophets* (New York, 1962).

7

THE CONTENT OF THE QUR'ĀN

A distinguished Biblical theologian of this century once terminated a long discussion on Bible interpretation by remarking: 'What I am trying to do in *Church Dogmatics* is to listen to what Scripture is saying and tell you what I hear.'[1] If that were all, would one need a million words in which to do so? His many-volumed work did not proceed so simply. For it was ruled by very strong principles about how the Bible should be received.

Even so, the idea has something to commend it, though 'listening' may well differ with every 'listener' and 'telling' with every 'teller'. Suppose a Christian tries this way with the Scripture of Islam and resolves to 'listen' and 'tell' what he hears. He will be something of a pioneer. For the effort has been made all too seldom, given the hesitations aroused by so many factors in original Islam and its subsequent relationships. Or the effort has retreated in the face of confusion, puzzlement or dismay. As any sensitive outsider knows, the Qur'ān does much to disconcert the alien listener, with its Arabic eloquence, its bewildering sequences and its sharp convictions.

But with a genuinely 'listening' will surmounting these, what shall we 'hear' and 'tell'? What may Christian reading of the Qur'ān mean for the reader with a mind to hear and understand? What might his report be? Ridding himself sincerely of prejudices that would deter, and of aspirations that might predispose him to read by his own lights, what will he take the Qur'ān in its whole consensus to 'say' to him, and to all?

Answer can well begin by noting that, strictly, it is not the Scripture 'saying' anything. It is God. The Book is only reporting. Whenever the orthodox Muslim quotes the Qur'ān, he uses the formula: *Qāl Allāh* ('God said . . .') or *Qaul Allāh* ('The saying of God . . .'). The point is important. The Prophet, in the trust

[1] Quoted in S. W. Sykes (ed.), *Karl Barth: Studies of his Theological Methods* (Oxford, 1979), p. 55.

of *Waḥy* and *Tanzīl*, was 'reciting'. In origin and in essence the speech is God's and God's alone. The Qur'ān is *kalām Allāh* 'the word of God'. There is nothing in the Islamic Scripture comparable to the Psalms in the Hebrew tradition. Still less is there anything analogous to the Book of Job, with its tempestuous human address to God and its passionate accusation of the divine. Apart from the Opening Surah, *Al-Fātiḥah*, in which God is adored in direct human praise, the only praise and petition in the Qur'ān occur in narratives, like those of Noah (54.10), of Hūd (11.56), of Abraham (60.45), of Moses (20.25–28), of Muḥammad (17.80), of emigrants to Mecca (59.10), of any Muslim (46.15), or of the Seven Sleepers of Ephesus (18.10). Even here, the stories which contain these prayers *to* God are understood as within God's speech to men. The Qur'ān, in this paramount sense, is of God and from God. It is God who speaks, and all human speaking in the Qur'ān, whether that of the Prophet, or of previous prophets, or of figures in life, is by the initiatory command: *Qul*, 'Say . . .' making what follows the divine command by the divine utterance.[2]

That active, authorizing divine reality is the central fact of the Qur'ān. If we allow ourselves the usage, 'The Book says . . .', then what it says is that God is, God rules, God creates, God sends, God guides, God ordains, God has mercy, God judges. The entire witness of the Scripture is to the sovereignty, the majesty, the transcendence, the knowledge, the power, the compassion, the exaltedness, the sublimity of God. That witness is forever summarized in the call most familiar to Muslims, *Allāhu akbar*, though, perhaps strangely, the two words together are not found in the Qur'ān.[3]

Allāhu akbar defines the Qur'ān. 'Greater is God', supreme beyond all comparison, so far so that no actual 'comparison' can ever be ventured. Grammatically the phrase remains always without a 'than'. None could be conceived appropriate even to name. Hence the value, in English, of making the comparative

2 *Qul* ('Say') occurs some 330 times in the Qur'ān. The command to speak is, in turn, an index to the fact that the whole Book is, essentially, an 'imperative'. It is that which must be heard and must be obeyed. The divine relation to the world is that of governance and control; the human relation to God that of obedience in *islām*.

3 The two words occur in sequence in 9.72, 29.45 and 40.10, but not in the grammatical form of the cry of praise. These verses say that God's pledge of bliss is 'greater' than all else, that recollection of Him is a 'greater' thing, and that God's disdain of the unbelieving is 'greater' than their own.

emphatic 'Greater is God', rather than 'God is greater . . .' which might seem to be waiting for completion of sense.[4]

If the divine reality is the central fact of the Qur'ān, the central emphasis within it is the reality of will, rather than of nature. Will and nature cannot, it is true, be finally separated and therein lies a deep hope of Muslim/Christian thinking. But emphasis, as the Qur'ān has it, is vital. The crux of revelation has to do with obedience, rather than with curiosity. It means to command and so to enlighten. Light, as powerfully in Surah 24, is indeed a right analogy: 'God is the light of the heavens and the earth . . .' (v. 35). But worship and guidance are its meaning, not the satisfaction of speculation or the unravelling of mystery. It is the light of a sovereignty that warns, rules, controls, teaches, disposes, rather than the light of a philosophy that clarifies, inquires, reflects and wonders.

It follows that the Qur'ān impresses the reader with imperative and obligation. In the words of a recent exposition of its 'major themes':

> The Qur'ān is no treatise about God and His nature: His existence, for the Qur'ān, is strictly functional – He is Creator and Sustainer of the universe and man . . . God's existence . . . becomes *the Master Truth* . . . The aim of the Qur'ān is man and his behaviour, not God.[5]

That the point could be so unhappily stated may be taken to demonstrate its importance. God's existence can never be merely 'functional' to man. But certainly it is 'the Master Truth' because it is the master fact. Man emerges in the Qur'ān as the great addressee of God and God as the supreme arbiter of man. Creation is the stage, and history is the drama with revelation as the 'direction'. The authority and the authorship are God's, and man's is to do his allotted part.

The centrality of divine will in the Quranic world is underlined by consideration of an aspect of the Qur'ān's theology which hinges on an interesting feature of Arabic grammar itself. Except in narrative situations the verb 'to be' is rarely used of God in

[4] Nor is *Allāhu akbar* superlative. For that could mean He was 'the greatest' within a comparability.

[5] Fazlur Rahman, *Major Themes of the Qur'ān* (*Bibliotheca Islamica*, Chicago, 1980), pp. 1–3.

the Qur'ān.[6] The Names of God, as Muslim commentary knows them, usually occur in what grammarians call 'nominal sentences'. The verb 'to be' does not appear, as it does in English. Meaning is had by juxtaposition, by *mubtada'* and *khabr*, 'beginner' (lit. or 'subject') and 'information' (lit. or 'predicate'). Thus *Allāhu ra'ūf* ('God kindly'); *Allāhu al-Raḥmān al-Raḥīm* ('God, the merciful, the mercy-giving'). No copula 'is' occurs. Thus the most extended passage of divine Names in Surah 59.22–4, in literal English would read:

> He God whom no god but He, the knower of the hidden, and the evident, He the merciful, the mercy giving. He God whom no god but He, the king, the holy, the peace, the faith keeper, the guardian, the strong, the overwhelming one, the greatly aware. Glory to God [immune] from all their idolatrousness. He God the creator, the maker, the shaper. To Him the excellent Names. Praises Him whatsoever there in the heaven and the earth, and He the mighty, the wise.

With the exception of the final: 'there praises Him . . .' there are no verbal sentences in this passage. All the attributes are in grammatically 'nominal' sentences. This is in line with, or a parable of, the fact that in the Qur'ān the Names of God describe His activity rather than His essence, that is, they are 'nominal' in the theological sense also. While they characterize His action they do not define His nature. God acts towards mankind in mercy, compassion, tenderness, might, judgement. He is not, however, 'identifiable' with or by any of these. He retains an untrammelled freedom over against any sort of moral or spiritual necessity. Man may hope for His mercy but cannot have it ensured to him. God may relate as 'loving'; He may not be said to *be* 'love'.

Since, so understood, the divine Names have played so great a part in Islamic thought and in Muslim devotion, it is important to keep this essential distinction in mind. It belongs squarely with the 'functional' – to use Fazlur Rahman's term – that obtains in the Qur'ān. The names have to do with relationship – God's to us of sovereignty, ours to Him of submission. They are, as it were, denominators in divine/human encounter and that

6 One example would be 4.158, where the context is historical, namely the Quranic sequel, in rapture to heaven, of Jesus' arrest. There God, it is said, 'was mighty and wise'. These, power and wisdom, interestingly, are just the very descriptives Paul uses, in a quite contrary sense, in reference to the Cross of Christ as being 'the power and the wisdom of God'.

encounter means Lordship commanding servanthood, humanity acknowledging submission.

Other significance in the relationships the Names denote will call for notice later. This of human obligation responsive to divine claim is paramount. It is what the listener hears, first and last, from the Qur'ān, the theme of all the warnings, sendings, guidings, remindings, enjoinings, that the Scripture recites and records.

The listener might then be liable to assume that he is hearing also the inferiorizing of man, that the Qur'ān with its strenuous witness to the sovereignty of God leaves no dimension of autonomy to man. But, on the contrary. Here a fascinating paradox comes into view. Man, to be sure, has no ultimate autonomy – a fact which is a major element in Islam's witness to contemporary secularity. Man is indeed tributary, a creature made, not for self-sufficiency, but for liability beyond the self. Yet, being so, he is strangely dignified and ennobled.

'It suffices me for honour that I should be Your servant. It suffices me for grace that You should be my Lord' – runs a much-loved saying in Islam.[7] It is plain from the Qur'ān that man is in no way a law unto himself. But his being under law to God is a summons to his own will. The very appeals of the Scripture bear witness to this, as do the long sequences of prophethood. *Islām* itself, as a term and as an obedience, is an act of will. If it were automatic, like the behaviour of atoms or planets, it would not be necessary.[8] Unless it were willed, it could not be mandatory. Man could not be, as he is in the Muslim Scripture, the addressee of God, if he were not free to be the respondent. In this sense it takes freedom to be *muslim.* Theologians, it is true, have wanted to hedge this fact around, seeing unbelief as fated and true *taqwā*, or 'Godfearingness', as always a mercy from heaven. Christians should be the last to minimize or miss these paradoxes of grace. Yet the fact remains that, however enabled by God's own decree, faith is by an act of will for which the Qur'ān unremittingly appeals by reminding men of all that makes it mandatory, desirable and urgent, both by argument of nature and by force of revelation.

The largest proof of this human liability is the reality of

[7] From one of the many editions of *Ṭahārat al-Qulūb*, ('Purity of the Hearts').

[8] Though there is a non-volitional *islām*, as many modern writers affirm, in the amenability of nature to natural law. One may say that chemical reactions, or planetary movements, or even mathematical formulae, are a form of subordination to divine will. But they differ from a religious, intelligent, moral conformity such as only humanity can bring.

idolatry itself – the reality which is the burden within all prophethood and, in negative terms, the essential reason for Muḥammad's mission. That man is free to be an idolator, to press to the most heinous degree his disavowal of God and Lordship, is the Qur'ān's own measure of what his dignity must be. This is what any intelligent Christian hears the Qur'ān saying, as he 'listens' to the implication of its central quarrel with the pagan Meccans. There is absolutely no point in prophets if such 'unruliness', as we must call it in the *Jāhiliyyah*, is not the perversion of a God-intended destiny in man for a true worship.

By the same token, we have to reckon in the Qur'ān with a quality of divine sovereignty that admits of this degree of disregard. The thought that God could be 'vulnerable' to man has always been anathema to dogmatic Islam. Yet it is hard to see how a sovereignty for which idolatry matters, a Lordship which *shirk*, or 'associationism', defies, could be otherwise. We can hardly have divine summons to man and divine indifference about response from man, unless we are somehow to let both be absorbed into baffling enigma where there could be no room for the passion of the Qur'ān and the thrust of Muḥammad. The God whom we *must* acknowledge is the God whom we *may* ignore. What may this say for His forbearance, His mercy and compassion, as well as for His power?

This, of course, is all bound up with the theme of creation, of Creator and creature, for which the Qur'ān often reserves its highest eloquence and its most poetic invocations. Man is the being to whom *khilāfah*, or 'dominion', is given (2.30) and this authority to be over nature is an entrustment anticipating conformity to the divine law. This *amānah* (33.72) is what distinguishes man from the lowlier creation, and an arrogant behaviour with it is the chief index to his perversity, and so, further, an evidence of the divine 'stake' placed, precariously in man, by the fact of creation. According to the celestial counsels which accompany the heavenly decision for the 'risk' of man, the angels were well aware of a seeming divine folly, or whimsicality, in God's venture with man. According to 2.30f. they all demurred fearing the blood-shedding and the follies to be expected from the frailty and fickleness of the creature to be. When at length the angels defer to the hidden wisdom of God, or at least to divine determination, they bow to 'worship' Adam in acknowledgement of his stature in the created world. Only Satan (*al-Shaiṭān*) persists in his repudiation of man, and of God's proposal in man, and by this defiance is outlawed. He then becomes the 'accuser' whose mythic role in history is so to disorder humanity by his machinations as to be able to demonstrate, though only *post facto*, the foolish divine miscalculation that mankind is seen to be. So, in turn, it becomes man's task, by *islām*, to give the lie to the liar and thus vindicate the divine entrustment which Satan so envies and, envying, scorns.[9]

That implicit 'gamble' about man, drawing on a long Hebraic mythic theme, rides with the constant sense in the Qur'ān of 'issues' turning on man's ways. His God-awareness is continually threatened by his God-forgetfulness. He is *ẓalūmun jahūlun*, as 33.72 says, 'wildly bent on evil', 'perverse and illdisciplined', a creature of wilfulness, refusing the right in both mind and motive. One of the most telling features of the Qur'ān's account of man, as the Prophet's mission saw it, is this waywardness and defiance of good, of which ingratitude and arrogance, assertiveness and hardness of heart, are the dark confirmation. The sensitive reader may sometimes feel that its accusation of mankind is too readily linked with occasions in Muḥammad's career and cause. But there is no mistaking its human tragic realism. It is odd to recall that some observers have thought the Scripture of Islam had no sense of sin.

But honest frankness about the human scene is only the other side of convictions as to stature and destiny. Aberration is only recognized by guidedness. *Ẓulm* in the Qur'ān can be known for what it is because there is *Hudā*. 'Wrong' is indicted because 'guidance' avails. This belief in man's 'directedness' comes from the constant *dhikr* by which the Scripture reminds his conscience and 'nudges' his will. *Hudā* is the charter of his creaturehood, the frame of reference for his entrustment.

Man's consequent responsibility as creature and as 'disposer' of things within the limits of his mortal competence is evident on all sides in the Qur'ān. It almost warrants a reversal of the familiar proverb: 'Man proposes, God disposes'. For, Quranically, 'God proposes', that is, decrees and orders and legislates and, by that delegated authority, 'man disposes', effectuates and handles the obligations he incurs under God. While the vicissitudes of circumstance to which the proverb customarily

[9] This understanding of the role of Satan is in line with the allusion in Psalm 8 about 'silencing the accuser'. There each new-born child is a new token of the divine trust in humanity renewed. Were the trust withdrawn, humanity would become extinct. So, in turn, each new generation is engaged in the 'crisis' through which alone God's stake in creation is vindicated. In Islamic Pilgrimage the ceremony of the stoning of *Al-Shaiṭān al-Rajīm* recalls this duty to disown the falsifier of man in highly dramatic form.

refers are always present, there is nothing bizarre or dubious about the mandate man has within those circumstances, to technologize and to manage his habitat. The Qur'ān has the familiar theme of Adam and the 'names' of things, only it is God who teaches him what they are, not he that names them (2.31; cf. Gen. 2.19–20). Classification, of which this is the symbol, has always been basic to science. To be able to identify is to be able to harness. Everything from agriculture to chemistry, from the ploughman to the surgeon, turns upon 'naming' and the resulting disciplines of skill and competence. All this is man's capacity, understood as God-imparted and God-entrusted. Our day is only different in having developed it to awesome degree and, all too often, in neglecting its meaning.

Characteristic of Quranic concern in this area are the questions in Surah 56.58, 63, 68 and 71: 'Have you realized the seed of your intercourse . . . the soil of your ploughing . . . the water of your drinking . . . the fire of your kindling?' The verb means both 'to see' and 'to have a view about'. It is an invitation both to reverence and to alertness, in line with several other passages as, for example, the Surah of Iron, noted in chapter 6. The sexuality meant in 56.58 is, of course, the most crucial factor of all in man's creaturehood, the very ability and will to perpetuate his kind and, thereby, to perpetuate the divine entrustment to his species – a sort of 'trust upon trust'. There is no clearer token of God's fidelity with His creation and of man's responsible role within it than the mutuality of the sexes.

This aspect of the content of the Qur'ān is borne out in the continuous presentation of the natural order as a realm of 'signs' (*āyāt*). Phenomena in their endless sequence to the senses are there, says the Qur'ān, to evoke both attentiveness and gratitude. They confront us with an invitation which we may recognize in response or ignore in neglect. This option is the *la'alla*, the 'perhaps' of the Qur'ān, the word which introduces a fascinating variety of verbs: 'perhaps you may be grateful', 'perhaps you may understand', 'perhaps you may come to your wits', 'perhaps you may realize what mercy is yours'. More than a hundred times the term recurs. By it we are called to a relationship to nature and life which is truly 'sacramental', in that the order of the world, received and explored in human cognisance, properly conduces to reverence, wonder and thanksgiving, as attitudes of the human spirit.

This, one of the most precious areas of the Quranic worldview, unites what we may broadly call 'science' and 'religion', or *'ulūm* and *'ibādah*, in a very salutary way. The *āyāt* underlie all technical competence in that science proceeds by observation, by experiment, by data that are ascertainable by just that close reference to phenomena which *la'alla* enjoins. By such reading of the *āyāt* which nature affords to the watchful (but does not advertize to the lazy), knowledge, and so control, of the environment – physical, biological, chemical, economic – have been built up over the centuries. So, by the intelligibility of the *āyāt* around him, man with intelligence alert to them, has achieved and fulfilled that *khilāfah*, or dominion, which was his birthright. Without the 'sign-quality' of nature, it would have been a barren, even a mocking, gift. God, however, 'did not create the heaven and the earth and all within them in jest' (21.16; 44.38). Thus the ever dependable, ever fascinating, 'signs' of God in nature are His keeping faith with man as trustee and tenant.

But the same 'signs' which thus admit of the scientific empire of man also call him to religious reverence. The same signs. The point is important. There is no proper division between work and worship, between authority and submission. Where man takes his dominion, he must present his praise. The *āyāt* which educate the researcher, require the laboratory, and give rise to the economy, must also point towards the sanctuary. Whereas a crude paganism, such as that which all the prophets from Abraham to Muḥammad reproached, divinizes phenomena themselves, Quranic theism teaches a unity of divine will and mercy behind all plural things and so directs all instinct of dependence, wonder, praise and reliance towards that one centre of a right adoration. It will be fair to say that whatever else one finds, or fails to find, in Muḥammad and the Qur'ān, here is a vital religious dimension that must be saluted and possessed with satisfaction by all whose sense of God is fed by the bread and wine of Jesus.

It prompts us to come back to those divine Names (*al-Asmā' al-Ḥusnā*) to which earlier reference was made. In that earlier context, the point was how the Names are understood by theologians in Islam as, strictly, 'nominal', in the sense that they constitute no definition of the divine nature. They certainly give the theological mind no guarantee about God. They are to be used, as the orthodox formula goes, *bilā kaif*, 'without asking how?'[10]

[10] 'Without asking how?' was classical theology's way in the third Muslim century of giving back as an answer the problem of theological language. Names which, like all human language, have human connotation, could be used of God (since otherwise religious expression would be impossible), but, so used, they were not to be taken as implying anything dependable. They could be counters in worship without availing for

But they truly are 'used'. Invoking God, addressing God, being worshippers before God, are ever-present realities in the Qur'ān. The themes of praise and prayer are always central to its narrative and its exhortations. *Subḥān Allāh*, 'glory (or 'praise') to God' is the cry of Joseph (12.108), of Moses (27.8), and of all loyal Muslims (23.91; 28.69; 30.18; 37.159; 52.43; 59.23 where it is the antithesis of all pagan pluralism such as a true praise repudiates). *Subḥānaka*, 'praise to be Thee' (2.32 *et al.*), is also frequent, or the same word with '. . . my Lord' (e.g. 17.93) or '. . . to Him that created' (e.g. 36.36). The reiterated *al-Ḥamdu li-Llāh*, 'the praise is God's', comes dependably in varied situations in the Book, either as a spontaneous response or an insistent injunction. 'His is the sovereignty and His is the praise,' says 64.1

Here, surely, is a dimension of the Qur'ān in which the Christian must rejoice. To be sure, there is the implicit question as to the 'predicates' about God which lie deep within our worship. But it is fair to say that theology is always safest in doxology, and the truths which the Qur'ān salutes in *Ḥamd* and *Shukr* and *Tasbīḥ* are in large measure those we share – creation and creaturehood, parental care and family bonds, the mercy behind phenomena, the precedents of fidelity we inherit from patriarchs and prophets, and the providence we discern in our affairs. It may be that a sense of community in these areas will help us to care more wisely and duly for the questions that remain. 'Unite my heart with those who fear Thy Name' is one reading of Psalm 86.11(b).[11] Can it be a prayer, however cautious, which is right for the Christian who is aware of Quranic thanksgiving? Is it deliberately that the psalmist writes: 'one in heart . . .' rather than 'one in mind . . .'? Can there be a unity of spirit beyond, or even despite, a lack of unity in doctrine? Can a community of fellowship reach outside a community of faith? Is faith itself shared even when it is at issue? Much, no doubt, turns on what the psalm means, and what we mean, by 'fear' and 'Name'.

Holding that question in abeyance, another important aspect of the Qur'ān's habit of praise and of its 'naming' of God emerges. It is the fact that the Names, whatever reservations theologians

---

comprehension. The only way out of this futility is to cease supposing some divine reluctance to be 'nameable'.

[11] This is one reading of the Hebrew of Psalm 86.11. Some translations take the 'unifying' to be that of the worshipper's heart, but it is possible to read the prayer for 'oneness' as between people. How far is 'religion' *per se* a unifying thing or are the intellectual and spiritual diversities within its many forms inevitably divisive, as history seems to indicate?

may impose, do involve God and humanity in relationship. On all counts, this is a precious truth for us all. Human vocabulary can have practical relevance to God, if only because it is necessary for adoration that it should be so. Nouns and adjectives which have their connotation from people can be predicated of God. They may not be 'descriptive'. They are certainly 'referential'. Otherwise, all the Muslim attitudes and aptitudes of prayer and invocation would be impossible. So also would the divine activities of mercy and compassion. It is just here that for Christians the meaning of the Incarnation belongs, namely the human expressibility of God. The Qur'ān's apparent veto on ever conceiving of the divine Names as legible in a single personality in a Messianic situation does not disengage the Islamic Scripture from the significances of human speech as relevant to God. On the contrary, every Qur'ān reader is within a context in which what is human – speech, language, vocabulary, history – is expressive of what is divine – revelation, mercy, guidance. His relatedness to God, thanks to the Book, is only possible as the manward side of God's relatedness to him.

We can rejoice, then, that the divine Names do 'signify'. The idea of the rigorists somehow to disembarrass God of their implications looks, on reflection, to be ill-judged. If pressed, it would endanger the whole impact of the Qur'ān as a divine summons to man. And it would disown the truth that the summons is also a divine liability with man. The Names denote a significance in God reciprocal to humanity. Many do so in some degree, others quite completely. Take *Al-Shakūr*, for example (35.30; 35.34; 42.23; 64.17), used of God. 'Every patient grateful one' (14.5; 31.31; 34.19; 42.33) is a phrase linked with attentiveness to the *āyāt*. But what can be meant by the 'gratitude' of God? Only, surely, a delight in human thankfulness, a reflexive joy in man's capacity for religious response to the creation.

> Thus God, by so disposing the corporeal senses for our use, has given us a perfect model of the love we owe Him. He has included a revelation in our sensibility itself.[12]

Our religious thankfulness becomes in turn a clue to the grace that evokes it. We are warranted in saying that the Qur'ān's religious theism (the adjective is necessary) practises, rather than proves, the reality of God or, better, proves in the practice. God

[12] Simone Weil, *Intimations of Christianity among the Ancient Greeks*, ed. and trans. by E. G. Geissbuhler (London, 1957), p. 200.

is thus denoted by the attributes that our response confesses. Worship, we might say, is the only task, and the only legitimacy of theology, since it is only in their using, by us, that the Names signify. But this can only mean that the impulse to worship, in their terms, is truly possessed of His relationship as they denote it.

One can see this readily from the progression in various derivatives of the same verbal roots among the Names. That, for example, through *Al-Ghāfir, Al-Ghafūr, Al-Ghaffār*, develops from the simple to the intensive sense of 'forgiveness' in a dynamic quality. Clearest of all is the *Raḥmah* root within the *Bismillāh* itself. *Al-Raḥmān al-Raḥīm*, as noted earlier, is not bare repetition of the single R Ḥ M root. The Arabic form of the derivatives indicates a mercy which is characteristic of God essentially and so, in turn, a mercy actually engaged with human situations, He who *is* the *Raḥmān acts* as the *Raḥīm*. It follows that all our human experience can be described as a coming through to us of what God is known by. Operative in this way, perhaps the Names are not so 'nominal' as rigorists have supposed. In any case, what matters is that in 'listening' to the Qur'ān we should understand from its divine 'Naming' the profound 'association' between God and man on which it proceeds.

'Association' is, doubtless, a suspect word because of the Book's strenuous repudiation of all things idolatrous. But *shirk*, often so translated in English, and the cardinal sin by which man deifies earthly entities, is something else. It means a perverse will to rank alongside God the items of creation. Such pretension from the created order in no way deters God's condescension into the creaturely. On the contrary, it necessitates it all the more critically, so that the phenomena which the idolater misreads and enthrones may be truly credited, *via* the divine Names, to their true origin in sovereignty and mercy that are God's alone. Unless, as the Names do, we can truly 'associate' God, in wisdom, power and love, with the things of time and nature, how shall we escape 'misnaming' these as powers in their own right? The more emphatically we assert that 'there is no god but God' and give the lie to *shirk*, the more firmly will we associate all our experience with the benediction of His Names. 'God is our adequacy', says Surah 3.173.

In that confidence, man himself is uplifted, but only soberly and responsibly. The true worshipper acknowledges the truth of himself as constituted by his God relationship. The Qur'ān has us 'listening' to this in all kinds of ways.

Central among them is its steady underlining of the mystery

of our sexuality, as the trust of mortal continuity set within personal demise. Life persists though the generations pass. The creature is a procreator. The individual has the competence to pay to the future his debt to the past. But only by partnership – a partnership divinely ordained for 'love and tenderness' (30.21) and to be interpreted as among 'His signs'. In several passages the Qur'ān reflects reverently on the embryo's progress from conception into life (e.g. 22.5) and at the beginning of the famous Surah of Women (4.1) calls the hearers to a due awareness of God in respect of all 'that you [pl.] ask, or seek, of one another', adding, 'and the wombs'. There could hardly be a more inclusive prescript to write over the intimacies and the tensions of the love relationship, with its mingled themes of need and power, of bliss and risk, of giving and receiving. Love as the potency of birth and the venturing of selfhood has its sure context in the fear of God.

It is true that the Qur'ān does not take sex as sacramental in the Christian sense. It remains a contractual relationship. Nevertheless, aside from the matter of 'female slaves', the Islamic Scripture requires that the contractual status of husband and wife be the sole proper condition of sexual relationship. Intercourse is not properly to be had as a commodity or as an exploitation. It must be dignified and circumscribed by the marriage bond. Divorce, at male behest, may sever this. But that properly liberates both parties for alternative fulfilment, provided this in turn is legitimated by due contractual ties. Anything less constitutes *zinā*, on which the Qur'ān lays firm prohibition (17.32).

While realizing that something indefinably significant goes out of marital love where it harbours its own demise, the Christian nevertheless is wise to appreciate the Qur'ān's reverence for the married condition, albeit in consecutive experience. Plural marriage has been traditionally taken as permissible within a limit of four wives, from Surah 4.3, but not incontestably so.[13] While, historically, Islam has been a man's world and woman's role that of fertility (cf. 2.223: 'Women are your fields: go then into your fields as you please . . ; keep in mind the fear due to

[13] There is an increasing interpretation of 4.3, as a 'virtual' prohibition of plural marriage, since the proviso *alla ta'dilū* ('do them justice') is unattainable. However, there is continuing debate as to what sort of just treatment is meant. Some areas, material and financial, are entirely feasible, whereas things emotional are not. The old view is that equal attitudes to wives in plural marriage *is* feasible and the authority for plurality remains.

God'), it is important, in our common contemporary stresses, to maximize the Scripture's undoubted emphasis on reverence, justice, gentleness and dignity. In a very Hebraic way, the Qur'ān sees the 'knowledge' of intercourse ('Adam knew his wife') as finally a humbling mystery evoking both wonder and compassion. Surah 2.187 declares: 'They (your wives) are a garment for you and you for them.' The term here, *libās* ('garment'), suggests the physical as a parable of the spiritual. The intimacy that makes two one creates a seemly privacy. So, likewise, reverence belongs where, without it, all would be gross and shameful. The word *rafath*, used in 2.187, meaning 'everything that a man desires of his wife', is linked closely with 'what God has ordained for you'. What He has forbidden is *fāḥishah*, 'indecency'.

In Surah 7.189, there is an interesting passage on the single creation of male and female, on man's 'security' with his wife, their intercoursing (*taghashshāha*), her conceiving and the growing weight of pregnancy. The couple turned anticipation into prayer, asking for a healthy (male) child and pledging gratitude. When God fulfilled their desire, they turned back to trust in idols. There is more than a hint in this passage that the experience of sex and procreation points us Godward and that there is within the bond of marriage an awareness, however fragile, of God's undivided claim upon our worship.

That claim, of course, extends into and through all the life-cycle of what the Qur'ān, in 7.189, calls 'a wholesome one' (*sāliḥan*), healthy, to be sure, as every parent hopes, but also 'sound' in quality. Progeny means nurture; parenthood issues into education. We must appreciate the ethics, as well as the procreation passages, of the Book.

Manuals of education drawn from the Qur'ān are numerous, the memorized Scripture itself being the cornerstone. By that requirement of *Ḥifẓ*, or recitation by heart, the Qur'ān is a literal educator in itself and inculcates with the accents of its very syllables the accents of its morality. All is grounded in the divine justice and determined by the divine authority. It is solemnized by the divine judgement of the Last Day.

The Qur'ān's own 'manual' for a *ṣāliḥ* is Surah 17.22 to 39, the longest single passage of ethical directive, many of whose injunctions are repeated in Surah 16. They also recur frequently in isolation elsewhere. It may be good to rehearse the sequence in full. It begins with the obligation to worship and serve only God, and continues:

Show kindness to parents, whether one or both of them attains old age with you. Do not be round or impatient with either of them but speak kindly words to them. Lower to them the wing of humility tenderly and say: 'My Lord, have mercy on them, as they nurtured me when I was little.' Your Lord knows well what is in your hearts, if you be true of soul. He is all forgiving to those who seek Him.

Give to the kinsman his due and to the needy and the wayfarer. Do not squander your substance. Squanderers are brothers to Satan. Satan is ever thankless to his Lord. If you have to disappoint them while you are awaiting from your Lord's mercy the means to provide, then at least speak to them kindly.

Do not have your hand chained to your neck. Yet do not be open-handed to the point of excess or you will end up reproached and bankrupt. Your Lord gives with bountiful hand, and with sparing hand, to whom He wills. Truly He knows and observes His servants.

Do not kill your children for fear of poverty. We will provide both for you and for them. To kill them is a most grievous sin.

Come not near to adultery, which is foul and an evil way.

Do not kill any man, a deed God forbids, except for rightful cause. If a man is slain unjustly, We have appointed to next of kin the right of satisfaction. But let him not carry his vengeance beyond the due, for there is counter retaliation.

Handle the property of the orphan in all integrity, until he comes of age.

Keep your bond, for you are accountable.

Give full measure when you measure, and weigh with just scales. That is better and fairer in the end.

Do not pursue things you have no knowledge of. Hearing, sight and heart – all these faculties of a man will be held responsible.

Do not strut proudly on the earth. You cannot cleave the earth or match the mountains in stature. All such ways are evil with your Lord.

All this is given you by revelation of the wisdom of your Lord, and set not up any other god beside God.

Clear echoes here of the Hebrew Decalogue and fainter ones of precepts in the Gospels are readily audible and the whole is a summary of Quranic moral guidance and a clue to the personal values of Muslim readership.

For all such readers the sanction behind the Qur'ān's social and individual ethics is the conviction exerted by the Book itself. Tradition of the Prophet, as we have seen, enlarges and exemplifies, but it is essentially the Qur'ān which enjoins. Islam's is essentially an ethics of the word, of divine injunction and prohibition. This conviction-shaping power of the text, to which the long history of Islam is witness, stands in a pattern of many strands.

The political order we have fully studied in chapter 3. The state dimension (*daulah*) as we have seen, belongs with the Book's very texture, as a Scripture of Hijrah and *Jihād*, with its immediate history centred in these. Within that framework of active sanction, the Qur'ān's moral efficacy may be said to consist in four other factors – the ritual obligations of *Dīn* or 'religion', the corporate solidarity of the *Ummah*, or community, the hortatory impulse of *dhikr*, or reminding, and the inner incentives of *ta'abbud*, or 'devotion'. These are the enabling sources of a true *islām* and each of them in unison constitutes the Qur'ān's translation into personal life.

Islam stands squarely within the Judaic instinct in believing that divine authority exerts its claim, and human obedience exercises its obligation, in ritual terms. The pattern of *Dīn* (religion) is within the *Sharī'ah* or sacred law. In fulfilling it the believer acknowledges the divine will and by the rhythm of its regularity habituates himself to the divine will in other spheres also. For *Dīn*, properly understood, has no other 'reason' than that God ordains it so. The five daily prayers, the sequences of *Rak'ah* or ritual movement, within them, the annual fast of *Ramaḍān*, the annual pilgrimage, the periodic payment of *Zakāt* – all utilize a habit of discipline.

They also both create and assume the sense of solidarity. No other religion achieves corporate feeling quite so markedly as does Meccan pilgrimage and the focus of the single *Qiblah* in Islamic prayer. The togetherness generated in *Ramaḍān*, also, has the same distinctive quality.

Since, in the nature of things, it is community which determines community, the outsider esteeming the Qur'ān is hardly suited to penetrate what its *Ummah* aspect contains. Its role for the Muslim as *dhikr* (reminding), being so dominant in its text, is one that he is more likely to realize. Exhortation is the very pulse of the Qur'ān. *Dhikr* is among its titles. Its function is to guide by 'the straight path', *al-sirāṭ al-mustaqīm*. Man's forgetfulness is countered by reminder, his weakness by encouragement. Verbal revelation proceeds upon confidence in the word, not only to 'carry' meaning, but to excite action. Repetition avails not only in the realm of worship, but in the sphere of conduct, by habituating the mind to duty and disposing the will to regularity. The Scripture of Islam, we may say, educates not only by its precepts but by its rhythms.

With the hortatory in the positive goes the concern of the Qur'ān for warning against what is inimical. This is no more than consistent. To be sure there are many coming to the Qur'ān who find the minatory passages disturbing and daunting in their severity and look eagerly for the accents of redemption, both in the earthly scene and when the Qur'ān paints its desolating picture of eternal doom. These, sadly, are areas to give us pause. But it will be well to keep in mind the vivid literalism of the Meccan mind and aim to 'contain' what would otherwise dismay and repel within the positive intention of the Qur'ān's human concern. So read, even the strident anathemas and the sharp denunciations of the Book need not deprive us of its central emphases on divine sovereignty, justice and compassion.

More congenial will certainly be the fourth element in the pattern of the Quranic regulation of Muslim existence, namely *ta'abbud*, or religious devotion in its most spontaneous form. Chapter 4 has already made us familiar with this dimension as it 'possesses' the Prophet. But it is also deeply nourished by the possessing of the Qur'ān. There are several guiding terms and attitudes of soul in the Scripture which define what perhaps we may call the right 'Godwardness' on the part of the believer. 'Be spiritually the Lord's,' says 3.179, as we have noted in an earlier context. Here the very word *Rabb*, denoting God as the sovereign Lord and Nurturer of man,[14] yields a derivative *Rabbāniyyīn* (pl.) meaning (lit.) 'Lord-devoted ones', people who are duly God's.

That calling is underlined by the Quranic usage *ḥaqqa* with noun in construct, meaning 'the true, or the right, the authentic . . . piety, reverence', or the like. For example, 3.102 reads: 'You who have believed, fear God a true fearing', 22.78; 'Strive in God the striving that is true to Him', 57.27: '. . . a true caring [for prayer]', while in 39.41 pagans are reproached in that 'they did not esteem God a true esteeming'. The term *bi-l-Ḥaqq*, 'with truth', is frequent in passages concerned with personal conduct

[14] 'Nurturer' here is necessary. The old Semitic sense of *Rabb* is certainly 'Lord' with *'abd* ('servant') as the corresponding term for man. But there has been a growing instinct to find in the name a sense that belongs to the root *rabbā* (yielding *tarbiyah* 'education') suggesting the care and rearing of dependent life, and so the bringing into maturity of that which is not yet full grown. The poet-philosopher, Muḥammad Iqbāl (d. 1938) gave wide currency to this reading.

and religious forms. The Qur'ān sets great store by sincerity, using the word *ikhlāṣ* and derivatives steadily. *Mukhliṣīn lahu al-dīn*, 'sincere before Him in religion' (7.29 and six other passages) or *'ibād Allāḥ al-mukhiliṣīn*, 'God's sincere servants' (37.40 and four other verses) enjoin integrity.

There is an interesting progression in three significant characterizations of the human soul. In Surah 12.53, Joseph, recalling his temptation in 'the house of the Egyptian', says, 'Truly the soul is prone to evil.' The phrase, *al-nafs al-ammārah*, occurs only here. It means that man is under a bias, is aware of an inward 'impelling', and these are 'toward evil'. This liability to temptation means that true goodness is always a *jihād*, a struggle. Another sole usage in 75.2 confirms this. *Al-nafs al-lawwāmah* means 'the soul under reproach', the self-accusatory soul which knows not to pretend its own innocence. The two lead into the blessedness of *al-nafs al-muṭma'innah*, 'the soul at rest', the rest of true quality. This adjective and its cognate verb are rather more frequent. Surah 89.27 is taken to refer to the Prophet: 'O soul at rest, return to your Lord, serene in the serenity [of God].' 'It is in the remembrance of God that hearts are at rest,' says 13.28.

The experience of *iṭmi'nān*, or rest of soul, may be understood by reference to two other themes of personal religion in the Qur'ān, namely 'refuge' and the 'open breast'. 'I seek refuge with God' is a plea which comes in the two final Surahs of the Qur'ān, though they certainly reflect the earliest 'atmosphere' of Muḥammad's listening audience. God as 'our refuge' is, of course, a long-echoed theme of Semitic faith. As the soul, ill at ease, considers its fears, its doubts, its sins, its follies, it learns to shelter from them in the mercy and majesty of God. A trio of stragglers after the Hijrah realized, says 9.118, that 'there is no shelter [*malja'* here] from God save in Him'. A deep theology, potentially, lies in that phrase. Refuge in the Qur'ān is *from* all things evil and untoward, *by* or *through* the divine grace. Both the term and the theme kindle an immediate sympathy in the Qur'ān reader whether he be inside or outside Islam. For we are akin in our frailty and share as one humanity the daunting features of the world and the inner stresses of the heart.

Sharḥ al-ṣadr, with its antonym of the narrow heart, is one of the Qur'ān's most intriguing metaphors. 'My Lord, open for me my breast,' prayed Moses, 'and facilitate what I have in hand' (20.25). Surah 94.1 addresses Muḥammad: 'Did We not enlarge your breast . . .?' making authentic his experience and call. This is the enabling which counters and overcomes the sense of oppression from the hostile people when his 'breast [was] straitened by the things they say' (15.97). 'The opening of the breast to *islām*' (6.125 and 39.22) may be said to mean this realized affinity between believer and belief, between liberty and surrender.

These, and other, elements of personal religion in the Qur'ān can be summed up in a 'desiring of the face of God' (*ibtighā' waj Allāh*) in humility and awe. Though 'everything on the earth is transient', as 55.26–27 has it, 'the face of your Lord abides, majestic, glorified'. 'Shall I desire other than God as Lord, when He is Lord of everything?' the Prophet asks in 6.164, and the question may well reverberate through all our assessments of the Qur'ān, keeping in mind that humility which it steadily commends, and its figures exemplify, in awareness of God (cf. 11.23).

We are far from exhausting in these pages the theological content of the Qur'ān, and some areas we have deliberately left to silence lest the great positives should be denied their opportunity or their proper recognition discouraged. For, in any open relationship with Islam, it is those positives which must avail to carry us beyond the dissuasives we register. This they can only do when they are allowed their true occasion. It is in their relevance that we have agreed to set all response to Muḥammad.

Can there be other than a ready confidence that the Qur'ān may truly be seen as a Christian's territory of meaning across whole stretches of its significance as to God and man? The truths we have reviewed we loyally possess. Their site-ing, if we may so phrase it, in the local arena of Mecca and Medina, in the prophetic personality of Muḥammad, and in the idiom of the Book of Islam, should not deter us from the satisfaction of their truth and the sharing of their relevance now. We receive in the Qur'ān a powerful and telling reinforcement of Christian conviction as to the reality and rule of God, the divine creation, the earth tenancy and investiture of man, the divine liability about Him, the intelligible trust of His signs, the interacting claims of worship and dominion, the solemn joy of sexuality, and the awe of our personal being as lived 'in the light of His countenance'. Whatever the reservations we still have to make, and allowing the fact that predicates about God differ within their agreements, we are not thereby deprived of a community of belief with the people of the Qur'ān which is authentic in its content and urgent in its significance.

Before turning to the further tasks this conclusion imposes, there are two remaining questions. Were we right in proposing simply to 'listen' to the Qur'ān, and are we justified in what some would accuse as a 'selective' treatment? Communication from the Book to those who, like ourselves, simply peruse, can only be from page to mind. Perusing is not a communal experience, nor does it receive the impact which belongs to its proper recital. The Qur'ān is meant to be heard, read aloud, reproduced (we might almost say) in the *tajwīd*, or chanting, which is the sole music of Islam. Then the Muslim possesses it and is possessed by it in a way that no external study can experience.[15]

While that is true and we are wise to know our ignorance and impoverishment, the meanings we have discerned are not impaired. It is simply that they lack, in our receiving, the resonance they bring to Muslim ears. The Qur'ān's being confined, with us, to our own mental capacity to relate to its contents without benefit of the aura its community knows, only makes that capacity more crucial and the willingness within it more keen. On that condition we are right to aim at knowing those contents, even though 'contents' are far from being a complete or satisfactory formulation of what the Book is to Muslims.

Our other query has to do with selectivity. Is it fitting to assess the Qur'ān in this way in order to 'appreciate' its meanings? Are we only wanting to find what we seek? Will Muslims 'appreciate' this kind of appreciation or will they not, rather, require an entire acceptance? Some, of course, will. But there are many 'selections' made from the Qur'ān by Muslims, either for the help of outsiders or for their own pursuit of interests, poetical, liturgical, exegetical, or thematic. In any event, no reading can be without presupposition. We cannot bring our minds and at the same time evacuate them. What matters is that presupposition should not be prejudice, or, if it be prejudice, be prejudice in the right direction. For too long, a wrong Christian prejudice has virtually sealed off the Qur'ān from attentive encounter or doomed it to barren neglect.

Further, has our treatment, in fact, been 'selective'? Our claim for it sees it as the gist or consensus of the Book considered thematically. Its findings tally with comparable efforts within Islam to read the essence of the Qur'ān. These, whether theirs or ours, are efforts consistent with the Book's own invitation, its call for *tadabbur*, or penetrating reflection (4.42; 47.24). This plea is made, in fact, to pagans and miscreants, if we have to be so classified. So we are only following the Qur'ān's own desire when

15 There have lately been interesting developments in professional recording of the Qur'ān. See, for example, Labib al-Said, *The Recited Koran*, trans. by B. Weiss and M. A. Rauf (Princeton, 1975).

we give ourselves, with full intelligence and unclosed mind, to its contents.

And if that intelligent study necessarily moves from Christian sensitivity, that too is what the Qur'ān commends: 'Let the people of the Gospel decide [judge] by what God has sent down there' (5.47). The task continues.

8

DECIDING BY THE GOSPEL

'Jesus and Muḥammad are friends in heaven. Let us be friends on earth,' pleads Dr Muḥammad Daud Rahbar.[1] By every means. The plea is sweetly in line with the Pakistani writer's instinct, taught by bitter experience, to try to locate all issues in poetic, even playful, context, rather than risk the asperities and confusions liable to attend intellectual and theological debate. We do well to stay in its temper even if we cannot quite so readily assume that this is all that need be said.

'If you greet your brethren only,' said Jesus, 'what do you more than others?' (Matt. 5.47). He was breaking out of Semitic custom confining salutation to the proper breed.[2] So, greeting there must be and friendship in the things on earth. Islamic and Christian faiths do not have sealed frontiers. Nor does separate religious community make us a different humanity. As chapter 7 has argued, and documented, there are wide areas of religious meaning which we truly share. The expression of their sharedness is precisely mutual greeting on their ground.

Yet friendship, so grounded, must be true to its quality. There are deep Islamic, as well as strong Christian, reasons for excluding mere sentiment and vacuous goodwill. The people of the

1 Quoted from the cover jacket of Muḥammad Daud Rahbar; *The Cup of Jamshid: A Collection of Original Ghazal Poetry* (Cape Cod, Mass., 1974). The reference later is to the author's long experience in the cause of intellectual scholarship and liberty in respect of religious issues. He indicates that it is often more profitable to proceed by humour and hint than by direct militancy.

2 The Semitic greeting *Shalom, Salām*, is normally restrictive, belonging to the right community of which, received and given, it is a pledge. See E. W. Lane, *The Modern Egyptians* (Everyman edn, London, 1908), p. 203. 'Should one salute, by mistake, a person not of the same faith, the latter should not return it: and the former, on discovering his mistake, generally revokes the salutation.' Lane was writing in the 1830s. But attitudes die hard.

Gospel must decide by the Gospel. Only so will their response to Muslims be alert both to Muḥammad and to Christ.

But what will 'deciding by the Gospel' mean as enjoined by Surah 5.47? At once there is the question about what 'the Gospel' is, the *Injīl* of Jesus to which in several passages the Qur'ān refers. Islam believes it to be a body of teaching, now no longer extant, which Jesus brought, as God's word, to his time and place. As such, it entirely conforms to the Qur'ān – a fact which makes its being no longer available irrelevant, since the Islamic Scripture comprehends, confirms and enlarges it. On this score, deciding by the *Injīl* will be synonymous with deciding by the Qur'ān.

This, however, does not end the matter. For it is 'the people of the Gospel', *ahl al-Injīl* who, according to 5.47, are to do the deciding. They believe themselves in trust with a Gospel which is not teaching alone, orally delivered, but the good news of a whole personality, in Messianic fulfilment, achieving the salvation of the world in the grace of the love that suffers. *Injīl*, so understood, is much more than verbal guidance; it is 'the power of God unto salvation'. The Christian, then, is bound to take the obligation of 5.47 as one which invites him to set the whole significance of Muḥammad within the criteria *that* Gospel provides and by which its 'people' must judge. No sensitive Muslim could wish it otherwise. The whole long, rich experience of what the New Testament calls 'God in Christ' is not to be set aside by any restrictive reading of the word *Injīl*. Nor would there be any point in reckoning with the Qur'ān by means of a referent considered invalid wherever it did not approve – which is the case on a rigid Muslim view of what the *Injīl* is.

By New Testament criteria, then, what are we to say of Muḥammad and the Qur'ān? What decisions can 'the people of the Gospel' properly reach, having agreed to surmount all the deterrents to decision which suggest that the effort itself is ill-judged or futile, that differences are theologically insuperable or an obstacle to practical relationships? Without honesty at their core how will relationships ever be practical?

The hope in this chapter is to face the Christian dissuasives about Islam which were briefly anticipated in chapter 1, and to do so, not in traditional terms of explicit controversy about abrogation, the 'Īsā/Jesus question, the argument about the Cross, or religious finality and the rest, but rather in the more unifying terms of Islam's own convictions about both God and man. It will be found that full justice is done this way to all that is at stake in traditional controversy about Christology and salvation. But there can be hope it will be also better justice, in that it will be a search for areas of religious reference where we can be at one, where the intentions, as distinct from the partisanships, of Islamic and Christian conviction may be said to meet. If we can set our spiritual 'dissatisfaction' with Muḥammad irenically in the context of considerations manifestly his own, and central to his *Rasūliyyah*, shall we not have more hope of their point being taken and their significance understood? For it will be a significance vitally relevant to Islam's own conviction about itself as chartering humanity on behalf of God, and not merely to Christianity's interests in its self-defence.

Perhaps we may even surmise that this stance will be closer to the mind of Jesus. Concern for ourselves, he taught, must always be concern beyond ourselves. That to lose is to find may be a truth for systems as well as for souls. If we can forsake the love of controversy we may truly find its duty fulfilled. We must draw as closely as we can to the Islamic reasons which warrant our continuing commitment to Christ. 'Ourselves your servants for Jesus sake' (2 Cor. 4.5), was Paul's formula. In our context this must mean the liveliest concern for divine imperatives constituting human meanings – as Islam believes – and, for that very reason, a careful witness to how imperatives and meanings relate in, and according to, Christ. Such witness, if rightly minded, will not neglect the warnings of Drs Adams and Hodgson, noted in chapter 1, about the autonomy of Islam. It will, rather, be the utmost respect for such autonomy. But it will also be a refusal to allow that the autonomies of religions have other than one humanity.

'Chartering humanity on behalf of God', 'divine imperatives and human meanings' – such, in summary, is Islam. If these phrases are in any way complete and we are right in locating ourselves firmly within the imperatives, the charter and the meaning, then deciding by the Gospel would seem to involve the Christian in three concerns: Is divine sovereignty complete?; Is prophethood ultimate?; Is man fulfilled? These are, plainly, the question of transcendence, the question of law, and the question of salvation.

There can be no denying that they are the vital questions of Islam and of *islām* under God, via the Prophet, for humanity. 'There is no god but God: Muḥammad is the apostle of God,' and man is to be *muslim* unto God. It is clear, too, that the questions are intimately related. For the Lordship of God speaks and claims through the vocation of the Prophet. The answer to both is the submission of man.

Further, to be squarely where these questions place us is to be deeply within all Christian concerns for Christology and the Cross. Loyalty to Islamic essentials brings us more vitally into Christian fields of meaning than anything else could – and more hopefully. It would be easy and necessary to insist, controversially, that the killing of the Banū Qurayẓah is worlds away from the Sermon on the Mount, or that the Jesus of the Good Samaritan and the Prodigal Son is unknown to the Qur'ān. But these, might prove provocative observations, tempting some into angry retort and their makers into self-congratulation. Then we might find ourselves somehow partisans of Jesus and be betrayed as his disciples by the easy fact of being superior as his admirers. Better far to let these areas of painful contrast be resolved within the larger themes of God and prophethood where Islam has proper recognition and Muslims occasion for a livelier sense of themselves. Can any of us go wrong if we begin and end with God?

The question, then, of transcendence. Is it, we ask, transcendent enough? The secularist, of course, will say, 'Wait! The prior question is whether theology has any grounds at all.' That, however, we will only come to in chapter 9 as useful for our practical relationships. The Qur'ān and 'the people of the Gospel' do not stay for the question 'Whether?' about God. He is. But they are much involved in the question 'How?' Theologies, and Scriptures for their source, are agreed about His being. They diverge in understanding the predicates they make of Him. This is the point we left latent in chapter 7 when freely assuming that the God of the Gospel, and *Allāh* of the Qur'ān are the same Lord. Emphatically so, as subject of all the predicates made. And one, too, in many of the Muslim/Christian predicates, such as Lord, Creator, Sovereign, Sustainer, in power, wisdom, mercy and truth.

But the predicates also differ powerfully. Since in grammar, predicates are to denote their subjects, there *is* a sense in theology too in which the subject 'differs' in line with any disparity in what is predicated. God, in the Qur'ān, is *not* 'the God and Father of our Lord Jesus Christ'. That is not a predication of Islamic doctrine. Carrying back that significance into the 'subject', *Allāh* means a 'difference' in how God is understood. So, likewise, with other dimensions of faith and with other 'adjectives', like merciful, gracious, holy, loving, which faith ascribes to God. These also have subtle distinctions within their common vocabulary currency.

But we reduce everything to chaos if we suggest that disparate predicates do not relate to the identical 'subject' to whom they are ascribed, as if there could be, in truth, 'gods many and lords many' corresponding to all the confused concepts, however numerous and contradictory. If that were the case there would be no point, and no hope, in proposing to reconcile the predicates. Certainly, again, there would be no point in 'mission', purporting to present a 'truer' faith, since, given disparate 'deities' said to be existent, all would have equal claim to credence. All intelligent faith, and all inter-theology, proceed upon the conviction that 'God is One'. Only this confidence warrants our concern with how we understand that unifying 'subject' of all our predicates and how we study these both in their sharedness and their disparity.

Thus, the answer to the vexed question, 'Is the God of Islam and the God of the Gospel the same?' can only rightly be 'Yes! and 'No!' Yes, as the common ground of all we say in partial unison: No, insofar as our convictions diverge. It would be foolish to make either the convergence or the divergence total, to identify altogether or to contrast only. A ruling sense of God's sublime Oneness will best serve us in confessing Him.

So we return, both cheered and alerted, to the question of God and His transcendence. But it will be wise to lead into it by taking first the questions of prophethood and man. This will allow us to end with the most ultimate issue and has also the expository advantage of enabling us to see more clearly what that issue is.

Muslim faith in the finality of Muḥammad as 'the seal of the prophets' means that he perfects and fulfils all earlier prophetic mission to man. But it means also a faith in the finality of prophecy *per se*. That which comes to climax in Muḥammad and the Qur'ān, namely guidance, teaching, directive, warning and admonition, is all there is. It constitutes entirely what is to be looked for from God, as the education of His creation in the experience of His will and His mercy. Prophecy – by which is meant not foretelling a future but forthtelling the divine word – is that in which God's relevance to man consists. It is the relevance of the Creator, whose will ordains and directs the human scene, whose sovereignty decrees how the creature shall live and relate to his fellows. It is a relevance which is essentially 'educational'. The prophets, we might almost say, are the tutors through whom that divine education of humanity proceeds. It is an education which enlightens, informs, guides, exhorts, warns, disciplines, prohibits and enjoins. Its gist is law, its pattern habituation, its goal obedience. All the world's a school.

Prophecy thus lives to bring and bring home the divine imperative. All our study of Muḥammad in preceding chapters confirms this understanding. The Qur'ān rings with the word *Al-Amr* – the command, the divine authority initiating and governing all things. The *Amr* descends through the seven heavens (65.12) that men may know that God is disposer over everything. That *Amr*, sometimes thought of almost as a hypostasis like 'wisdom' in the Wisdom Literature, energizes the whole creation, being the 'mandate' by which the creation comes to be. 'He only says: "Be!" and it is' (6.73; 16.40; 36.81; 40.68). 'He gives the ordering of the *Amr* from the heaven to the earth' (32.4–5). The *Amr* is also closely linked in the Qur'ān with the Spirit (e.g. *al-Rūḥ min Amrihi*, 40.15) whence flows the revelation. Thus the creation of the world and the descent of the Qur'ān happen by the imperative of divine authorization, to embody the divine purpose. The *fiat*, or 'let there be', of God explains their mutual relation – createdness and guidedness – as meant for each other. This, of course, is in line with the significance of the *āyāt* or 'signs', and with the 'dominion' of man, as the sentient master within the created order *and* the recipient of the prophetic instruction to subdue that mastery to its true patterns.

It is God's 'mercy to the worlds' that man is not left in doubt or darkness about his meaning and its obligations. 'Light upon light' is his both through nature and in revelation. He is an authorized creature in an authorized creation, a warranted being under prophetic warrant. A divine imperative is both his origin and his destiny.

Such 'chartering', as we have called it, man under *Amr*, spells both dignity and duty. But, blessed as these truly are, they seem, by Christian criteria and their own implication, incomplete. Is 'education' man's total need? Should there, on prophecy's own showing, be something more than prophecy? Does law, by prohibition and injunction, make good its own intention? Or must there be dimensions to divine sovereignty greater than those of 'education' and 'command'?

These are the questions which arise from 'deciding by the Gospel'. Jesus, according to the Gospels, used the words: 'Yea, I say unto you and more than a prophet' (Matt. 11.9), in respect of the forerunner, John Baptist, the Yaḥyā of the Qur'ān. The phrase has a fascinating ring, beyond the immediate sense and context of the passage. One prophet more than another, in range, in honour, or in impact – this is a view with which Islam is familiar enough. Indeed, Muḥammad's finality clinches it. Yet something more than prophethood itself – how can this be?

It is that 'more' upon which the whole New Testament proceeds – the 'more' of Messianic action to redeem, the 'more' of God's loving engagement with the sequel to rejected 'education' of the world, the 'more' of a divine expressing of the Word, hitherto only spoken, but now in flesh and personality, in suffering and salvation. John's being 'more than a prophet' is *à fortiori* true about Jesus as the Gospels understand him.

Yet, this 'more' by which the prophets' task leads into the saving events of the Christ as 'the word made flesh' belongs entirely with all that they signified as to a divine engagement with human history. It is none other than the open logic of prophecy itself. It takes up the positive intention for a right world and fulfils it beyond the negations and frustrations to which the educational word is subject by reason of the perversity of mankind. That those negations are real and desperate enough is proved by the fact of idolatry itself and, therefore, by the whole necessity of Muḥammad's mission. Are we not then warranted in saying that the Prophet of Islam's very stature argues the sort of divine commitment to the human situation and its righting which the Christian sees implemented in Jesus as the Christ?

We put the matter in another way if we ask, simply, whether 'guidance' of itself suffices? That it is given is, as we have argued, a blessed pledge of God's relation and of our vocation. But what of its reception in the wayward world? Here, of course, we are squarely within the Hebrew dilemma of the law with which Paul wrestled so long. A divine imperative to us is the utmost tribute to our significance. Without it we should know neither meaning, nor reproach. Without these, life would have no worth, no quality, no benediction. We have every reason to bless the God of law and His *hudā* of discipline, the holy *Sharī'ah* of His definition of ourselves.

But, the more perceptively we acknowledge our liability to the sovereignty whose law, by its summons, makes us truly human, the more urgently we realize our compromise and our rebellion. We have it in us chronically to defy the law, to refuse its claims, to transgress its charter of our being. So real is this rebellion that it takes us into pseudo-worship, into existence 'excluding God', into idol substitutes usurping His prerogative.

Nor are these evils overcome by exhortation that deplores them. Nor yet by examples that avoid them. Nor yet by dire threatenings that condemn them. The human autonomy, needed for submission, is minded to withhold it. Habituation will not suffice to ensure conformity. We cannot ritualize ourselves into a true being. The solidarity on which we might rely to conform us with aid of numbers and tradition may itself only generate a collective mis-guidedness. Even within our actual, or assumed, conformity other evidences may lurk, of our hardness of heart, our proneness to pride, to merit, to self-congratulation.

What is there, in these circumstances, that is more than prophecy? What will *hudā* do about these reaches of evil that are immune to its appeal? Is it not clear that the question whether prophecy is really final is also the question whether God's sovereignty is fully vindicated in 'prophetic' terms alone? Must we not also say that the question as to the adequacy of the prophetic is the question about the nature of man? May it not be that to see prophecy as the ultimate is to underestimate *both* the human situation and the divine competence? In that event, the meaning of *Allāhu akbar* must be taken further.

'Deciding', this way, 'by the Gospel' may be resisted. But it can hardly be discounted within Islamic convictions about God. Indeed, in this realism, we are not reading by the Gospel only; we are reading by Islam, by the Qur'ān and its splendid assurance of divine ultimacy. There is, for both Muslims and Christians, no question 'Whether?' about the greatness of God. The question is 'How?'

The same conclusion seems to face us when we assess that confident recruitment of the political arm which we saw in chapters 2 and 3 to be the instinctive assumption of Muḥammad. The issue here, as we saw, is not some alleged declension. Nor is it sincerity. There is an inner consistency, given opposition as long and tenacious as that in the pre-Hijrah years, in reaching for means of enforcing victory if prophetic direction and warning are the final dimension of God's will. An education resisted, when its sanctions are divine and its contents sovereign, may well proceed to an imposed success. The 'prophetic' as operative in the Qur'ān has every right to become the political power. God's word in that sense is bound to have the last word. There is a reasonable logic in moving from teaching to constraint, from *balāgh* to *ḥisāb*,[3] when the prophetic has no further resources, no larger mandate.

[3] *Balāgh* ('communication') and *Ḥisāb* ('reckoning') are frequently expressed contrasts in both the Medinan and the Meccan period. *Ma 'ala-l-ra sūl illā al-balāgh*, 'the apostle has no responsibility other than giving the word' (24.54; cf. 5.99; 13.40; 16.35 and 82; 29, 18; 36.17; 42.48; 64.12). 'Upon Us [God] is the *Ḥisāb*' (e.g. 13.40). The final meaning of *Ḥisāb* is the judgement of the Last Day. But there is also a sense in which the 'reckoning' with the Quraish came in the post-Hijrah developments. The essential point is that there is a clearly understood distinction between the obligation to preach and the obligation to win – a distinction later merged into one objective.

This entire consistency within the Quranic scene, and in Muḥammad's prophethood, raises, however, profound issues both about God and about man. It involves those 'problematics' briefly sketched in chapter 3, about *fitnah* and *nifāq*, about militancy and hypocrisy. But it has to be read back further into what the Gospel would call 'the patience of God'. That which 'fails' educationally must proceed punitively, unless the 'lesson' has other resources of grace and long-suffering. The Gospel, at such juncture, reads differently. It has that strange logic at its heart which reads: 'I will send to them My Son, My beloved' (Luke 20.13). A strange logic indeed, in face of the brutal reception of a string of messengers refused by an obdurate humanity entrusted with God's, and nature's, vineyard. A strange logic, too, if all the Lord is seeking is the year's harvest of the soil. Clearly, in the parable, the sending of 'the heir' is a lifting of the whole level of relationship. The question that emerges from the situation of sinful 'autonomy'.is no longer the economic one – What about the yield? It has become the total one – What is your relationship to Me?[4]

That, too, is plainly where questions of disobedience to law finally lead. For, on this view of God, law and *hudā* are not an end in themselves. They are on behalf of a divine/human relationship they were intended to actualize between Creator and creature, between Lord and servant. When, therefore, they fail of their intention a new divine initiative takes up the added burden and redeems it. Here of course we are in the significance of the Incarnation and the Cross – a significance which, quite consistently, Islam excludes. Not a significance, however, which can be dismissed as unrelated to Islam's charter for man.

So the question to which the Gospel prompts us is whether we *can* expect such further dimension of the divine intention responsive to the human situation as law and *hudā* summon it in revelation, whether, in short, we can 'look for redemption'. It is a view of God which will decide, and be decided by, the answer. And a view of man too. The Qur'ān is committed to the confidence that man is perfectible by divine mercy complete in

[4] This lifting of the level of relationship seems clearly meant in the Parable (Matt. 21.33–44; Mark 12.1–12; Luke 20.1–19.) The story lets in a flood of light upon Jesus' own sensing of the issues of his ministry as confrontation developed between his teaching and the 'establishment'. It might be objected that the reading argued here runs across the final 'ousting' by the Lord of the vineyard of the obdurate trustees. That expulsion, fulfilled in the days of Titus, and known to the Evangelists, does not cancel the 'love gesture' in 'the beloved Son'.

Amr, in the *Tanzīl*, or descent, of revelation, in the appeal of nature's *āyāt*, in the sanctions of institutional Islam, and by the effective persuasion of political establishment. It is no stranger to the perversity of the human situation. It experiences that perversity only too well in the fact of *shirk*, the false appeal of idols, the rejection of the prophets, the deceptions of the sinners. But all these it sees as finally answerable and manageable by the sinews of statehood dedicated to the Prophet's cause as congruently God's. Its reading of humanity is realist enough, its sense of God robust enough. Whether there is not a costlier reach to both is the question from the Gospel.

'The people of the Gospel' decide there is, not only from the character of the Gospel itself but from two other considerations which occupy the Christian reader of the Qur'ān. These are the punitive emphasis there, and a parallel, yet questionable, exoneration of the established community.

The punitive in the Qur'ān has sometimes been a matter of dismay even to committed Muslims. There has been a tendency to explain the vivid details of the Quranic Hell as its way of communicating moral distinctions to the highly visual mentality of the Meccans, unused to abstracts like remorse or purgation. Even so, there is something desolating about these aspects of eschatology which, read in any other context, would seem almost like vindictiveness. Is the full value of human personality secure in the 'taskmaster' kind of concept which, from time to time, characterizes the strictures against evildoers and unbelievers? Divine requital seems then to be the ultimate in divine Lordship. The Gospel, to be sure, has its own dimension of requital, understood as the self-perpetuated rejection of the divine love. A salvation that is uncompulsive and free must leave room for an unyielded hardness of heart. There are certainly mysteries here for faith. But it is fair to ask whether the persistence and pathos of human evil do not argue a more resourceful divine initiative of grace.

That will involve us further in asking whether divine retribution can be so negative, so adamant, and in that sense so arbitrary, as Quranic passages assert. The 'justification' of God must surely come within those resources of grace and compassion in which we are all invited to believe. We do well to think hard about how we relate God and Hell. Too often Muḥammad's preaching appears to proceed in far too sanguine terms about damnation. The Qur'ān could well profit from the impatience of Job.

The other consideration has to do with the vindication of the custodial community of the revelation in the Qur'ān. The thrust for *al-fauz al-mubīn* ('the manifest victory') and *al-fauz al-'azīm* ('the great victory') in the Scripture tends, like all militancy, to take its necessities for granted. *Jihād* does not readily turn Hamlet-like against itself. It is the laggards and the timorous, not the ardent and the vigilantes, whom the Qur'ān reproves. This communal dynamic towards success is a natural feature of the political equation we have studied.

Its very assurance makes it largely negligent of the temptations of all 'establishments', and indeed of religion itself. Largely, but not wholly so. There are some passages in the Qur'ān which suggest that even success may have aspects that need forgiveness. Thus, for example, Surah 110:

> When God's help comes about, and conquest, and you have seen people coming crowding into the religion of God, then sing the praise of your Lord and seek His forgiveness. To be merciful was ever His wont.

The verbs are singular and addressed to Muḥammad, reputedly at the time of the taking of Mecca and the subsequent delegations acceding to Islam. The Surah is splendidly inscribed on the fine Mausoleum monument in Karachi to the memory of Muḥammad 'Ali Jinnah, founder of Pakistan.

But such a salutary reminder of the inherent moral compromises of victory is rare. Too often, as in the following Surah 111, with its imprecation against Abū Lahāb, the Quraishī leader, there is no mood to question the instinct of hostility. It is interesting that the normal Arabic word for 'conscience', *ḍamīr*, does not occur in the Qur'ān, not because there lacks any strong concept of 'justice', but because justice is so readily identified with the militant cause. 'Obey God and obey the Prophet' (4.59) is an imperative reiterated some fifteen times in nine different Surahs.

Within a community of obedience engaged on a mortal struggle, that merging of loyalties is natural. In the event it proved eminently effective. But the question presses whether there can ever be such a close 'association' between what is due to God and what is required by the campaign that is committed to His Name. The familiar faith in transcendence ought to be operative, not only in terms propositional, but in terms political. *Allāhu akbar* is a confession which should repudiate not only our idols but our enmities – and these, most of all, when they are 'justified' as being for His sake. There can be few things more blasphemous than crying '*Allāhu akbar*' with a clenched first, as God's partisans are prone to do.

The Qur'ān even startles the Christian reader with the phrase *ḥizb Allāh*, 'the party of God', *ḥizb* being the term normally used for political groupings (5.56; 58.22 twice). It is contrasted with *ḥizb al-Shaiṭān*, 'the party of Satan' (58.19 twice). It is confident who are the victors and the vanquished, who are the gainers and the losers, and uses these denominators frequently to warn of doom or to celebrate and serve success. It would be inconsistent with the steady political alignment of things Quranic to expect it to be otherwise. The temper of the Qur'ān in this context is the natural consequence of the political equation we explored earlier. What is disconcerting is the absence of self-interrogation and of a sense of the need to suspect interests that are so readily taken to be God's. Even the note of *istighfār*, of which Surah 110 is a moving example, is understood by some to mean, not a deep 'forgiveness-seeking' (the root sense), but rather a 'protection-seeking', a defence against a malice that is outward, stimulated by victory, rather than a pardon that is inward for what victory may have entailed.

This is not to say that Muslims fail of all critical self-awareness in this context. Muḥammad Kāmil Ḥusain, for example, in his *Qaryah Ẓālimah*,[5] developed a powerful if oblique, examination of Islamic political assurance in the setting of an imaginative study of the factors making for the communal conspiracy against Jesus in the Gospels. These factors he identified as the perverse collective interests of the Jewish and Roman 'establishments', whose 'expedience' overrode conscience and 'justified' transgression.[6] He ends with a very sombre view of the degree to which collectives and 'causes' can be held to ethical criteria when these

[5] Published in Cairo, 1954, translated into English as *City of Wrong* (Amsterdam, 1958; New York, 1964). The author reconstructs imaginatively the way in which the disciples of Jesus reacted to his arrest. He uses Quranic quotation to help them argue a forcible rescue only to have Jesus countermand this. The implied criticism of Quranic militancy is unmistakable.

[6] The same author, in his *al-Wādī al-Muqaddas* (Cairo, 1966), translated into English as *The Hallowed Valley* (Cairo, 1977), reiterates the same sceptical view of the amenability of institutions to the sort of restraints which conscience would impose on personal actions: '. . . how to bring life, conscience and creed into one. This is the eternal problem of humanity. The effect of individual purity on the refining of the relations between man and community is less than its influence within the person himself. As for its impact on the inter-relationships of communities – that is a frail thing and hardly to be depended on.'

impede their demand to succeed or deny their religious mandate. The stand of individual conscience seems to him a frail gesture against the current of collective will. Yet he sees it as the only hope of righteousness. Rarely in the Qur'ān does one find a plural imperative like *utī'ū* ('obey'), *jāhidū* ('strive'), qualified by a singular imperative: 'consider', 'stay', 'think again'. May it be that the different sensitivities of the Qur'ān and the New Testament here arise from the fact that, as 'story-telling' faiths, the one history is that of 'manifest victory', the other of manifest grace through death and resurrection?

The place of self-accusation in religious ends goes deeper than this question of the compromises of force exerted in its name. It has to do, further, with an awareness of the presence of evil in religion itself. It is true that there is no political revolution, not even that against idolatry, which is really revolutionary enough. Political possibilities are always within factors more ultimate than they can reach. There has to be the 'hidden victory' beyond the 'manifest' one. To assume about human nature, and, on the basis of the assumption, to put all else to rights, is to be finally undone. 'Deciding by the Gospel' brings us into a lively realism about the human equation. It requires us to recognize that we may well be farthest from God in the very pretence of obeying Him, that there is a demerit in all meritoriousness, that much penitence is self-congratulatory, that piety may often be a subtle form of pride. Religious rightness, in our own eyes, may, in God's eyes, be the utmost idolatry. *Allāhu akbar* can never well be made to read *Islāmu akbar*, or any other 'establishment' naming His name.

It is for this reason that we can never attain a standing where we are exempt from grace, or beyond the need to seek and find forgiveness. Personal salvation can never be equated with collective success or achieved by external institution. These may have a minor role to play and are in no sense an area that faith can disregard. But their potential and their pitfalls, either way, only take issues of truth and salvation deeper still into the final questions of human remaking and redemption. If one could ever imagine an Epistle of St Paul to the Meccans, these would be the concerns it would expound. If one could visualize the preaching of Jesus post-dated into the markets of the Quraish this would be its burden.

Hence the inquiry with which we began whether, within prophethood alone, the meaning of man is comprehended, whether what remains didactic and hortatory suffices for his real predicament, whether what institutionalizes itself politically accomplishes his salvation. Those are the queries which the Gospel, with all its respect for the prophetic and its own teaching element, compels us to raise. If the very honesty of our acknowledgement of Quranic concerns leads us into these other dimensions we are confirmed in the view, which the Gospel certainly takes, that there is need for 'more than prophecy', and that this 'more' is because of a more radical despair and hope, of man.

This means, in turn, a larger expectation of God. If we can get this into clearer focus we shall have taken final measure of what 'deciding by the Gospel' involves in respect of the firm and loyal theism of Islam. It involves a theological decision. But that decision is within all the praise, the *Ḥamd*, the *Tasbīḥ*, which Islam so steadfastly offers. That Muslims and Christians in their spiritual relationship should thus be driven back, together, into the meaning of the greatness of God ought to be to both the most congenial of obligations, the most reconciling of tasks. What, in a word, is the nature of our faith in God?

Here in the final area of our convictions, and the relating of them, there must be a due sense of awe and mystery. Without these there can be no worthy theology. We must esteem God a true esteeming, as Surah 6.91 has it. But how? A patient Christian study of how the Qur'ān does so always leaves a clear impression of entire transcendence. For its own sake that sense of God as exalted beyond all relation to man needs to be balanced by a due sense of God's engagement with the human world. Where there is so strong a 'distancing' of the divine from the human something vital is forfeited by 'sovereignty' itself. The Christian, accordingly, wants to bring into the tremendous Islamic conviction of God in total command and utter supremacy the dimension of grace and participation with man, without which majesty alone cannot be a 'true esteeming'.

It may seem strange to speak of 'distancing' of God from the human scene in the Qur'ān when a verse like 50.16, declares: 'We are closer to him than the jugular vein,' and when the *Bismillāh* itself emphasizes mercy in double stress. But the 'nearness' is that of vigilant watchfulness, before which nothing is concealed, so that God 'knows what man's soul whispers within him'. That unfailing awareness in God of every secret of the heart scrutinizes us closely and inescapably. It belongs with the constant imperative of divine law and guidance which, as we saw, is the essential 'function' of the Scripture. It is not understood as a divine engagement with our sorrows and our yearnings. Rather it is a divine reckoning with our duties.

In that form the very 'nearness' may constitute 'remoteness' precisely because it has to do with our submission. It belongs with the interests of God in man concerning compliance, obedience, surrender and the law. But can we legitimately speak of the interests of man in God, and the human plea for compassion, tenderness, long-suffering and grace? The instinct of Islam here, following loyally the Qur'ān, has always been to decline such dangerous thoughts lest the sheer Lordship of God should somehow be diminished by them. 'Exalted be He above all that you associate.' Humanity is certainly warranted in having hopes for God; it would be presumptuous to believe that they had 'rights'. We cannot properly think of a divine pathos over mankind since such implied 'involvement' with us denies His transcendence.

We must be clear that this Quranic 'esteeming' of God as utterly immune from man in this way was taken in good intent. It was so, in vigorous response to the folly and evil of idolatry. God, in His absolute unity and rule, had to be strenuously dissociated in a society like Muḥammad's from all pagan divinization, from all easy intimacies which such paganism harboured between gods and situations, between worship and fertility, between deities and tribes, between heathen powers and popular festivals. Only by radical repudiation of such rites and notions could the sole Lordship, the universal sovereignty, the inclusive mercy, of *Allāh* alone, be proclaimed and enforced. All intelligent theism stands in that faith in the unity of God, whether Muslim, Jewish, or Christian.

But did Muslim theology somehow forfeit, by that very zeal for a contra-pagan unity, the other dimension which properly belongs with transcendence, namely the divine supremacy that is vindicated, over against evil, by the reach of divine love? Has Islam suffered, in consequence, a tragic loss of what we must call divine 'association' with humanity in grace, just because it was so urgently called to denounce divine 'association' with idols? A Christian reckoning thinks so. In thoroughly sharing the radical 'dissociation' from idolatry, we must aim to reverse the resulting 'dissociation' from humanity which a Quranic theology asserts. Is not God's transcendence most truly 'esteemed' when we find it vindicated, not only against pagan idols, but against human sin? For sin is a larger flouting of God's sovereignty than plural worship. The confession *Allāhu akbar* can rejoice in redemption even more than in a disowning of the idols. For there is no idolatry more pernicious than the human perversity which begets it.

Deity immune from human tragedy, compassionately inviolate, sending not coming, summoning not suffering – has been the consistent theme of Quranic *Tauḥīd, Tasbīḥ* and *Shahādah*, the steady confession of Muslim unitary faith and praise – consistent in its logic and its loyalty. But is it truly consistent? Can divine sovereignty, understood this Quranic way, be consistent with the Qur'ān's own doctrine of creation? Or its faith in revelation and prophethood? Or its conviction about *Sharī'ah* as man's charter for society? Or its understanding of external nature as awaiting man's reverent custodianship?

All these clearly argue a divine 'interest' in mankind in every sense of that intriguing word. The created world, on the Qur'ān's firm showing, is not a divine jest (21.16 and 44.38), not a divine 'hobby', not a divine enigma, not a divine 'toy'. That way lies deism, and the Qur'ān is passionately theist. The divine power and purpose continually sustain and 'will' the world, seen as the arena of divine intention, the issue of a perennial *Kun fa yakūn*, God's 'Let there be and there is'.

This is the deep and unifying truth which we all share. There is no doubt of our common Muslim/Christian theism.[7] Where we differ is about the divine involvement this entails. It seems clear that God cannot create and be as if He had not. Or, in a New Testament term, creation itself is *kenosis*, risk and liability. He now has the world on His hands, in His hands. It is a divine enterprise hinged on man, an intention on God's part, staked in a human concurrence, a necessary human *islām* to which the divine calls and the human responds.

This response, however, cannot be automatic, if it is to be human. It cannot be guaranteed, if it is to be free. It cannot be brought, if it is inevitable. One need not send prophets to puppets. The Creator, then, is 'involved with mankind' by the very nature of His creation. That which we are given to understand is 'desired' by Him has, by its nature, to be 'willed' by us. Can we then believe in this sort of divine creation and *also* in divine immunity? It would seem not.

The same logic seems inescapable in respect of revelation and law-giving. For these are continuous with creation and give expression to how purposive it is. One cannot enjoin and be as if one had not, or be unconcerned about the response to one's legislation. Moses, bearing the Torah from Sinai descends into the squalid folly of the golden calf. The law, interpreting creation

[7] No doubt, that is, that we share it. Doubt about it, as shared, from the side of secular humanism, or contemporary agnosticism born of man's perplexity or pride, will concern us in chapter 9.

and enlisting the creature, means this radical risk and so a divine stake in mankind.

That the stake is by no means assured of its intention is evident from all such idolatry, from *shirk*, from all human attitudes *min dūni Llāhi*, living 'to the exclusion of God'. Hence, again, the urgency of prophethood, of the Qur'ān itself understood as the uncreated word of God in heaven, enshrining from eternity that speech of God which is adjuring the waywardness of a society sold on idolatry. Could there be a surer index to the fact that there is truly a divine travail about the human scene?

There is really no question between Islam and Christianity about divine involvement in the human situation. The question there is has to do with its measure and degree. Muslims, almost in spite of their theism, have generally exempted God in transcendence from the real engagements of creation and man. They have confined His relevance to law, to guidance, to exhortation, to judgement. 'Deciding by the Gospel' enlarges that relevance to grace, to Incarnation, to suffering love, to redemption. Islam broadly disavows these as unfitting to divine sovereignty. The Gospel lives by them. But they can hardly be excluded from those deep implications of Quranic theism so firmly present in the Book's robust witness to creation and its human charter.

Why, then, this Islamic reluctance for the measure of divine sovereignty which the Gospel draws from the same premises about creation and Lordship? Perhaps the historical answer takes us to the circumstances of the locale in Mecca. For those circumstances, speaking humanly, made crass paganism the central concern in the prophetic assertion of God. Muḥammad's mission would have been radically different had he been struggling against pluralism in the ghats of Varanasi on the banks of the Ganges, or within the Messianic climate of confusion with which Jesus had to deal. We must try to see patiently beyond the factors which concerned Muḥammad's immediate mission when interpreting his mission 'to the worlds'.

Whatever the historical answer, the spiritual answer to our question has to do with the desire to exalt divine glory. It is the view that divine condescension somehow compromises divine transcendence. God's sovereignty must reserve itself, will send rather than come, confine itself to prophets rather than give itself in *Logos*-love. It must retain a final capacity to be arbitrary, lest its patterns being taken as dependable would begin to be presumed. It must not relate to humanity so that creaturehood could develop 'rights' instead of pleas, claims in place of hopes. Its self-reservation, duly acknowledged by an always submissive worship, will be the truest sanction of its laws and the surest index to its sovereignty.

Behind this instinctive sense of things theological in the Qur'ān and in Islam lies the conviction that there can be no place for suffering in deity. For 'suffering' seems to imply some external source inflicting it, some exposure to 'other' power, some inferiority that can be 'subject' to constraint. And these are manifestly excluded by the very concept of 'God', and of sovereignty. God must surely be 'impassible', as the term goes. Christian 'Articles' of faith assert the same, and for the same reasons when such implications are meant. None of us can believe, or would believe, in a theism compromised by such patent inner contradiction.

But when we see the travail of God as *within* His nature, then we are not believing in what doctrines of 'impassibility' rightly mean to exclude. There are then no external 'superiors' conceded as more 'ultimate'. Quite the contrary. Given the meanings we have studied in creation and the prophets, God would be denied His sovereignty far more radically if we denied Him, even for devout reasons, the power to make good His sovereignty against all evil by the outgoing, outdoing, majesty of love. That being so, concern for divine immunity may be, paradoxically, a rather faithless confession of the divine unity.

Some old Christian writers used to put this point by asking for a 'theodicy'. The word is less often heard these days. It means the 'justification' of God. Behind the terms lies a strong – and surely God-honouring – sense of the divine responsibility. If one takes creation seriously one cannot exonerate God from the content of human history. Or one might if one could embrace all that is, and has been, in the verdict. 'It had been better if it all had never been'. Such a sentiment would be not only an idle posturing; it would also be the most despairing denial of God. Muslims and Christian alike could have no truck with it.

But to 'accept' what is, in history, in ourselves, and still to derive what is from a purpose of personal, divine intention, is honestly to ask where that intention proves itself, holds itself steady, reassures its doubters, counters its enemies – in a word, achieves itself. Islam prefers not to ask too searchingly, falling back on the evident facts of prophethood and law, of *Ummah* and *Daulah*, of Scripture and Tradition, as sufficient token of the divine due to history and man, leaving more disturbing questions to inscrutable will or indubitable power. For it is never good to be over curious or over intense.

But this is not finally a matter of 'curiosity'. It is a matter of what can be divinely credible. Nor can it be fair to dismiss as intense what takes God in His own Quranic seriousness. If we have begun to understand Job, or Jeremiah, or Paul, 'theodicy' will be for us the fullest tribute to divine reality, the surest honesty in worship.

There is no doubt where Chistianity finds it. The 'justification' of God is *via* the love of Christ. It stands in the humility of the Incarnation, in the redeeming grace of the Cross. To substantiate that confidence in positive terms belongs elsewhere. Our obligation here was to 'decide by the Gospel' as 'the people of the Gospel' must. We see that the full acknowledgement of Muḥammad, to which we are coming in chapter 9, must entail a Christian concern for a larger, more loving, comprehension of divine transcendence and, as its sphere, a deeper estimate of human nature and its answer in that which is 'more than prophecy'.

There remains one final observation here. It will be clear that this chapter has left to silence the traditional fields of Muslim/Christian controversy. It is hoped that it may also be clear that we have done them wiser justice this way. It is not that the Holy Trinity, the divinity of Jesus, the meaning of the Cross, the mystery of the Eucharist, the integrity of the four Gospels, the doctrine of the Holy Spirit, and many contingent matters, are not vital. It is that they are better left latent here, within the positive and often common themes of Islamic faith and devotion. At the end of the day there is only one question. It is the question of God. The question of Muḥammad can end nowhere else.

9

READY FOR RESPONSE

It is significant that the personal name 'Muḥammad' occurs only four times in the Qur'ān. Throughout, he is known by the title *Al-Rasūl*, 'the apostle,' or by the less frequent *Al-Nabī*, 'the seer'. The way in which the title almost entirely displaces the individual name must be seen as a token, in the Qur'ān, of a personality wholly taken up into a religious destiny. Of the four instances, only one (33.40) has to do with a personal circumstance, namely the sad fact that the Prophet had no surviving male heir: 'Muḥammad is not the father of any man among you.' The other three (3.144; 47.2 and 48.29) insist that Muḥammad is no more than a mortal messenger with the same brief lease on life of all his predecessors and that his message is truth from the Lord. The last adds that 'his followers, while severe against those who deny God, are merciful to one another'. The Qur'ān and Muḥammad belong together[1] – and are together inseparable from the custodian community of faith, power and worship, to which, in partnership, they gave existence. It is only in that total context of Book and people that an 'answer' to the 'question' of Muḥammad can be reached.

Hopefully, we are now ready for the question, after careful review of all the aspects of Muḥammad's Islamic actuality in Quranic *Waḥy*, in Hijrah and statehood, in Tradition and devotion, in ethical and spiritual definition of Muslim society and culture. Christian response to the main theme of his prophethood has surely to be a positive acknowledgement of its significance,

[1] Abdul Hamīd Siddīqī writes in his English translation of *Saḥiḥ Muslim* (New Delhi, 1978), p. 1: 'Muḥammad and the Holy Qur'ān are, no doubt, two separate entities, but they are both so closely allied that we cannot conceive of their independent existence. It is through Muḥammad that the Holy Qur'ān has been vouchsafed to us, and it is in his august personality that we find its visible expression'. While this fairly expresses the situation, it would, if pressed, fall foul of the vital orthodox doctrine of the 'uncreatedness' of the eternal Qur'ān.

as reviewed in chapter 7. But that lively sense of its relevance is left taking strenuous issue with the guiding principles of action by which the message was reinforced. Such strong, if critical, Christian affinity with the Qur'ān via the Prophet is long overdue. But its sincerity in no way relieves us of the necessity to maintain our steady witness, for Islam's own sake, to religious dimensions which must always elude the power-equation.

The thrust of these chapters, then, is that the Christian conscience must develop a faithful appreciation of the Qur'ān and thereby participate with Muslims in Muḥammad within that community of truth as to God and man, creation and nature, law and mercy, which they afford. But such community in truth will never cease to stand in need of those measures of grace and love, of sin and redemption, which are distinctive to the Gospel and which must remain incompatible with the original assumptions of Islamic *Jihād*.

There will doubtless be immediate rejection of this positive, critical position by many Christians and by many Muslims too. There will be those among the latter who will say that the prophethood and the principles of Muḥammad can in no way be open to discriminating judgement of this kind. They are inseparably joined and sealed by divine sanction. Among the former many will find truth community with the Qur'ān quite excluded by their dogmatic lights and inadmissible by their instinctive loyalties. To all these, either way, their consciences and decisions of mind and will.

But the decision these consciences dispute is not to be denied a conscience of its own, rooted in the sense of things, both Quranic and Christian, which have been explored in the previous chapters. It is a conscience firm in the conviction that its acknowledgement of Muḥammad rests on authentically Christian/Biblical grounds *and* that its instinct to make central the power-question is what the New Testament vitally requires of it. It may thus claim to be loyal to Christ no less by what it welcomes than by what it disavows. And each for the other's sake. What remains irreducibly at issue, for the Christian, about Muḥammad in no way detracts from what waits authentically for confession and assent. The crux of either is what he did with prophetic experience at the watershed of crisis.

There is significance in the fact that it is in this context of prophetic travail with danger that the Qur'ān is most expressly aware of what we might now call 'inter-religion', a point where all concern for God, on human part, seems to converge. It is a rendezvous with suffering. The key passage is in Surah

3.138–148. After affirming that the Qur'ān is a clear manifesto and guidance for humanity, it reflects on prophetic pain and makes a familiar plea for constancy and stout-heartedness. This is reinforced by steadying recollection of brave precedent from the past. The kinship of religion, clearly, is a fraternity of wounds. But how should these be taken?

> If wounding has befallen you, the people [opposing you] have had their own wounds too. These days We [God speaking] make it turn out that way among people so that God may know who are believers and make witnesses of you. . .

After stressing how the will to die had been present even before the crunch had come, the passage goes on to emphasize that Muḥammad, mortal like all his predecessors in prophecy, fully shares this situation of peril in vocation and even his demise in battle would be no cause for Muslims to turn and flee. No one dies prematurely in God's disposing of conflicts. The choice is between eternal reward for the martyr and temporal illusion of ease for the recreant. The passage goes on:

> Many a prophet there has been with whom have fought thousands and thousands of men and these did not flinch at what befell them in the way of God. They did not weaken: they did not give in. God loves those who endure. Their only word was to say: 'Our Lord, forgive us our trespasses and our excesses in the course of duty. Help us to stand firm and give us victory over the unbelieving people.'

Here and in several similar passages the Qur'ān places Muḥammad's mission squarely within what it believes to be a well-nigh universal pattern in which the prophetic experience of a destiny with truth becomes the prophetic experience of a destiny for conflict in which a physical victory is won. We are saying that a Christian verdict freely perceives Muḥammad's destiny with truth and by the same Christian discernment takes issue with the rest. It does so for the double reason that rejection of truth has deeper reaches of evil than such victory touches and that there lives in the Gospel of Christ a different precedent of prophetic word and wounds – so different that we call it no longer only prophethood but 'Sonship'.

But we should be clear that we can apply this category of assessment, taken from Jesus and the Gospel, only if we are ready to understand the divine 'cause' present in the message of Muḥammad as the messenger. If we were to see that message as no more than the Prophet's initiative or devising or worse, we would have no right to hold its sequel in action to criteria other than those of human opportunism and success. If the claim that Islam is *Fī Sabīli-Llāh* ('in the way of God') is to be deplored in its historical campaign, it cannot well be dismissed in its essential witness. For it was just that witness which merited a different active translation. The Christian must be honest with both terms of his decision. Only the worth of the prophetic experience which leads into the suffering warrants us in questioning the shape of Muḥammad's reaction to it.

Before we move from this vital clue it is fascinating to note how it pervades the central cleavage within Muslim unity – that between Sunnī and Shī'ah. This division of the household of Islam is not only early, critical and permanent. It is directly derived from this issue of truth and travail. The 'manifest victory' to which initial Islam was committed, in both idea and action, by post-Hijrah success was necessarily denied to those 'unsuccessful' factions into which Muslims inevitably fragmented under the first three Caliphs and beyond. For where personal rivalries emerged, tribal and local tensions grew, and the success criterion – politically sanctioned – dominated, 'success' could not possibly be the experience of all. On the contrary, 'failure' was bound to be the experience of some – 'failure', that is, of Muslims prizing 'success', and seeking it, no longer over ignorant pagans but over their own kindred in faith.

So came the Shī'ah experience of acute non-success. Sunnī Islam, under the Ummayyads, continued, broadly speaking, in the success tradition of Hijrah Islam. But the Shī'ah, denied and frustrated, fell back upon a theology of suffering which developed the theme of the 'immaculate' *Ahl al-Bait* ('the people of the house') (Surah 33.33), the righteous ones whose innocent sufferings possessed a merit which could avail for the redemption of the unworthy and for a deep emotional release and compensation.

The abiding presence, within the fellowship of Islam, of this profound minority verdict against Sunnī 'victoriousness', is greatly significant. It registers a deep dissociation of experience from the assumptions by which the Qur'ān is guided. That it takes place within the very community of that Scripture, and so early after its origins, is eloquent indeed. Even this most successbent of faiths has not escaped a sharp, internal, abiding reminder that, in this all too human world, truth cannot be unambiguously immune from tragedy nor properly married with establishment, as Sunnis readily suppose by warrant of the Hijrah, and of their early history.

What is further significant about this phenomenon of the

Shī'ah is that the focal point shifts from the Prophet to the house of 'Alī, and most of all to Ḥusain, the younger grandson of Muḥammad. Of course, the centrality of the Prophet and the singularity of his role in the Qur'ān are never in question. But the emotional focus passes to the 'sufferers', 'Alī, Ḥasan, and Ḥusain, to the tragedy of Karbalā'. Even the Prophet, in the Passion Plays of the Shī'ah, commemorating the Shī'ah martyrs, laments the tribulations of Ḥusain as sorrow *par excellence*, far outweighing all the woes of his own *Sīrah* and, for example, his grief at the death of little Ibrāhīm, his infant son by Mary the Copt.

It is fair to ask how the revelation might have been if there had been a Karbalā' inside the Qur'ān. As it was, this dimension came only within subsequent Islam. While the Sunnī mind, by Quranic sanction, excluded it, the Shī'ah had to brace themselves to take it. To do so they had to turn to other sources for their understanding of vicarious suffering – sources whose complexity we cannot here unravel. Insofar as the Qur'ān could avail them by arguable citations about hereditary 'virtue', and redeeming innocence, they pleaded it, but only against the run of Sunnī exegesis and the Sunnī mind. These, for their part, were in no mood to admit into their reckoning notions denied, as they saw it, by the patterns of Muḥammad and the emulation these deserved. The emotional focus of Shī'ah devotion, within the faith of Muḥammad's prophethood, is, therefore, to 'Alī, the deferred Caliph of a sadly chequered Caliphate, to Ḥasan immolated in Medina, and to Ḥusain, the tragic victim of the massacre perpetrated against Muḥammad's precious line on the dark Tenth of Muḥarram, 680. That intense shift of heart's allegiance from the Ummayyad heirs of the Prophet's own prosperous activism to the martyrs of his family must be read as the voice of sharp dissent, within Islam itself, from the cult and creed of 'manifest victory'.

That fact is only the more eloquent in the light of the paradox that Shī'ah awareness of vicarious dimensions in suffering and of the mystery of tragedy arises only in the context of an activism that was political. Ḥusain's expedition to Karbalā' was a bid for power, a challenge to the accession of Yazīd after the death of the formidable Mu'awiya, Caliph in Damascus from 661 to 680. The 'Alid cause, as a whole from its origins, had been fully Islamic in being fully political. The massacre at Karbalā' became the focus of the Shī'ah 'passion' cult only because it was the bitter climax of a politics that failed, and because the military brutality of the victors could with justice be seen as the ultimate symbol of inhuman malevolence. The cynic would say that militarily speaking the bid for power was the casualty of imperfect 'intelligence' about support. In any event it was defeat which constituted it a symbol.

It is this circumstance which has always made it difficult for the Christian to associate with Karbalā' as Shī'ah devotion does, meanings akin to those of the Cross of Jesus or of Gethsemane, where suffering has contrasted sources in hostility to teaching, not in military encounter, and where a cosmic forgiveness may be seen to spring from a forgiveness supremely active in the event itself. Or do we dissent from Shakespeare's verdict: 'I am afeared there are few die well that die in a battle . . . when blood is their argument.'[2] Let us agree that there is much perplexity here which we cannot resolve. The point is that Muslims know from their own internal history the inadequacy of 'manifest victory' as the fulfilment of religious meaning or the condition of spiritual truth. We are back with the utter necessity of clinging to the Christ-criteria of what is 'more than prophecy'.

But that loyalty does not deny us the glad recognition of what prophethood, like that of the Qur'ān, declares and serves. In the broadest terms, it means the rule of God, the reality of divine power, wisdom, mercy and justice. It means the strong permeation of the human scene with a consciousness of God, His claim, His creating, His sustaining, His ordaining. That awareness by which Islam lives is sure enough to contain all those issues the Christian must be minded to join when he studies the predicates of his New Testament theology. But those arguments, as we have seen in chapter 8, will obtain *within* a recognizably shared theism warranting community across disparity.

It is intriguing how, even at random, one can state Islamic truths of God and man in words borrowed from Christian writers totally innocent of any knowledge of Islam or intention to handle it. They are, as it were, *muslimūn* in spite of themselves and, equally, because of themselves as Christians.

Take T. S. Eliot:

The soul of man must quicken to creation . . .
Shall we not bring to Your service all our powers
For life, for dignity, grace and order
And intellectual pleasures of the senses?
The Lord who created must wish us to create
And employ our creation again in his service
Which is already his service in creating.

[2] *Henry V*, Act iv, scene 1, lines 149, 151.

Here, in *The Rock*, are the *āyāt* of the Qur'ān and man the responsive deputy to God, the procreator within a creation not his own.

> Visible and invisible, two world's meet in Man:
> Visible and invisible must meet in his Temple . . .
> . . . the work of creation is never without travail;
> The formed stone, the visible crucifix,
> The dressed altar, the lifting light,
> Light
> Light
> The visible reminder of Invisible Light.[3]

'The visible crucifix' will not be there in the Taj Mahal of Aligarh, nor in Jerusalem's Dome of the Rock. But Islamic architects, masters of line and light, have rich works of creation as 'visible reminders'. *Al-Ẓāhir wa-l-Bāṭin*, 'the visible and hidden' (57.3), are attributes of the divine. The Surah of Light (24) hails the 'light upon light' of God and links it with houses He has permitted to be fashioned where His Name may be celebrated.

Or consider Thomas Traherne when he ponders

> . . . how great a Lord gave us so great a dominion:
> We shall think it abominable to be treacherous
> and unfaithful in the midst of His dominions.

And again:

> The sun in your understanding illuminates your soul, the sun in the heavens enlightens the hemisphere. The world within you is an offering returned, which is infinitely more acceptable to God Almighty, since it came from Him that it might return to Him. Wherein the mystery is great. For God hath made you able . . . to give and offer up the world to Him, which is very delightful in flowing from Him, but much more in returning to Him . . . the voluntary Act of an obedient Soul.[4]

Of course, there are Christian nuances here. But 'unto Him is our returning' reverberates through the Qur'ān, not only in reference to death but in the meaning of praise and surrender. And certainly the Islamic Scripture is full of the sense of divine bounty and the 'outstretched hand' (e.g. 5.64) and the 'grand perhaps' of a human gratitude in intelligent cognisance of the 'signs'. Traherne has an unknown sympathy with a Muslim poet of the nineteenth century who writes:

[3] T. S. Eliot, *The Rock* ix, in *Collected Poems* 1962 (London, 1963), pp. 181–2.
[4] Thomas Traherne, *Centuries* (London, 1980 edn), p. 103 and p. 99.

O Ghālib, the beauty and grandeur of the flower enhances the perception of the beholder: it is necessary, therefore, that the eyes remain open in all circumstances.[5]

For did not Traherne insist:

> Men's lips are closed, because their eyes are blinded . . . But did they know all the blessedness of their estate, O what a place full of joys, what an amiable region and territory of praises would the world become . . .
>
> Man hath a dominion over all the rest and God over him. Above all, man discovereth the glory of God.[6]

When the great Ibn Khaldūn was a youth in the service of the court of Tunis his work was to be 'master of the signature', namely to write, between the formal opening and the text of all official documents, the words: 'To God the praise, to God the thanks.' Man the master with this signature was the Quranic teaching.

Richard Hooker – again at random among Christian theorists and himself something of a Christian Ibn Khaldūn – agrees:

> God hath His influence into the very essence of things, which without influence of deity supporting them their utter annihilation could not but follow. Of Him have all things both received their first being and their continuance to be that which they are . . . By every effort proceeding from the most concealed instincts of nature his power is made manifest.[7]

Such sentiments read almost like a paraphrase of the Qur'ān, a Scripture quite unknown in seventeenth century Bishopsbourne in Kent.

These affinities with Quranic themes on God and man are everywhere in the Fathers, Eastern and Western. A perceptive reader of Augustine's Confessions has often cause to write Quranic parallels in the margins. Or there is Gregory of Nyssa, explaining why man comes into the creation only when all is prepared for his 'dominion'.

> When, then, the Maker of all had prepared beforehand, as it were, a royal lodging for the future king (and this was the land, and islands and sea, and the heaven arching like a roof over them) and when all kinds of wealth had been stored in

[5] Verse of Mirza Asadullah Khan Ghalib, died 1869. See Muḥammad Sadiq, *A History of Urdu Literature* (London, 1964), pp. 176–204.

[6] Traherne, p. 101 and p. 68.

[7] Thomas Hooker, *Laws of Ecclesiastical Polity*, v, 56.5 and 48.2.

this palace . . . he thus manifests man in the world, to be the beholder of some of the wonders therein, and the lord of the others.[8]

Surah 79.28–33 was unknown to Gregory:

> He raised the canopy of heaven and set it in poise. He made the night a cover over it and he brought forth its high noon. And then He laid the expanse of the earth, bringing forth waters and pastures therein, and He made fast the hills to be a joy to you and to your flocks.

The cautious will say that these celebrations of nature and man, and man's gracelessness in slighting them, are far from resolving all that is theologically at stake between those who share them. Such caution is proper. But their being partial does not prevent their being real. Given the readiness, much may grow from them. They have ripe potential for relationship.

'Ripe', we have to say, because they are beset by much neglect or contradiction in the contemporary world. To face this is to come to another important aspect of any Christian response to the Qur'ān and its people, a response that is not simply discursive about the past of our doctrines but active about their future.

To be alert in saying, as we have throughout, that Muḥammad's great achievement has been to bring about a vast human practice, or ruling consciousness, of God's reality as Lord, is to ask about its continuity in the world of our time. To believe so surely and to pursue to stoutly a divine charting of our existence is to meet head-on the secularizing factors of the day. The West, of course, has known these more intensely, for reasons of history. The Islamic world, in general, confronts them, in technological terms, more at second hand. But it does so at a more rapid rate and with more concentrated impact. It would seem that the sort of consequences experienced in the Western world are likely to be universal. Any Christian relation to Islamic theism, and so to all issues about Muḥammad, has lively occasions here.

Briefly the situation is that Muḥammad's whole emphasis on a total liability to God, on man's accountability beyond, on his transcendental reference both of guidance and of judgement, seems questioned by man's confident 'self-reference', in the things of technology and the exercise of an autonomy which appears to function and fulfil itself without any necessary relation outside nature, for scientific data, and outside society, for moral steering. Where does the greatness of God come in, given the

[8] Gregory of Nyssa, *On the Making of Man* (*De Opificio Hominis*), II, 1, p. 390.

seeming adequacy of man? Certainly God is not to be accounted great by dint of keeping us small. His greatness, if we are to credit it, must be of the sort to leave room for ours. *Need* we read the 'signs' of nature religiously when we apparently can succeed so well in merely reading them efficiently? Can we not manifestly have the mastery implicit in 'dominion', without acknowledging the 'servanthood'?

Does not modern man conspicuously assume this, without dire consequences except those of his own folly, ineptness or haste? Will not his ruin, if it comes, be as self-made as his success? Either way, is it not all self-enclosed? Is civilization celestial obligation? Is history subject to providence and *hudā*? What should we make of the seeming non-intervention of God in our current affairs? Science has certainly tended in popular terms to a recession of the immediate sense of God, and in sophisticated terms to a bland or puzzled renunciation of it.

All theism confronts this issue, but Islam, it might be said, most of all, because its theological emphasis is so strongly imperative, so requirement oriented, so instinct with divine directive, so obligated to an authoritarian heaven. Christianity has perhaps been more minded to appreciate what we might, perhaps oddly, call the diffidence of God, the degree to which He might patiently leave His purposes within the vagaries of human behaviour, not by any kind of abdication, but by the quality of His long-suffering. Islam, with its powerful understanding of the divine *Amr*, has the options associated with 'the Word made flesh' less readily.

For some the proper reaction to secularity is a vigorous reassertion of divine imperatives, both cultic and moral, a more resolute enforcement of the Prophet's word and will, a rigorous obedience to the once for all Qur'ān. Examples of that 'zealot' response are everywhere to hand for the observer of Muḥammad's people. They are at once both alarmed and confident and the qualities abet each other. They see the external works of technology as digestible, its interior mentality of suppositions a menace to be banished. One recent writer on education says that the Arab, Muslim world must do with science what Arabs do with melon seeds, namely chew the nut and spit the rind away.[9]

It must be questioned whether the matter can be so naively

[9] Ziauddin Sardar, *Science, Technology and Development in the Muslim World* (London, 1977), p. 130, The 'rind' is the scientific temper, the 'nut' is its efficient works.

settled. Scientific thinking is not dispensable in this way, nor its implications such as can be jettisoned by dwellers in metropolis. We must learn more intelligently the meaning of *Allāhu akbar* in the world of oil terminals and tankers, computerized communication and space shuttles.

The secret, more wisely, is in the Quranic/Biblical understanding of man as both servant and master, both tenant and trustee. The raw material of his dominion has to be the fabric of his consecration. The rightness of his authority lies in the faithfulness of his submission. The God who, in the Qur'ān, leaves man in no illusion about his idols yet also leaves with him their actual repudiation is the same God who claims from our generation an undivided worship yet waits for it uncompellingly. Stated in summary form, the essential mission of Muḥammad was to 'let God be God'. That same call may be seen to be the crisis of contemporary man. The Christian has every reason, conceptual, compassionate and contemporary, to recognize how vital that call is in the common world, how kin to the Biblical claim, and how relevant to what he believes to be the goal of the Gospel. To see this in no way ends our quarrel: it could mean that we continue it as a quest.

This all too summary conclusion as to the content of Muḥammad's prophethood brings us back to its method. For the one, we said we should have an expectant recognition. This, in broad and summary terms, is now complete. For the other, we said there must be a steady taking of issue. To this we must now turn. It has to do with a Christian disquiet about Islamic power-assurance, taught by the contrast of the Gospel's patterns.

Let us be clear that all prophetic religion is necessarily combative, committed to *Jihād*. The question is in no way 'Whether?' It is always 'How?' 'All strength is known,' as Kant observed in his *Metaphysic of Morals*, by the hindrances which it can overcome.'[10] Prophetic faith intends to change the world. Unlike mystical religion, or Asian attitudes of mind, it struggles to restore, to rebuke and correct, to condemn and save. It aims to recruit *mujāhidīn* ('strivers') after its own heart. Such recruitment, as with the Companions of the Prophet, is vital. The Church, too, is 'militant here in earth'. In either case, the struggle is by and for a divine revelatory action believed to inaugurate and require it.

Our other sphere of relation to Muḥammad, therefore, as Christians, will be a Christian response to what we must indicate

[10] Immanuel Kant, *Metaphysic of Morals* (Berlin edn, 1797), vi, p. 405.

as, to us, the qualities, the limitations, and the paradoxes of prophetic action in the service, during the *Sīrah*, of prophetic message. As we have seen in chapters 2 and 3, the Prophet's story has the merit of focusing these most sharply. But first, in this context, a few points of response by way of summary, to those areas of prophetic personality considered in chapters 4, 5 and 6.

As Tradition monumentally shows, example was among the most potent forms of Muḥammad's recruitment to the struggle for Islam as well as its age-long school in later centuries. Here a Christian verdict must surely be to leave the 'criticism' of Tradition to Muslims[11] and recognize in the whole phenomenon the form of Islamic ideology. This will be the only properly religious response, leaving to academic historians their pursuit of questions of research. Even where sayings and actions, attributed to Muḥammad, have been, or may still have to be, doubted, the possession of them by the Muslim community has to be seen as the shape of their own aspirations and ideals.

It is possible to detect a symbol of this in the pattern of *Isnād* or attestation which, from early centuries, Muslims adopted in the ordering of Tradition. *Isnād* rested on a careful system of reportage by 'Companions' known to have companied with Muḥammad and themselves well attested both as to character and contact. Hence the unbroken chain of human linkage which carried back the *matn*, or matter, of the Tradition to the Prophet himself, and the careful vetting of the biographies of these reporters in their sequence. In this way the authority and veracity of the Tradition rested, not so much on intellectual inquiry whether its details were eligible in themselves, as on the proof that the community, through its mentors, had them in circulation. In other words, the authenticity was finally their right currency, rather than their content 'neutrally' assessed. Whether or not we take *Isnād* this way as a symbol, there is no question that Tradition was the means by which Islamic ideals took both example and mandate from the action and personality of the Prophet. Tradition, it might be said, has been a kind of ethical immortality for Muḥammad within the behaviour of his people.

As such the Christian's relation must be to anticipate and serve the direction the moral interpretations of Islam may take

[11] The most famous of the great traditionalists, Imām al-Bukhāri attributed his vocation to a vision he received in which he saw the face of the sleeping Prophet, Muḥammad, infested with flies, which he, Al-Bukharī, wafted away with a fan. The flies were the spurious traditions and the fan his rigorous editorial scholarship.

in the contemporary world, closely tied as these are with the community's reading of Muḥammad. We must realize that our effort to come to terms positively with the Prophet involves us in issues only they can decide about themselves. It would be idle, not to say irresponsible, to react to the Muḥammad of history in neglect of the Muḥammad of present, and progressive, ideology within Islam. Decisions, both theirs and ours, over historical reference, refer to more than history.

The same is manifestly true of the Sufi love of Muḥammad which we explored in chapter 4. Here we are on still more sacred ground. It would seem that there is, and has to be, an interiority in all faiths where the outsider cannot really penetrate, where the inward meaning is, by its nature, proper to itself. The Christian might desire, for deeply compelling reasons, to enter into the Sufi devotion to Muḥammad with the sympathies and dimensions of the New Testament devotion to Jesus and his own personal discipleship to Christ. But the likenesses which arise from the strains of mysticism which are recognizably common will not easily accept the distinctive features that belong to the Christ story. We have to concede that the ground is pre-empted that Jesus might occupy, The *imitatio Muhammadi* is one, the *imitatio Christi* another.

Even so, it is heartening to realize in retrospect on chapter 4 that there are implications for theology in the cherishing of Muḥammad within Islam very significant to the Christian mind. We come to realize that thoughts of the divine 'pleasure' in the revelatory medium which, for us, underlie the whole meaning of Jesus' Incarnation have this strong Sufi place within Islam itself. Piety, not to say, philosophical yearning, has undertaken what classical Islamic theology forbad and ventured a devotion, with an accompanying thought structure, which sees a divine mediation via personality as well as speech, and exalts divine agency into something akin to divine presence. That this should have happened within so rigorous a system as Islam and with arguably Quranic approval is remarkable and offers to Christian thought a lively area of religious meaning to develop in relationship.

No doubt it is possible roundly to dismiss mysticism as unwarranted 'Asianizing' of Muḥammad and a compromising thing on every score, both cultic and institutional. But the *Mutawaḥḥidūn,* the Wahhābis and other accusers of such compromise, do not monopolize Islam. Other Muslims register religious needs and impulses which they can never satisfy as long as they forbid to the soul the love it means to bring. That Muḥammad should be the *Quṭb*, the axis, of such devotion is, within Islam, the proper consequence of his role in the Qur'ān and a religious development directly from it. It will not be the part of Christians to join forces, as it were, with the rigorists in decrying it. For, in this territory of faith, what Muslims find in Muḥammad as the soul's loved and lover, brings them close to those same factors in experience which, for the Christian have meant discovering in Christ the personal rendezvous with God. Those factors are summed up in the old words of the psalmist: 'My soul hath a desire . . .' (Psalm 84.2). Its satisfaction is very differently found by Christian and Muslim. But the yearning has a kinship. The rest must be witness.

The reticence necessary in the theme of chapter 4 need not attach to the question in chapter 6. It is right for Christian response about Muḥammad to help Muslims towards a freer, livelier, view of his role in prophethood. Both they and we must surely understand Muḥammad as recipient in terms that allow employment to the full of his powers of will and mind, so that *Waḥy* does not have its way by some kind of surreptitious infusion of words to be uttered apart from any living engagement with their sense before or during their infusion. The Qur'ān does not need for its authority this thesis about its inspiration. Its worth is more evident for being rid of this incubus. We do not believe that Muḥammad had never heard of Joseph or Moses until the names came to him in the first *Waḥy* that referred to them. It is neither right nor necessary to believe that *Allāh*, as a term, was put upon Muḥammad's lips as something never before in all his thoughts, when his own father had the name 'Abdallāh, and there were the *Ḥanīfs* reaching for a unitary faith in his father's generation.

It is right on every intelligent score to understand the Scripture as coming to him in a context of personal thought, experience, travail and activity. This is no way diminishes the revelatory status. On the contrary, it helps to its appreciation. One can, no doubt, find in the Greek tradition and in Plato's *Dialogues*, the idea of 'divine' inspiration coming only in total passivity, where 'truth' is 'given' with all rational and conscious processes suspended.[12] But all this is far away from the Quranic setting of

[12] For example, in *Timaeus*, 71, it is suggested that a person completely in his right mind has no capacity for prophetic inspiration, and in *Phaedrus*, 265, prophecy is spoken of as a frenzy or mania. Writing on the poets in *Ion*, 534, Plato thinks that when deity inspires, personal consciousness is suppressed. Divine energy overwhelms mental awareness. If we were to think this way Quranically it would point in the very unIslamic

prophetic struggle in the immediacies of time and place. Such Greek occasions of 'inspiration', *enthusiasmos*, needed some other interpreter than the recipient. Muḥammad, clearly, was his own. To depersonalize the incidence of *Waḥy* will not be the way to reckon appropriately with the Qur'ān or to understand the stature and personality of the Prophet. A wise Christian response to Muslim inquiry of us about him will be to encourage Muslims themselves, in the clear quality of their own Book, to see him fully within a living scene in mind and heart and not lips alone. Only then are the lips duly heeded. It is not for the Prophet to say, *from* the thoughts of his own mind, *Qāl Allāh*, 'God said . . .' But can he so say *without* them? We believe not; and we think too, that Muḥammad is only then rightly recognized and heard.

So we return, finally, to the issue of prophetic 'struggle' and the conclusions required of us in the light of chapters 2 and 3. It may be good to move from one of those rare incidents within the Qur'ān where imagination can readily visualize an actual Muḥammad in the market at Yathrib. It is a scene we might describe as wanting a solution. The Prophet is preaching and the audience, it seems, drifts away at the call of merchandise and diversion. Perhaps they are disinclined to concentrate. Or the pull of gains and bargains is too strong. Or the preacher's fervour sounds remote to their concerns. So they disperse and leave him standing (Surah 62.11), while he assures their fading earshot that 'the things of God excel pleasure and trade'.

Only a glimpse, but in its simple way a hint of the central burden: how make truth avail, and prevail? Here the hindrances are merely inattention, the competitiveness of the world, the distractions of the all too human scene. Preaching is stranded in a sort of gentle powerlessness wanting audience. But more, it wants obedience and, given heedlessness, this is remoter still. Also there is much more than the casual in the world. There is enmity to truth, hostility, outright rejection. One cannot merely cry out after these that 'the things of God are better'. The things of God are denied, distrusted, refused, maligned. The preacher, too, is not then 'left standing'. He is threatened, molested, persecuted and condemned.

That being so, there is also a paradoxical sense in which God,

---

direction of some sort of prophetic 'divinization', a sort of *pro tem.* suspension of Muḥammad's humanness. Then there is the sharp problem of the intelligibility to an audience of the message when delivered, not to say its repeated insistence on such intelligibility and the appeal for intelligent response. Should we then ban the intelligibility from the spokesman himself?

too, is in search of an audience He is denied, denied, that is, by virtue of human forgetfulness, a sort of historical inattention. Revelation, says Dr Sayyid Husain Nasr, is that which makes man remember what he has forgotten so that he may regain the beatitude he had before he fell into the prison of the senses.[13] Hence, of course, the term *dhikr* so often used by the Qur'ān of itself, as 'a reminder to the worlds' (38.87 and numerous other passages). Hence, too, the faithful sequence of the prophets and their intimate link, in the *Shahādah*, with the divine claim to the world.

Yet the necessity of *Jihād* suggests that what is wrong is something more than forgetfulness. Manifestly the reminder and the exhortation, calculated to correct it, do not suffice. The whole logic of Muḥammad's career is that the verbal deliverance of prophetic truth fails of satisfaction and must therefore pass to the post-Hijrah invocation of power. The realization of what is preached comes about not only in the proper attentiveness of the immediately faithful but in the effective surmounting of the long-time obdurate.

We put the matter in another way if we say that there is still a defiance in the human situation when the impact of teaching has had long earnest occasion to make good its message. Or it might be truer to say that the defiance was always there and that preaching has merely proved its persistence, its toughness and stubborn quality. Here on Islamic ground we are very much in line with Paul's comment that 'by the law is the knowledge of sin' (Romans 3.20). Directive understood to be from God and vested in His messengers encounters, and so discloses, in the human scene an unreadiness to be directed. There is, in this sense, the divine imperative and the human negative in a sort of confrontation. Revelation, as a speaking medium of the imperative, truly educates the human world as to God's will. But the lesson is that man, far from being apt to learn, defies the teaching. That this should be the experience of the 'final' prophecy makes it also a final conclusion. There can be no more resilient or resourceful 'education' still to come. That *the Qur'ān* should have unresponsive and antagonistic hearers is, on its own showing, the ultimate evidence of human disaffection against truth. Perhaps this, further, may be why what is final in prophecy must prevail in fact. The word becomes the struggle, the *dhikr* the *Jihād*.

13 Sayyid Husain Nasr, *Islamic Studies: Essays on Law and Society, the Sciences and Philosophy, and Sufism* (Beirut, 1967), p. 15.

It is clear that here is the whole crux of religion – the discrepancy between what ought to be (however derived and defined) and what is, how the discrepancy is overcome and what the forms of 'overcoming' do to the discrepancy. For they can so easily misread it or increase it. All that is at stake here quickly leads on to the suspicion that religion's greatest struggle is with itself. To have only a simple *Jihād* externally directed is to fail the truth. It is to ignore the enemy within, whom we may not even have identified or may have mistaken for a friend – the menace in struggle itself.

Just as, earlier in this chapter, we tried to set Muḥammad's preaching as to God and man in the context of modern secular technology and human autonomy, so now we must relate his confidence in *Jihād* to the contemporary religious scene. For the Christian response we are trying to determine, while obligated to the questions that require study, must also care for the issues that demand compassion and salvation. It is the massive actuality of Islam in the world in this new Hijrī century which properly dominates our thinking. This 'massive actuality' with Muḥammad as its mentor, has to inform all our decisions about him in a realism alive to the world. What does a mutual Muslim/Christian concern for the divine will, duly disciplining the human scene, require of both communities of faith? *Tauḥīd* and *Takbīr*, as the Prophet demanded them, mean this discipline, this identification of false idolatries and their repudiation in truly 'letting God be God'. In that broad consensus comes the claim of concrete situations, local and global, where respective liabilities belong. They have to do with politics and society, with the economic order, and issues of liberty, justice and compassion. They are concerns about poverty, about discrimination, about chronic imbalance in resources and living standards both between and within national states. They have to do with exploitation of natural and human resources, with pollution and the rape of nature, with the menace of technological vandalism and the cult of sheer efficiency. They raise questions of liberation, the role of woman, the control of science, the trust of environment, the value judgements – or lack of them – in the social sciences. And all verdicts in these fields stand under the shadow of contemporary competition in the means to nuclear holocaust.

However difficult the decisions in thought and action, and however disparate the incidence of what is at stake within our societies, there is nothing in current perplexity or crisis which does not finally return for its resolution to the inclusive question of God and His active worship. So at least Muslims and Christians understand. For both, the 'putting down of the mighty from their seats', 'the filling of the hungry with good things' alike have their prelude in 'magnifying the Lord'. These were celebrated in *Magnificat* as being only what such *Magnificat* could celebrate. *Allāhu akbar*, in its different way, has the same intent. Only within it can the contemporary significance of Muḥammad be wisely realized.

The imperative 'mood' he gave to it is, indeed, imperative. Without the sense of divine will, conjecture, evasion, indecision cloud the vision and paralyse the human will. Law from God is vital in all Semitic religion, where ethics and society are theologically accountable. New Testament experience of grace does not deny Sinai; rather it retrieves its moral, without its ethnic, intention by other means. We will be right to take Quranic law as the Islamic analogue to Sinai, and focus on its central intention to subdue the world to God, and to say that, as such, its chartering of humanity is a positive we should not neutralize because our theological predicates partially differ. Muḥammad is to be 'recognized' in the recognition of the claim he made that God be 'recognized' in right submission.

It is interesting to note how '*muslim*' in their temper, in this respect, are some recent Christian theologians of liberation. José P. Miranda, for example, in *Marx and the Bible*, writes, though no doubt unconsciously, in a quite Islamic way, when he speaks of 'a God whose being is to command us':

> He stops being God the moment his injunction ceases. And man has many resources at his disposal to cause this command to come to an end. He need only objectify God in some way. At that moment God is no longer God. Man has made him into an idol: God no longer commands man . . . To situate myself outside of the demand which God makes on my concrete existence is to speak of something else, not of God.[14]

Miranda goes on to show how this absolute command in which alone transcendence is really 'situated' (and not in mental categories of being) claims our entire commitment to justice for our neighbour. Here he is strongly in the company of Amos and of Isaiah and, many would believe, of Muḥammad also. Whether so or not, what is clear is that here we have deeply Islamic accents – idolatry as non-obedience, a theology not of curiosity

[14] José P. Miranda, *Marx and the Bible: A Critique of the Philosophy of Oppression*, trans. from the Spanish by John Eagleson (London, 1977), pp. 44, 40 and 43.

but of submission, the transcendence which commands. 'The question', says Miranda, 'is . . . whether we are seeking him where God himself said that He is.'[15] And 'where He is', for the Qur'ān, is in the 'thou shalt' of His will, in the *Qul* ('Say') of His revelation. *Ẓulm*, in the Qur'ān, is the crucial evil of withholding what is due. The essence of wrong is the denial of God's rights and these are not rationally established, so as to be within our adjudication, but divinely prescribed so as to command our submission.

There is point in thus 'capturing' the gist of *islām* from a source outside it and despite the obvious disparities. For, if it is accepted, it bears eloquently upon our acknowledgement of Muḥammad. It is certainly New Testament grace and the struggles of Mexican liberation theology which give to Miranda his characteristic passion. The Qur'ān has its own world. But the partial parallel does avail to underline the vital place in an honest theology for the imperative 'mood' by which Islam lives. In the command to 'let God be God' we can hardly fail to recognize each other.

But it is just this significant 'agreement' and not some bent for insensitive hostility which requires a Christian's reservation about Muḥammad. The reasons have been evident in chapters 3 and 8. Command is not the only 'mood' of divine relationship to mankind. The Gospel presents what we must call a divine 'indicative', an initiative of self-disclosure on God's part by which His relation to our human situation is not only in law and education, but in grace and suffering. Christians therefore believe that they have to 'let God be God' in just those initiatives which Islam excludes – initiatives which bring God into the pathos of His creation as man's devising has wronged it. Such grace does not compromise the divine authority. Rather it spells a divine liability for man that is blessedly fulfilled.

If it is asked whether, as human, we have any right to make theological judgements which turn, like this, upon the 'satisfaction' of our creaturely ideas, when the very essence of 'revelation' is to be absolute and arbitrary, the answer must be that our warrant is His image in ourselves. May it not be that He reveals Himself by letting us identify the clues by which we have to 'test' His sovereignty? As such they must surely take in our human tragedy. Our 'demands' on Him – as the Book of Job struggles to believe – will then be the context in which we truly measure and accept His demands on us.

[15] *Ibid.*, p. 57

This, beyond Job's struggles, the Gospel rejoices to believe. Our sense there that God is love does indeed meet our deepest human yearning but, so doing, most surely vindicates the divine supremacy. That double conviction is the significance of Christ. It is a question – to borrow an earlier quotation – of 'seeing God where He Himself has said that He is'. The place, for us Christians, is where 'the Word is made flesh', in the ministry and Cross of Jesus our Lord.

But neither of us should be entrenched in purely assertive positions about 'where' according to our faith 'He has said that He is'. Either way, the human significance has somehow to be translated into experience and 'realized' in life. For that, as we have seen, Muḥammad relied confidently on the legitimate role of the power-structure. Much in Christian centuries has proceeded by the same confidence. But Christian origins, in line with the grace-dimension 'where God is', defined the relation between society and salvation as being inside the state's governance but not within its auspices. There is a greater militancy.

When Jesus replied to a questioner, 'Render to Caesar the things that are Caesar's and to God the things that are God's' (Matt. 22.21; Mark 12.17; Luke 20.25), he did not mean that Caesar's realm was one of divine indifference, an autonomy absolved of all transcendent reference. On the contrary, he meant that the things of God, in their inclusiveness, cannot be identified with the interests of Caesar or entrusted to his ways.

It was Muḥammad's understanding of 'the things of God' which, after the Hijrah, put away the distinction. In his own person he saw them compatible. If, restoring Jesus' principle, we question or regret the Caesar in Muḥammad, it will only be for the sake, in their Quranic form, of those same 'things of God', which move us to acknowledge him.

CHART OF READING

Bibliography relating to Islam and Muḥammad in general is much too rich even for partial listing here. Relating to the immediate theme of the title it is almost nil. The notes that follow are designed only to facilitate the reader's own pursuit of a wider familiarity with the overall field *and* of an alert reckoning with the decisions a Christian is expected to reach.

An invaluable bibliographical source, carefully annotated and indexed, is that of J. D. Pearson, and others: *Index Islamicus 1906–1955* (Cambridge, Heffers, 1958), with *Supplements, 1956–1960* (1962); *1961–1965* (1967); *1966–70* (Cambridge, Mansell, 1971). Since 1971 the Supplements have continued as a Quarterly, numbering 7 vols. to 1983. See also, C. J. Adams, *Reader's Guide to the Great Religions* (New York, Free Press, 1965).

For the themes of chapters 2, 3, 5 and 6, see A. Guillaume, *Life of Muḥammad* (Clarendon, 1955), being his translation of Ibn Isḥāq's *Sīrat Rasūl Allāh*, the earliest of the lives of Muḥammad by traditional historians. A 19th-century presentation, based on Ibn Isḥāq, and still a valuable work, was Wm. Muir, *The Life of Mahomet and History of Islam* (4 vols., London, 1856–61; new abridged edn, Edinburgh, 1923; revised edn. A.M.S. Press, New York, 1975).

D. S. Margoliouth, *Mohammed, and the Rise of Islam* (Putnam, 1905), is a scholarly example of the older, Western biography admitting no extenuation. A quite different, and invaluable, initiative was W. Montgomery Watt, *Muḥammad at Mecca* (Clarendon, 1953), and *Muḥammad at Medina* (Clarendon, 1956), in which, by study of the first adherents to Islam, their tribal and economic data, he aimed to explore the material background of Islamic origins. These two books were distilled into Watt's *Muḥammad, Prophet and Statesman* (Oxford, 1961). M. Rodinson, *Moḥammad* (Allen Lane, 2nd edn. 1971, trans. from the French by A. Carter) took clues from Watt in aiming to 'reconcile early experiences with the Marxist theory of the social causality of the lives of individuals'. Rodinson arranged his presentation under 'Birth of a Prophet, of a Sect, and of a State', with special care for 'a prophet in arms'. His approach has not, in general, found favour with Muslim writers.

An indispensable source, bearing especially on chapter 6 here, is Tor Andrae, *Muḥammad, the Man and His Faith* (trans. from the German by T. Menzel, Harper, 1960). This work studies the inner experience of Muḥammad's prophethood with a penetrating scholarship.

Among notable biographies by Muslim authors see: Muḥammad Hamidullah, *Le Prophète de l'Islam* (2 vols. Paris, 1955), and the same author's *The Battlefields of the Prophet Muḥammad* (Woking, 1957); Muḥammad Husain Haykal, *Life of Muḥammad* (Arabic) trans. into English by American Trust Publications (New York, 1975), A. Yusuf Ali, *The Personality of the Prophet Muḥammad* (Ashraf, Lahore, 1931); Abd al-Rahman Azzam, *The Eternal Message of Muḥammad* (trans. from Arabic by C. E. Farah, New York, 1965), M. Zafrullah Khan, *Muḥammad, Seal of the Prophets* (Routledge & Kegan Paul, 1980)– the author is a renowned legist and a former Judge of the World Court, Geneva; Muḥammad Shibli Numani, *Sīrat al-Nabī* (trans. from Urdu by Pakistan Historical Society, Karachi, 1975), Zayn al-Abidin Rahnama, *Payambar, The Messenger* (trans. from Persian by L. P. Elwell-Sutton, Ashraf, Lahore, 1964) – based on Ibn Isḥāq but written like a novel. Mention may also be made of a recent work in German by a very esteemed author, Annemarie Schimmel, *Und Muḥammad ist Sein Prophet* (Dusseldörf, 1981).

On Tradition still the only introductory work for the general reader is A. Guillaume, *The Traditions of Islam* (Oxford, 1923).

On the Qur'ān itself readers are well advised to consult a variety of translations of which the most serviceable may be A. J. Arberry, *The Koran Interpreted*, (Oxford, 1964); N. Dawood, *The Koran* (Allen Lane, 1956); A. Yusuf Ali, *The Meaning of the Illustrious Qur'ān* (Lahore, 1957); and Muḥammad Asad, *The Message of the Qur'ān* (Gibraltar, 1980).

In the area of chapter 4 the best source is C. E. Padwick, *Muslim Devotions* (SPCK, 1961), a careful distillation of the content and temper of Muslim prayer manuals and the acts of devotion they inform. See also Annemarie Schimmel, *As Through A Veil: Mystical Poetry in Islam* (Columbia, 1982) and her *Mystical Dimensions of Islam* (Chapel Hill, 1975). J. C. Archer, *Mystical Elements in Muḥammad* (Yale University Press, 1924), is an older work conjecturing the possible sources of Muḥammad's sense of mission.

There is an increasing literature relating more or less explicitly to the concerns of chapters 1, 7, 8 and 9, though almost nothing on the precise theme of a Christian view of Muḥammad. Two World Council of Churches publications present Muslim–Christian dialogue, namely S. J. Samartha and J. B. Taylor, *Christian-Muslim Dialogue* (Geneva, 1972), and *Christians Meeting Muslims: W.C.C. Papers on Ten Years* (Geneva, 1977). A source trans. from the German is Annemarie Schimmel and A. Falaturi, *We Believe in One God* (Burns Oates, 1979) – see their chapter 4. In French Y. Moubarac's *L'Islam et le Dialogue* (Cénacle Libanais, 1972) and his *Verse et Controverse, Les Musulmans* (Beauchesne, Paris, 1971).

Three Muslim works in the field of secularity and its challenge, faith and technology and Muslim contemporary response, are Sayyid Husain Nasr, *Islam and the Plight of Modern Man* (Longman, London, 1975); Gai Eaton, *King of the Castle: Choice and Responsibility in the Modern World* (Bodley Head, London, 1977); and Fazlur Rahman, *Major Themes of the Qur'ān* (Minneapolis, 1980).

Books on contemporary politics in the Islamic world are, of course, legion. Two recent ones with their bibliography may be noted here, namely: A. J. Cudsi and A. E. H. Dessouki, *Islam and Power* (Croom Helm, 1981), and E. Mortimer, *Faith and Power: The Politics of Islam* (Faber, 1982).

GLOSSARY

Adhān: the call to prayer, made five times daily from the mosque, with the summons: 'Come ye to *Ṣalāt*, come ye to good.'

Amr: grammatically, 'the imperative'. The term denotes the authority of divine initiative by which the world came into being, the revelation happened, and the believer is guided and motivated.

Asbāb al-nuzūl: the 'occasions' of the Qur'ān's being given to Muḥammad, the circumstances in his career at which its incidence took place, as noted in Tradition.

Āyāt: the 'signs' of God evident in the natural order as the stimulus of science and the spur to gratitude and worship of God. The same term is used for the verses of the Qur'ān.

Balāgh: the content of Muḥammad's message, as distinct from any reckoning with its reception: the divine communication.

Bismillāh: the invocation of the Name of God in the phrase: 'In the Name of the merciful Lord of mercy', with which every Surah of the Qur'ān (except No. 9) opens, and which prefaces all Muslim acts of piety.

Daulah: the political order, the state, in alliance with *Dīn (q.v.)*, the organ of Islamic power.

Dhikr: one of the titles of the Qur'ān, meaning 'reminder' or 'recollection', and the practice of remembering God and His will in Muslim devotion and in Sufi technique.

Dīn: religion in general and religious duties in particular comprising the five 'pillars' or 'body' of Islamic duty, namely: *Shahādah, Ṣalāt, Ṣaum, Zakāt* and *Ḥajj* (*q.v.*). *Dīn* also means 'judgement', as in *Yaum al-Dīn* 'the day of judgement'.

Fiqh: jurisprudence, as expounded by the several Schools of Law.

Fitnah: what opposes and so 'tests' believers. When the first Muslims were a minority, it meant 'persecution': after success and 'establishment' it meant 'sedition'. *Qatl* (slaughter) is a lesser evil than *fitnah*.

Ḥadīth: the 'tradition' of the Prophet, as derived from his 'Companions' and treasured as a second source of law after the Qur'ān.

Ḥajj: the statutory pilgrimage in Islam, with the rites at Mecca, and its environs, during the pilgrimage month, and mandatory at least once in a lifetime.

Ḥanīf: a seeker after true religion, such as Abraham in the Qur'ān: (pl.) *ḥunafā'* a group of monotheists prior to Muḥammad's day in the Arabian context.

Ḥaqīqah: the 'reality' of, or within, Muḥammad as being, in mystical devotion, the repository of the divine light and wisdom.

Ḥaram: 'shrine' or 'santuary': the sacred enclave at Mecca housing the *Ka'bah* (*q.v.*) and the focal point of pilgrimage.

Ḥirā': the mountain in the Meccan region traditionally associated with Muḥammad's inaugural visions.

Hubal: the name of one of the pagan idols in the *Ka'bah* at Mecca, and a patron of the Quraish.

I'jāz: the state of being 'matchless', or 'inimitable', attributed to the Qur'ān as a surpassing eloquence mediated to an 'illiterate' Muḥammad: the evident 'miracle' of the Scripture.

Īlāf: the organizing, or marshalling of the Meccan caravans (Surah 106).

Imām: in Sunnī Islam, the leader of the mosque prayer: in Shi'ah Islam the due successor to Muḥammad in authority to rule and guide the true community.

Īmān: faith, the act of believing and obeying, correlative to *Dīn* or practice. Properly indistinguishable from *islām* but sometimes actually absent from bare 'surrender' (cf. Surah 49.14).

Islām: the historic faith of the Muslim: *islām* (as a common noun) means the act of 'submission' to God's law and will.

Jāhiliyyah: the time of 'ignorance' before Islam. In some modern usage it may also denote an unworthy form of Islam as practised by alleged compromisers of its purity.

Jihād: 'struggle', or 'militancy' on the part of the Muslim against inner evil and, more generally, against lands, peoples, or powers, not yet brought under Islamic control.

Ka'bah: the cube-shaped structure in the centre of the *Ḥaram* at Mecca, around which pilgrims circle in the pilgrimage ritual: the focal point of Muslim prayer: its location associated with Adam and its building with Abraham.

Kāfirūn: 'unbelievers', those in a state of denial and repudiation of revealed truth.

Kalām: (lit.) 'speech': the term used to denote scholastic theology in Islam.

Khalīfah: man as the 'deputy' or 'vicegerent' of God, set over the created order as 'manager' and 'trustee'. Used politically of the successors to Muḥammad's empire.

Maulid: the birthday of Muḥammad, celebrated in popular religion by special prayers and benisons, which are disavowed, however, by the purists.

Miḥrāb: the niche in the wall of the mosque which orients worshippers in the direction (or *qiblah*) of Mecca.

Muhājirūn: (lit.) 'emigrants', those who participated in the Hijrah, or emigration, from Mecca to Medina in 622, when Muḥammad opted for the political order.

Munāfiqūn: those guilty of *nifāq* or 'hypocrisy', the people who feigned allegiance in merely prudential response to Muḥammad's success while actually subverting his mission.

Murū'ah: the 'virtue' of 'manliness', much admired and enjoined by Arab society: the courage in tribal loyalty which Islam garnered into the religious cause.

Muslimāt: Muslim women (pl. of *muslimah*), believers (fem.).

Muslimūn: Muslim men, the believers in the faith.

Qatl: 'killing' or 'slaughter' – a lesser evil, in the context of the cause of Islam, than *fitnah*, or chronic disaffection against the faith (Surah 2.217).

Qiblah: the direction of prayer towards Mecca.

Quraish: the dominant tribal group in Mecca and the custodians of the *Ka'bah* to which Muḥammad himself belonged.

Al-Raḥmān al-Raḥīm: the two most frequent of the 'Names' of God, forming the *Bismillāh*, and derived from the root meaning 'mercy'. The relation of the two words is that of 'essential' to 'operative'.

Rasūl: the dignity and title of Muḥammad as 'apostle' sent by God and for God. It yields the abstract *Rasūliyyah*, or 'apostolate', 'messengership'.

Risālah: (from the same root as *Rasūl*), the fact and the content of the *Rasūliyyah*, the 'message', and the 'mission' with it in their inseparable quality.

Ṣabr: the quality of 'patience', or 'steadfastness', in which the true believer abides under adversity, pending divine retrieval of his fortunes.

Ṣalat: the prayer rite in Islam, the liturgy of actions and words by which God's sovereignty is acknowledged and obeyed, and the community of Islam is realized.

Ṣaum: the act of fasting in Ramadān, the fourth 'pillar' of Islam, in which food and drink are withheld by the believer during the daylight hours of the month.

Shahādah: the 'witness' or 'confession' of Islamic faith in the words: 'There is no god but God: Muḥammad is the *Rasūl* of God.'

Sharī'ah: the sacred law of Islam, as yielded by the Qur'ān and the *Ḥadīth* (*q.v.*) and the lesser sources.

Shī'ah: the followers, initially, of 'Alī, fourth Caliph: the segment of Islam which 'seceded' from the Sunni, or 'orthodox', majority in respect of authority, exegesis, politics and devotion.

Shirk: the cardinal sin of pagan plural worship, the evil of 'association' by which the sole worship of God is distorted by idolatry. Those who thus deny God in diversified trust and celebration are the *mushrikūn*.

Sīrah: the 'course' or 'sequence' of the Prophet's story, gathered and rehearsed in tradition.

Ṣūfi: the general term for the 'mystic' in Islam. Originating early in ascetic patterns of devotion. Sufism developed into a rich and subtle variety of esoteric ideas and techniques.

Sunnah: the corpus of tradition, housed in *Ḥadīth* (*q.v.*) which constitutes the second source of *Shari'ah* (*q.v.*) on the basis of 'non-repugnancy' to the Qur'ān.

Tadabbur: the careful reflection on the Qur'ān which it demands of the reader: intelligent and perceptive exegesis.

Tajwīd: the art of Quranic recital by which the beauty of the text is saluted and cherished and heard.

Takbīr: the saying of *Allāhu akbar*, 'Greater is God': the believer's act of 'magnifying' the Lord, i.e. affirming the divine greatness.

Tanzīl: the 'sending down' of the Qur'ān upon Muḥammad: the mysterious bestowal on him of the words and the content of the Scripture so that he recites *verbatim* the substance of the heavenly Book.

Taqlīd: the blind citation of past authority, the 'hideboundness' of conservative traditionalists as deplored by 'reforming' thinkers.

Taqwā: the fundamental Muslim quality of 'God-fearingness', the 'awe' that recognizes duly the divine glory and the human fealty.

Tasbīḥ: the act of glorifying God in the words: *Subḥān Allāh*, 'praise be to God'.

Taṣliyah: The 'celebrating' of Muḥammad in response to the directive in Surah 33.56, where it is said that God Himself salutes and celebrates the Prophet and believers are summoned to do so also. The words are: 'May God send down blessing upon him and give him the greeting of peace.' This formula is abridged in the letters (SA'WS) in devout writing after every mention of Muḥammad's name.

Tauḥīd: the affirmation of the unity of God, the 'making' of God 'One' against all pluralism and idolatrous *Shirk* (*q.v.*).

Ummah: the single community which Islam constitutes, the totality of Muslims, beyond, or despite, the frontiers of 'nation' or 'national State'.

Ummī: an adjective meaning 'illiterate', the sense of which, in the case of Muḥammad, is rather that of being (prior to the Qur'ān) without a Scripture among a Scriptureless people, i.e. the Arabs.

Waḥy: the phenomenon of the recipience of the Qur'ān as undergone by Muḥammad. The term includes both the 'revelation' received and the 'inspiration' under which it came. These two are not distinguished in Islam, in line with what is believed about the text and language of the Book.

Zakāt: the payments due from Muslims (only) on their income, for use 'in the way of God': the third 'pillar' of Islam.

Ẓulm: the evil, or wrong, of withholding what is due: injustice, tyranny, violation of rights, and – most of all – atheism and unbelief as the denial of God and His claims.

N.B. The termination '-ūn' in all plural Arab nouns will read '-īn' when not in nominative case. The corresponding feminine plural, in all cases, has the termination '-āt'.

INDEX

Quranic Passages cited